Lynne Attwood received her doctorate in Soviet Studies
the Centre for Russian and East European Studies, Univer
She is the author of *The New Soviet Man and Woman: Sex*
the USSR, and has contributed to a number of other books r
Union and Russia. In the past she has taught Russian Stu
at the University of Texas at Austin, and at Humberside
now Lecturer in Russian Studies at the University of Man
teaches a course on Russian and Soviet cinema.

Also by Lynne Attwood

The New Soviet Man and Woman: Sex Role Socialization in the USSR
(London, Macmillan, 1990; Bloomington, Indiana University Press, 1991)

RED WOMEN
ON THE SILVER SCREEN

SOVIET WOMEN AND CINEMA FROM THE
BEGINNING TO THE END OF THE
COMMUNIST ERA

LYNNE ATTWOOD

with Maya Turovskaya, Oksana Bulgakova, Elena Stishova,
Dilyara Tasbulatova, Marina Drozdova and Maria Vizitei

TRANSLATIONS BY LYNNE ATTWOOD AND KIRSTEN SAMS

Pandora
An Imprint of HarperCollinsPublishers

Pandora Press
77-85 Fulham Palace Road
Hammersmith, London W6 8JB

Published by Pandora Press 1993
10 9 8 7 6 5 4 3 2 1

Text by Lynne Attwood and selection © Lynne Attwood 1993.
Original contributions © Maya Turovskaya, Oksana Bulgakova,
Elena Stishova, Dilyara Tasbulatova, Marina Drozdova, Maria Vizitei 1993
Translation of contributions from Russian into English © Lynne Attwood

Lynne Attwood asserts the moral right to
be identified as the author and compiler of this work

A catalogue record for this book
is available from the British Library

ISBN 0 04 440561 8

Typeset by Harper Phototypesetters Limited,
Northampton, England
Printed in Great Britain by
Mackays of Chatham, Kent

CONTENTS

LIST OF ILLUSTRATIONS

PLATE SECTION 1

Nikolai Batalov and Lyudmila Semenova in *Bed and Sofa* (Abram Room, 1927)

Sergei Stolyarov, Lyubov' Orlova and Jimmy Patterson in *Circus* (Grigorii Aleksandrov, 1936)

Lyubov' Orlova in *Circus* (Grigroii Aleksandrov, 1936)

Vera Maretskaya in *Member of the Government* (A. Zarkhi and I. Kheifitis, 1939)

Tat'yana Samoilova in *The Cranes are Flying* (Mikhail Kalatozov, 1957)

Maya Bulgakova in *Wings* (Larisa Shepit'ka, 1966)

Nina Ruslanova and Vladimir Vysotskii in BRIEF ENCOUNTERS (Kira Muratova, 1968/88)

PLATE SECTION 2

Zinaida Sharko in *Long Farewells* (Kira Muratova, 1971/1987)

Natal'ya Negoda and Andrei Sokolov in *Little Vera* (Vassilii Pichul, 1988)

Leila Abashidze in *Turnabout* (Lana Gogoberidze, 1986)

Aiturgan Temirova in *Snipers* (Bolotbek Shamshiev, 1985)

Sofiko Chiaureli in *Some Interviews on Personal Questions* (Lana Gogoberidze, 1979)

Inna Churikova in *I wish to Speak* (Gleb Panfilov, 1976)

Raisa Nedashkovskaya, Nonna Mordyukova and Rolan Bykov in *The Commissar* (Aleksandr Askoldov, 1967/1988)

Nonna Mordyukova in *The Commissar* (Aleksandr Askoldov, 1967/1988)

INTRODUCTION

'She writes books, and there's no milk in the fridge . . .' mutters the hero of Gleb Panfilov's film *The Theme* (*Tema*), prowling round the errant woman's apartment. 'Women intellectuals . . . they will be the death of society . . .'*

The Soviet Union was the first country in the world to decree that women were fully equal to men. To establish this in law was one thing; to bring it about in reality was quite another. From the start, the revolutionaries had to deal with a legacy of profound male chauvinism and misogyny. The extent of this is evident from old Russian proverbs: 'When the hair is long, the brain is short,' one chuckles; 'I thought I saw two people walking down the street, but it turned out to be a man and his wife,' jokes another. If women's equality were to become more than just a legal fiction, such attitudes would need to be transformed.

The cinema was an obvious vehicle for such a transformation. Its potential role as an agent of socialization had been noted almost from the first film showing, and not only in Russia. In Britain, in 1917 (coincidentally, the year of the Russian Revolution), the National Council of Public Morals expressed anxious concern about 'the profound influence upon the mental and moral outlook of millions of our young people' which films were able to exert.[1] In the Soviet Union, in contrast, the tone was less one of anxiety than of hopeful anticipation. The cinema was the newest form of popular entertainment, and most readily adapted to the needs of a workers' state. It was untarnished by the bourgeois stigma which weighed so heavily on the theatre ('those sometimes amusing games with dolls . . .', as Soviet film-maker Dziga Vertov disparagingly described the latter).[2] Its reliance on new technology made it a particularly appropriate art form for the industrial age. Unlike books and newspapers, it could reach the entire population; the illiteracy rate at the time

---

* *The Theme* was made in 1979 but not released until 1985.

was almost 80 per cent, and as one contemporary observer put it, 'The cinema is the only book that even the illiterate can read.'[3] Its novelty value would also increase its impact. This was especially the case in the countryside and in the Moslem republics of the south, where films had made few inroads before the revolution, and where support for the new government was at its weakest.[4]

The cinema would, then, be a powerful tool in forging a 'New Soviet Person', committed to socialism and to the new socialist government. Lenin impressed this fact on Lunacharskii, the Commissar of Education: 'Of all the arts', he told him, 'for us the cinema is the most important.'[5]

How did Soviet film-makers interpret their new task? Was the 'New Soviet Person' to be free of traditional gender stereotypes? Did the cinema propagandize women's equality, did it attempt to challenge those ingrained notions of women as inferior creatures? What role did women film-makers play in the creation of new female images?

For all the interest shown by Western scholars in the Soviet cinema, there has been remarkably little discussion about its relationship to women. Neither the images of women which have appeared on screen, nor the experiences of women working in the film industry have come under much scrutiny. This book takes a step toward filling that gap. It also does so at a timely juncture, when the seventy-four year history of the Soviet Union has slithered to an end.

The subject is tackled from two different angles. In Part I, I provide what could be called a view from 'the outside': a broad introduction, from a Western perspective, of the history of the country, its cinema and women's place in both. For readers who are new to Russian and Soviet Studies, this will provide the necessary background for the chapters that follow. It will introduce them to the principal works published in the English language on the Soviet cinema, as well as looking at some of the discussions appearing in the Russian press since *glasnost'* opened up its pages to more critical debate.

Parts II and III provide a view 'from the inside'. In the past, our knowledge of the Soviet Union came solely from Western scholars or journalists, who slipped 'behind the iron curtain' to send reports back home to a leery world. The Soviet people had no chance to talk for themselves. The notion that they were unknown and unknowable – 'a riddle wrapped in a mystery inside an enigma', to borrow Winston Churchill's phrase[6] – was a mainstay of Cold War politics, something wilfully perpetrated by Western governments. At the same time, Soviet restrictions on the flow of information to and from the country also made it difficult for those who lived there to publish honest accounts of their own experience.

This is no longer the case, and this book is able to offer a unique study of women and film in the former Soviet Union 'from the horse's mouth'. The chapters in Part II have been written by Soviet film critics, who are (with one exception) still living and working in what was the Soviet Union. Part III consists of interviews with women directors, camera-operators and script-writers.

Before its disintegration, the Soviet Union was the largest country in the world, and contained within its borders more than a hundred different ethnic groups. This fact was suddenly brought to the attention of the West with the outburst of hostilities between different groups, and the media interest which focused on them. The mistaken assumption of the past, that 'Russia' and 'the Soviet Union' meant the same thing, was dispelled. 'Russia' was just one of the Soviet republics, albeit the largest and most powerful; and life in Russia was not synonymous with life in the country as a whole. The huge cultural, historical and religious variations in different parts of the Soviet Union were bound to have an impact on the images of women being presented on screen. Accordingly, the book looks at the cinema in a variety of republics. There is a contribution from Dilyara Tasbulatova, a film critic from Kazakhstan. There are interviews with women directors from Georgia and Uzbekistan. The script-writer Maria Zvereva relates her experience of working for an Estonian director. Nor has the demise of the Soviet Union as a single state made ethnic issues any less important. In fact, they are certain to dominate politics in the new Commonwealth of Independent States.

It is hoped that readers will find this book a rich feast. However, a few words of preparation are necessary in order to aid digestion. Firstly, readers who are unaccustomed to texts translated from Russian may find the writing style in Part II a little unusual. Russian writers have a tendency towards the poetic, the lyrical; language is not just a vehicle for conveying ideas, but is something to be enjoyed in itself. When translating the articles, I felt the need to make some adjustments to the style to ensure that the texts were always accessible to an English-language readership. However, I was careful to do nothing which would actually distort them; nor have I re-cast the articles in an 'English' mould. I feel sure that readers will soon adapt to, and enjoy, the stylistic differences.

The second point is that while I reject the old cliché about people in what was the Soviet Union being 'unknown and unknowable', I do feel that readers should bear in mind that people's understandings of the world around them are formed largely by the historical and cultural contexts in which they live. Otherwise they may be puzzled by some of the views expressed by the book's contributors, particularly regarding feminism and socialism.

The views of Soviet women have not, for the most part, fit comfortably into a Western feminist framework. Although the reasons for this will become clearer as the book progresses, I will offer some suggestions at the outset as to why this should be. Following the October Revolution in 1917, the new Soviet government took on itself the role of champion of women's rights. The government defined what equality between the sexes meant; and, as the years went by, it sometimes adjusted the definition to make it fit the changing economic and social needs of the country. There was an official women's organization, the Committee of Soviet Women. However, its main function was to represent the interests of the Communist Party rather than of Soviet women. The emigrée writer Tat'yana Mamonova contends that it was even told who to send to international conferences, and what statistics they could quote there.[7]

Unofficial women's groups were not allowed. When a dissident feminist group did emerge briefly in Leningrad in 1979 and produced a journal called *The Almanach: Women and Russia*, it was brought to a quick and decisive end with the arrest and exile of its members. The issue of women's rights was, in short, appropriated by the Communist Party and its bureaucratic apparatus. Since these were viewed with scorn by much of the Soviet population, anything connected with them was compromised.

Meanwhile, women had to struggle with two virtually full-time jobs. After working all day in the office or factory, they went home to a second shift of cooking, cleaning and childcare, while their husbands lounged in front of the television. If they ever had time to pick up a magazine, it invariably told them how fortunate they were to be living in a society which had their interests so much at heart, and how their very fulfilment and happiness rested on this combination of roles. It is not surprising that many women became cynical about the very notion of equality.

Yet there is another, rather paradoxical point to be made about the family. Even though it made so much extra work for women, it was also one of the few places in pre-*glasnost'* days where one could talk openly and freely, and where people were valued as individuals instead of members of the mythical 'mass' promoted by Soviet ideology. Hence while Western feminists were turning a critical eye to the family as a focal point of male oppression, their sisters in the Soviet Union saw it as a place of refuge against state oppression.

Readers will find, then, that many of the contributors to this book have a list of priorities which is rather different to their own. Instead of demanding equality in the workplace, they want protection from jobs which consist of heavy physical toil. Instead of insisting that men take an equal share in housework and childcare, they call for a reduced workload for women outside the home so they can devote more time to life inside it. Instead of demanding to be treated as human beings, they dream of the luxury of being treated 'as women'. We will find such arguments voiced even by the women film directors interviewed in the final chapter, who have had to show remarkable strength and dedication to penetrate the walls of what is still regarded as a male bastion.

It is worth bearing in mind the point that Maya Turovskaya makes in the first of her contributions to this book. Women of the former Soviet Union and women of the West are confronted by the same circle of problems, she suggests. Our attention, however, is momentarily focused on different points on its circumference.

If the notion of women's rights became compromised in the Soviet Union, how much more so did that of socialism. Several of the contributors repudiate even the early years of the revolution, a period which many of us in the West still see as brave and exciting. Elena Stishova, for example, after describing the vibrant characters in a script for a film by Esfir' Shub, then shocks us with her suggestion that a few years later, with the onset of Stalin's 'Terror', these same brave revolutionaries would be clamouring for innocent blood. Marina Drozdova, discussing the portrayal of an old Bolshevik woman in a recent documentary film, argues that her adherence to the abstract ideals of the revolution was the first step along the path to anti-humanism. *Glasnost'* has unleashed a feverish re-analysis of Soviet history, and the term 'totalitarianism' figures strongly in this. But while we may find its application appropriate to the Stalin years, it comes as a surprise to find the term applied to some of the greatest films and film-makers of the 1920s. We do not have to agree with these definitions (and it should be noted here that the chapters do not represent the views of the editor). We should, however, try to understand the context in which they have developed.

Part I, *Woman, Cinema and Society*, provides a framework for the discussions which follow. It charts the development of the Soviet cinema, and women's part in this process. It looks at the changes in women's rights and obligations in different periods of the country's history, and at the cinema's role both in reflecting and propagandizing these changes. It also looks at some of the recent re-interpretations of early Soviet cinema and society from within the country. Finally, it turns to the rather disturbing new portrayals of women which began emerging in the Gorbachev era, and attempts to find an explanation for them.

Part II, *Woman on the Screen*, is concerned with Soviet responses to the images of women portrayed on film. The first two contributions are by Maya Turovskaya, one of the best known Russian writers on film and theatre, who has taken part in a number of international film festivals and conferences. Her first chapter (Chapter 9) looks at the background to what is referred to in Russia as 'the Woman Question'. Having grown up herself in Moscow in the 1920s, hers is a personalized history of the problems confronting women, and the ways in which they were reflected in the literature and films of the day. Her second chapter (Chapter 10) discusses the concept of 'Women's Cinema', which provoked considerable controversy in Russia and the former Soviet Union.

Chapter 11 is by Oksana Bulgakova, who, although originally from Russia, has lived and worked in east Berlin for several years. She looks at the Russian version of the 'film-star', contrasts her with her Hollywood counterpart, and shows how she has changed in the different periods of the country's history.

Elena Stishova, head film critic of the journal *Iskusstvo Kino* (*Art of the Cinema*), has written Chapter 12. She looks at the almost mythologized image of Soviet womanhood portrayed on screen, paying particular attention to the heroine of Aleksandr Askoldov's film *The Commissar.*

Chapter 13 leaves Russia and heads south-east, to Kazakhstan. Dilyara Tasbulatova looks at the 'Woman of the East' and her portrayal on the screen.

The final chapter of Part II is by Marina Drozdova, a young film critic from Moscow. She looks at cinema of the *perestroika* era, and particularly at the sex scenes which became an almost obligatory part of every new film. Drozdova contends that these had little to do with eroticism as such. In contrast to Freud's notion that sexual urges are often sublimated into other activities, Drozdova suggests that in the Soviet situation, the myriad frustrations citizens had to deal with were sublimated into sex.

Part III, *Woman Behind the Camera*, explores the experiences of women who work in the cinema. It begins with a look at the structure of the film industry. Maria Vizitei, a recent graduate of VGIK (the film institute in Moscow), then discusses the training women undergo at this institute, and at the particular problems they encounter when they try to break into the more male-dominated areas of the industry.

The final chapter is based on a series of conversations with women who have either already made their name in the film industry, or have at least secured a foot-hold in their chosen professions. They talk about their successes, their failures and their hopes for the future – not just for themselves but for a new generation of women film-makers emerging into a vastly different world.

I would like at this point to acknowledge the help I have had from a number of people in getting this project off the ground. Particular thanks are due to Siân Thomas, a television researcher and producer now based in Moscow. She was the associate producer of 'Women in Soviet Cinema', a series of two programmes screened in Britain by Channel 4 in 1990, and her work on this project convinced her that the subject was worth exploring in greater depth. It was she who set the book in motion, then, and opened the door to the Soviet film world for me. She introduced me to a number of crucial people in the film industry, and helped with some of the interviews in Part III. She was also responsible for much of the picture research. It is no exaggeration to say that without her help this book would not have been written.

Thanks are also due to the Russian members of KIWI (Kino International Women's Federation) for arranging my visit to Moscow in the summer of 1989 to attend the Moscow Film Festival. I would also like to thank the Union of

Cinematographers for making their library available to me during this visit. Dorethea Holloway was kind enough to invite me to 'Femme Totale', a festival of Soviet women's films which she organized in Dortmund, Germany, in May 1989. Kirsten Sams has earned my utmost gratitude for her help with the translations, often at very short notice, and at times which were far from convenient for her. Last but far from least, I would like to thank the contributors to the book, and the many other women who took the time to talk to me during the Dortmund festival in May 1989, the XVI Moscow film festival of July 1989 and the XVII Moscow film festival of July 1991. They have given me a far richer understanding of what life is like for women in the former Soviet Union, especially for those who choose to work in this male-dominated profession. I hope this book will do the same for its readers.

Regarding the transliteration of the Russian names, film titles, etc., from Russian into English, I have broken from my usual system in three particular circumstances. When a Russian name has a clear English version, I have kept to the usual spelling: hence, Maya, for example, instead of Maiya; and Maria instead of Mariya. Similarly, if a Russian name has consistently been spelt in a certain way in English, I have used this: hence, Eisenstein rather than Eizenshtein, Yeltsin instead of El'tsin. Finally, when I have been quoting from an English-language source, I have, of course, retained the transliteration used in that source.

Lynne Attwood

PART I

Woman, Cinema and Society

LYNNE ATTWOOD

The first ever moving picture arrived in Russia in May 1896, as part of the festivities surrounding the coronation of the last Tsar, Nicholas II. It consisted of a compilation of short scenes made in France by the Lumière brothers: people walking along a Paris street, a train pulling into a station, workers leaving a factory, a small boy stepping on a hose and spraying the gardener with water. After its première in the capital, St Petersburg, it was shown in music halls across the country, to the delight and alarm of audiences. The writer Maksim Gorkii, reviewing the phenomenon for his local newspaper, wrote prophetically that: 'Without fear of exaggeration, a wide use can be predicted for this invention . . .'[1]

The old order in Russia was on its last legs, though blissfully unaware of the fact. The cinema, on the other hand, was just beginning. Hence, as Russian society went through its epic transformations, the camera lens drank them in like the eyes of a curious child. Soviet film critic Neya Zorkaya talks of the powerful visual record the early film-makers left us of life in Russia in the years leading up to the revolution: the contrast between the opulence of royalty and the poverty of the workers, between the palace tables piled high with food and the carts in famine areas piled high with corpses.[2]

But films do more than simply reflect society. They can also help to shape it - something of which the post-revolutionary Soviet government, embarking on the creation of a new society, was well aware. The chapters which follow, then, seek to explore the dialectical relationship which developed between Soviet society and the Soviet cinema. They sketch the historic changes taking place in the Soviet Union throughout the seven decades of its existence, particularly in relation to women. They explore the development of the cinema, and the role it played in reflecting, interpreting and influencing these changes. Above all, they look at the representation of women on Soviet screens.

One of the distinctive features of Soviet cinema has been the symbolic use of the human form to convey certain abstract ideas: the motherland, liberty, Bolshevism, and so on. Soviet film scholar Yurii Davydov calls this the 'screened image of an idea', the portrayal of 'abstract ideas (or concepts) . . . clothed in the flesh and blood of real individuals . . .'[3] Indeed, this was not confined to the cinema but permeated all forms of Soviet visual art. As Victoria Bonnell explains, the Bolsheviks had to find a rapid means of legitimizing their rule in the wake of the revolution; they felt that 'the success of this effort depended on the creation of compelling visual symbols and rituals designed to reach people – many of them illiterate or semiliterate – who were accustomed to the elaborate pageants and visual imagery of the Old Regime and Russian Orthodox Church'.[4] We will be paying particular attention to the symbolic use to which the female figure has been put in Soviet films throughout the country's history.

1 THE BACKGROUND

What kind of society was Russia at the time of the cinema's first appearance? In a nutshell, it was an autocratic monarchy scarcely out of the feudal period, headed by a Tsar who still believed that he ruled by divine edict. This notion did not go unchallenged, however. Toward the end of the nineteenth century, a number of underground political movements had begun to take shape; despite huge differences in philosophy and method, they were united by a common desire to bring to an end the Tsar's ultimate authority.

Populism was one such movement. It promoted a rather vague and gentle socialism, seeking an alternative to the state through the establishment of communes. Since Russia was predominantly rural, the peasantry were seen as the necessary starting point in attempting to bring about change. Accordingly, idealistic young urban students donned peasant outfits and set off for the countryside like socialist missionaries. Women were particularly prominent in this movement, training as teachers, midwives or nurses and going off to live amongst the peasants. Others stayed in the cities and took jobs on factory production lines in order to make contact with urban workers. Some modelled themselves on Vera Pavlovna, the heroine of Chernyshevskii's 1863 novel *What is to be Done?*, who escaped from a patriarchal family by means of a fictitious marriage and went on to set up a sewing co-operative for poor urban women.

The populists, then, adopted a peaceful approach to socialism. In contrast, a number of terrorist groups also came into being, the members of which felt that social change could only be achieved through violence. It was one such group, the People's Will, which carried out the assassination of Tsar Aleksandr II in 1881, assuming that revolution would surely follow. It did not, and five of the plotters - including a woman, Sof'ya Perovskaya - were hanged for the act. As with the populists, women formed a fair proportion of the activists in the terrorist movements.

This was less the case with the Social Democratic Workers' Party, the

principal forum of the Russian Marxists. Although it included a number of
women members, few were actively involved in leadership or policy-making.
Aleksandra Kollontai was an exception, engaged in a long battle to convince
male comrades that transforming gender relations was an essential part of
transforming society. Yet even she saw the 'Woman Question' not as an issue
in itself, but as part of the struggle for socialism; feminism in and for itself
was a bourgeois phenomenon, which had little relevance to Marxists. The
oppression of working-class women was part of the broader oppression of the
working class, and could be dealt with only within the context of class struggle.

In 1905, a literal class struggle broke out. Factory workers in the capital, St
Petersburg, had staged a peaceful march to the Winter Palace to ask for better
working conditions and a basic platform of civil rights. The Tsar was not at
home, and his troops – unaccustomed to such a crowd – panicked and fired.
Hundreds, possibly thousands, were killed.[1] The result was a wave of strikes
and uprisings across the country, which reached even into the Tsar's armed
forces. The Tsar's power was temporarily suspended as Soviets, or Workers'
Councils, took over much of local government in the cities. By the time the
Tsar regained control, he had been reluctantly forced to allow the
establishment of a kind of parliament, the Duma. Its franchise was extremely
limited, however, with only the wealthy and propertied allowed to vote.
Theoretically, this could include women, but few actually passed the strict
property criteria. The only way the working class could express its grievances
was through strike action. In 1914 there were more than 4,000 strikes by the
time Russia entered World War I that summer.[2]

This, then, was the background against which the Russian cinema was born.
As we noted, when the first 'moving pictures' arrived from France in 1896 they
were greeted with enormous enthusiasm; all the same, an indigenous film
industry did not develop immediately. It was French film-makers who first
flooded the market, setting up studios in Russia as well as importing films from
home. Then, in 1907, came their first local challenge, in the form of Russian
photographer Aleksandr Drankov. Drankov is not known for any great
cinematic achievements, but his studio did have one notable success – it
persuaded the writer Lev Tolstoi to overcome his initial reluctance and submit
to the camera lens. The resulting footage was rediscovered two decades later
and used by the female documentary film-maker Esfir' Shub in her 1928 film
The Russia of Nicholas II and Lev Tolstoi. Drankov also produced what is generally
held to be Russia's first feature film, *Stenka Razin*, in 1908, about the leader
of a peasant uprising in the seventeenth century. This choice of subject-matter
does not indicate a sympathy with revolution, however. Drankov fled to the
United States after the Bolshevik takeover in 1917.

The cinema in its early years was no competition for other forms of art.

Russian literature was in the midst of its 'Silver Age', and was producing some of the most acclaimed writers in history, such as Lev Tolstoi, Anton Chekhov and Maksim Gorkii. The theatre was also going through a great period of experimentation under the guidance of innovative directors such as Konstantin Stanislavskii and Vsevolod Meierhold. Nonetheless, this new upstart alarmed the practitioners of other arts. Theatre workers saw it as a direct challenge to their profession and tried to protect themselves by carving out a separate space for the newcomer. Their own role would be to provide cultural and educational entertainment, they decided; cinema's strength lay in its appeal to more primitive emotions. As N. Lopatin wrote in 1913, 'if the cinema shows us a villain, it is a real villain; and you detest him from the first glance, from his hat down to his savage black beard'.[3]

In the summer of 1914, Russia entered World War I. For a while the war unified the population (as wars have a way of doing), and the strikes and demonstrations came to a halt. Before long, however, it had turned into a disaster. It consumed the country's resources, and brought desperate hunger to the civilian population. The army was poorly equipped and badly led, and by the end of the first year, some four million soldiers had died.[4] The Tsar had insisted on taking over its leadership himself, against the advice of his ministers, and so its failures reflected badly on him. Meanwhile, domestic affairs had been left in the hands of the empress, Aleksandra. Her growing attachment to Rasputin, the womanizing monk who was reputed to possess supernatural powers, did nothing to improve public confidence in the royal family – especially when Rasputin began to exert considerable influence over government affairs.

Against the background of mass poverty and growing discontent, the rich were growing steadily richer. In Leon Trotskii's eloquent words, 'Enormous fortunes arose out of the bloody foam. The lack of bread and fuel in the capital did not prevent the court jeweller, Fabergé, from boasting that he had never before done such flourishing business. Lady-in-Waiting Vyrubova says that in no other seasons were such gowns to be seen as in the winter of 1915-16, and never were so many diamonds purchased . . .'[5]

Gowns and diamonds were also abundant on cinema screens. The costume drama had become the most popular type of Russian film, and its biggest star was Vera Kholodnaya, black-haired and ashen-faced, who made her first appearance on screen in 1915 at the age of 22. She became the symbol of female beauty and enjoyed almost a superstar status, something hitherto unheard of in her country. The characters she played did not demand much from her as an actress, however. As V. Khanzhonkova notes, 'in almost all her films, the actress played the same role – that of a passive suffering woman'.[6] This woman invariably came from a humble background, was briefly propelled to the heights of wealth and status, and then tumbled down to poverty and death. The stories were primarily an excuse for lavish sets, costumes and scenery, and above all for that great new status symbol, the automobile. It zoomed onto Russian screens, in the words of Zorkaya, with its 'bright head-lights piercing the night darkness; that symbol of luxury, that novelty of the century'.[7]

In the world beyond the film theatres, there was little luxury in the lives of ordinary people. Even the shelves of bread shops had become empty. Strikes and demonstrations began again, after the brief respite caused by wartime patriotism. Yet little of this intruded into the fantasy world of the cinema. The feature film was generally intended to offer escapism, not a record of reality. There were exceptions, however. Evgenii Bauer, to give one example, tried to combine social comment with entertainment in a number of his films. In *A Child of the Big City* (1913), a humble seamstress is rescued from poverty by a wealthy gentleman, who, finding her naïveity and gaucheness refreshing, installs her in his luxurious town house. Her naïveity soon vanishes; the opulence of her new surroundings corrupt her. Before long, the pretty plaything has become a power-hungry monster, deserting her benefactor for a succession of more eligible providers. While the squalor of the working-class life from which she sprang is not romanticized, nor is the indulgent egotism of the aristocracy. Yet Bauer's films were not representative of his era. Even though most films were set in the present, it was, as Zorkaya notes, 'a fancy and rootless present', which paid no heed to the war, nor to the growing likelihood of revolution.[8]

2 REVOLUTION AND CIVIL WAR

The first revolution came in February 1917. Bread demonstrations had turned into riots in the capital (which had been renamed Petrograd after the start of the war, since St Petersburg sounded too Germanic) and the Tsar's troops were ordered to fire at the crowd, but refused to do so. The Tsar's authority collapsed; it had ultimately rested on military force, and if he could no longer command the army, he could no longer govern. Accordingly, he was forced to abdicate. Members of the Duma formed themselves into a Provisional Government, declaring that they would function as caretakers until proper elections could be held.

Like the Duma, the Provisional Government was a middle-class institution which consisted mainly of landowners and factory managers. On the grounds that it could not possibly represent the interests of the working class, the old St Petersburg Soviet reassembled its members. Its example spread to other cities. In the beginning, the Soviets claimed for themselves only the role of watch-dog: they would keep an eye on the actions of the Provisional Government and make sure that it did not ignore the needs of ordinary people. However, before long they had begun to take over much of local government. The situation became, as Lenin described it, one of 'Dual Government'.

The cinema halls were still showing the old-style costume dramas. However, with Tsarist censorship lifted, a new kind of film also hit the bill-boards – 'pseudo-revolutionary films', which were little more than sensationalized and eroticized portraits of the royal family. Titles such as *Grishka Rasputin's Amorous Escapades, The Secrets of the House of the Romanovs, Mysteries of the Secret Police* and *People of Sin and Blood (Sinners from The Tsar's Village)* were obviously intended to titillate the public rather than inform them.[1]

There was also a new breed of more serious dramas. Zorkaya singles out for praise two films released in 1918 starring Vladimir Mayakovskii, the young actor and poet who virtually became the spokesman of the revolution. These were

The Young Lady and the Hooligan, directed by Evgenii Slavinskii, and *Creation Can't Be Bought*, by Nikadr Turkin.[2] Although the stories were imported from abroad, it is evident why they found a resonance in revolutionary Russia, where the working class had found a new power through participation in the Soviets. Both films were about young men from the working class who fell in love with women from the intelligentsia. In this new society the worker was a hero, and could evidently make claims on what had formerly been beyond his reach.

To the Russian Marxists, the events of February 1917 constituted a bourgeois rather than a socialist revolution. According to classical Marxist theory, a socialist revolution would come only when capitalism was fully developed. This was hardly the case in Russia; the February Revolution had merely released the country from feudalism. Accordingly, the Marxists assumed it would be some time before their hour came.

However, time turned out to be in short supply. The Provisional Government had badly misjudged the public mood. Its members thought that the revolutionary ferment in the capital had been directed not against the war but against the Tsar's inept handling of it. With them in charge, things would go better. In fact, people were fed up with the war itself, and were not prepared to wait any longer for the social reforms which were desperately needed. The Provisional Government found itself confronting chaos: peasants grabbed land from their former masters; soldiers deserted *en masse* from the army; relations between factory workers and managers deteriorated; and the food shortages in the cities grew ever worse. Supported and encouraged by the Marxists, the nation declared its priorities – 'bread, peace and land'. If the Provisional Government could not provide this, then the solution had to be – as the banners at demonstrations urged – 'All Power to the Soviets.'

So, only eight months after the Provisional Government had taken over, it was toppled by a second revolution. This took place in October 1917, in the name of the Soviets and under the leadership of Lenin. Lenin had originally been a member of the Social Democratic Workers' Party, but it had split into two after a dispute over what level of commitment could be expected of party members. Lenin wanted all members to take an active role, and his supporters became known as the Bolsheviks, which means simply 'those of the majority'. His opponents, the Mensheviks – 'those of the minority' – felt that it was enough for most members to just pledge their support. This was a crucial difference, since the more relaxed expectations of the Mensheviks could have generated support for a mass party, in contrast to Lenin's small vanguard of revolutionaries. But it was the Bolsheviks who seized the initiative when it became increasingly obvious that a slow passage to socialism was not going to work.

They inherited a country on the verge of collapse. Agricultural production was at an appalling level, there was not enough food to feed the cities, inflation was rampant and wages scarcely covered living costs. The Bolsheviks did, as promised, take the country out of the war, but they plunged it into a civil war instead. The Red Army found itself pitted not only against indigenous White forces (the Russian counter-revolutionaries), but also against troops sent from the West in an attempt, as Winston Churchill so delicately phrased it, to 'strangle Bolshevism in its cradle'.[3] The new 'workers' state' also found itself, ironically, with an increasingly small number of workers. They had formed the backbone of Bolshevik support and were the most willing recruits to the Red Army, so although they were needed to build up the industrial base of the country, they were also the first to be sacrificed to the war effort. Many of those who were not sent to the front fled to the countryside instead, in the desperate hope of finding food.

Conditions were far from conducive to the building of socialism. All the same, the Bolsheviks did make moves in this direction in their first months of power. The Decree on Land expropriated landlords and divided up their large estates between the peasants. The Decree on Workers' Control planned for the democratization of the factories by increasing the powers of workers' committees. The judicial system was to be transformed, with judges elected by the people and serving in 'people's courts'. There was also a decree on the democratization of the army, which would abolish ranks, military insignia and all other forms of army hierarchy, and provide for the elections of officers by soldiers. Laws were amended to ensure women's full equality. Yet the Bolsheviks were severely hampered by a shortage of resources and the more immediate problem of dealing with the Civil War. Few of the new laws were put into effect. Of those which were, many were soon abandoned.

The Decree on Land did survive. However, this was little more than an attempt on the Bolsheviks' part to oversee a process which was already underway: peasants had begun helping themselves to their former masters' land from the moment the Tsar abdicated. The Bolsheviks were far from delighted about the new arrangement, even though they made a show of supporting it. Many peasants settled into family or small-community production, and produced little more than was needed to meet their own needs.[4] This meant there was not enough to feed the city workers and when the food shortage in the cities grew acute, the Bolsheviks were forced to take brutal action. They despatched troops to the countryside, on orders to requisition anything that seemed surplus to the peasants' own needs. The peasants responded by producing even less.

The moves which were made to establish women's equality were more impressive on paper than in reality. Like Marx and Engels before him, Lenin linked women's inferior position in society to their exclusion from the public sphere of work and their confinement to the private sphere of the household. It was necessary to draw them *en masse* into the workforce, and establish a network of state services - laundries, canteens, childcare institutions and so on - to take over the work they normally did at home. This would provide the basis for equality. There was an acute shortage of labour during the Civil War period, which made the first of these principles easy to fulfil. However, there was not enough money in the state coffers to do much about the second.

In any case, with all the other problems the new government had to contend with, women's rights were not seen to be a pressing issue. A more immediate concern was to consolidate the gains of the revolution, and to secure the population's support for the new government. A Women's Department, or *Zhenotdel,* was established within the Communist Party (as the Bolsheviks now called themselves), not to campaign for women's rights but to draw them into the political community. A plethora of women's magazines also appeared, such as *The Woman Worker* (*Rabotnitsa*), *The Woman Peasant* (*Krestyanka*) and *The Woman Kommunist* (*Kommunistka*), not to educate women about feminism, but about communism. The fundamental division in society was seen as that between the bourgeoisie and the proletariat: 'The division into men and women ... has no great significance'[5] the Bolsheviks declared, with one exception - that only women could bear children. Motherhood was presented to them as a moral obligation; it was essential that, in the words of Aleksandra Kollontai, they 'guarantee a steady stream of workers for the worker's republic'.[6]

Despite the crisis situation in the Civil War years, the Bolsheviks somehow found the time and energy to seriously address the role of the cinema in this new society. The film industry was nationalized on 27 August 1919, and was placed under the control of the Commissariat for Enlightenment - a clear indication of its main purpose. The private cinema had been a tool of commercial profiteers; to borrow Mayakovskii's poetic description, 'capitalism (had) covered its eyes with gold'.[7] Now it would be a tool for educating workers and peasants, and encouraging their support for the new system. In other words, it would be a vehicle for government propaganda.

The term 'propaganda' did not have the pejorative meaning it has acquired in the West. The Bolsheviks saw themselves as a vanguard party with a legitimate educational task. In any case, this was a time of war; it was essential to win people's support by whatever means were available. The cinema had great novelty value, and was also thought capable of exerting a peculiarly powerful psychological influence. As Richard Taylor has noted, films are screened in the ideal circumstances for this to happen: people sit in darkness, their attention focused on a single source of light; they are alone but at the same time part of a mass, sharing a common experience. This makes them 'uniquely susceptible to mass emotional reactions'.[8]

This was the conclusion reached by Lev Kuleshov, who became one of the most notable film-makers of the 1920s. He spent evening after evening in cinema halls merely observing audience reaction. He chose the cheapest cinemas where 'the public was less educated and reacted more spontaneously to what they saw'. He decided that films had almost a narcotic effect on them.[9] Such a power could not be squandered on salon dramas. The new society required 'a new, revolutionary cinema . . . which would sweep away all the traditions of cinematography with its ersatz-psychological dramas, with its sugary-sentimental "kings" and "queens" of the screen'.[10] It would be based on 'realism', the analysis of social reality – or, in the words of Russell Campbell, 'sociology . . . with a human face'.[11] The educational theorist Nadezhda Krupskaya, Lenin's wife, spoke in similar terms. She contrasted the Soviet cinema with that of the capitalist countries, where the ruling class 'aims . . . to create images which dull the consciousness of the masses'. The Soviets, on the other hand, 'use the cinema as a tool of knowledge, to enable people to understand the reality which surrounds them'.[12]

This was evidently not what the pre-revolutionary film-makers had in mind. Even before the private film studios were taken into state control, more than half of them had fled Bolshevik territory and settled in towns controlled by the counter-revolutionaries. Odessa, on the coast of the Black Sea, became the virtual Hollywood of the independent film community. Drankov, the founder of the first Russian film studio, was to be found wining and dining in the city's clubs and cabarets, until he moved on to the United States. Vera Kholodnaya went there too, but Odessa was the end of the road for her. Less than a year after she arrived she died in an influenza epidemic which swept through the overcrowded city. Despite her 'defection', her funeral, attended by thousands of mourners, was shown on Soviet cinema newsreel; her old films also continued to appear on Soviet screens long past the revolution.[13]

All the same, 'realism' was to be the hallmark of the new cinema, though there were some disagreements as to what this actually meant. Lenin interpreted it in a literal sense. He thought that newsreel was the best way of delivering the government's message, since it was undiluted by plots and narratives.[14] Audiences had other ideas, however, and their tastes obviously had to be taken into account. The short 'agitation films' of the Civil War period were a compromise, aiming to deliver a political message within the framework of a simple but entertaining plot. Vladimir Gardin's 1921 film *Hammer and Sickle*, for example, as its name suggests, sought to encourage solidarity between industrial workers and peasants. It told the story of Andrei, an impoverished son of the soil, who goes off to Moscow to find work. After a stint in a factory he finds himself caught up in the revolution, fighting in the Red Army. He eventually returns to his village as a committed revolutionary, and sets about exposing a local kulak (a rich peasant) who has been hoarding grain while his fellow villagers suffer the effects of famine. Other films used similar stories to try and dispel religious superstition. [15]

By 1921, the Civil War was over. The Bolsheviks had emerged as the only political force in the country, and had extended their control to almost all of the territory of the former Russian Empire. Yet victory must have seemed somewhat hollow. There was nothing to buy in the shops, and a burgeoning black market had developed around even the most essential needs. The cities had witnessed a dramatic depopulation, and agricultural output was lower than it had been under the Tsar. The popularity of the Bolsheviks was falling even amongst some of its most loyal former supporters. Something had to be done.

3 THE 1920s

In 1921, the New Economic Policy, or NEP, came into being. One of its primary aims was to give peasants the incentive to produce more grain. A tax system was introduced to take the place of requisitioning; the peasants would now only have to give up a fixed proportion of their surplus crop, and could sell the rest at market. For this to be an effective incentive, there would need to be something for them to buy with their earnings. The system had to offer a reasonable supply of consumer goods. In an attempt to revitalize the economy, it was decided to resurrect private enterprise in light industry and the service sector. Until recently, the official word was that this was always seen as a temporary measure, a regrettable side-step away from socialism which would end once the economy was back on its feet. However, with the onset of *perestroika* – which had much in common with the NEP – this position was revised, and the view put forward that shortly before his death, Lenin had come to see the NEP as a possible path to socialism instead of a move away from it. We will return to this later.

The NEP did bring some improvements to the economy, but it also bred much resentment. Many of the old Bolsheviks who had fought in the Revolution were aghast at what they saw as the reversal of socialist aims and the resurrection of capitalist features. A new breed of entrepreneurs known as Nepmen emerged, who were concerned above all with their own profits and who flaunted their new wealth with fancy clothes and in private restaurants. Meanwhile, other people sank into unemployment and poverty.

Women were hit particularly hard. They formed a disproportionate number of the new unemployed since their extra domestic responsibilities made them the least productive, hence the most expendable, workers. Nor were Nepmen inclined to put their money into relatively uneconomic ventures like crèches and canteens. Lenin's preconditions of women's equality, then – their entry into the public sphere of paid work, and their liberation from the confines of the private household - had even less hope of realization in the 1920s than they had during the Civil War.[1]

Nor did relations between men and women receive much attention. Only Aleksandra Kollontai considered this to be a political issue. She discussed love and sexual morality both in her political writings and in a series of short stories, calling for the liberation of love - the 'winged Eros' - from the confines of the old bourgeois family structure. This did not mean that she advocated free love, although this charge was certainly levelled at her. What she meant was that marriage in capitalist society reduced women to the status of property owned by their husbands, and that sex had become little more than a commodity. She wanted to free it from these economic controls.[2]

In some ways love could, indeed, be said to have liberated itself from the family, though not as Kollontai intended. The upheavals brought about by the revolution included a transformation in sexual relations. Brief liaisons were the norm amongst revolutionaries in the Civil War years, and this situation continued into the 1920s. It was exacerbated by the introduction of the so-called 'post-card divorce', which allowed one partner to notify the other by post that their marriage was over. Some men now found marriage an easy way to persuade a woman into sex, knowing that they could terminate the relationship when she got pregnant or when a new woman caught their fancy. Marriages contracted before the revolution also became increasingly fragile. Since women were still weighed down by family and domestic duties, they had fewer opportunities for self-development than men; as Trotskii noted, many wives were rejected and abandoned by their 'new' husbands who now saw them as backward and primitive.[3]

The growing number of impoverished women on the one hand, and the emergence of a new class of entrepreneurs with money to spare on the other, resulted in the reappearance of the 'oldest profession' in the new society. Sex may no longer have been a commodity sold in the bourgeois family, but it was certainly sold on the streets.

Lenin was not happy about this new sexual profligacy. He railed against what he saw as an erroneous equation of communism and sexual freedom - 'the famous theory that in communist society the satisfaction of sexual desires, of love, will be as simple and unimportant as drinking a glass of water'. Of course, he conceded, thirst must be quenched: 'But will the normal man in normal circumstances lie down in the gutter and drink out of a puddle, or out of a glass with a rim greasy from many lips?'[4] Until young people were ready to start families, he said, they should sublimate sexual energy into sport and intellectual pursuits. Kollontai's concern with sexual relations did not go down well, and earned her an unjustified but lasting reputation as the principal advocate of the 'glass of water theory'.

Things were rather different in Central Asia. There the Bolshevik argument that women's inequality was not an issue in itself was rather less tenable. Central Asian women were treated as little more than property, first of their fathers and then their husbands. The veil was still worn, polygamy practised and girls sold into marriage when they were scarcely out of childhood. Obviously, the *Zhenotdel* could not draw women into the political community here unless it first introduced radical changes in family relations. Yet the price women paid for challenging male authority was high. Hundreds were murdered by husbands and brothers when they 'shamed' the family by throwing off the veil, or even by just organizing literacy classes.[5]

Despite the privatization which took place in the NEP period, the film industry remained largely in the hands of the state. A number of film theatres returned to private ownership, however, and their primary concern was profit rather than propaganda. There was, accordingly, a dichotomy between the kind of films being made and the kind being shown. The montage experiments of the so-called 'leftist' directors, such as Eisenstein and Vertov, proved indigestible to the average taste. For the most part, audiences preferred the old Russian costume dramas and imported Americana. So while film history was being made in the studios of the 1920s, the people it was aimed at were hanging portraits of Vera Kholodnaya on their walls, and laughing at the antics of Charlie Chaplin and Buster Keaton.[6]

These non-revolutionary interests were fed by the 'bourgeois' film magazines which had either survived from before the revolution (despite Bolshevik decrees which banned publications opposing the revolution), or had even come into being after it. *Kino-Zhizn'* (*Cinema Life*), first published in 1922, was full of such unrevolutionary material as photographs of old stars, advertisements for cosmetics and debates on which were more popular, romances or detective stories.[7] Even on the tenth anniversary of the October Revolution, in 1927, the country's leaders were dismayed to find that most of the cinemas in Moscow were showing foreign imports instead of films about the revolution.[8]

Some Soviet film-makers began to think that their first priority should be to wean the population from its unhealthy diet of foreign films, even if this meant scaling down the revolutionary and artistic content of their own productions. Accordingly, there was a new spate of psychological dramas of the pre-revolutionary tradition, produced in post-revolutionary studios. The 'leftist' directors, however, wanted the cinema to make a complete break with the past, and were not willing to compromise. They thought that film makers should be trying to educate public taste rather than pandering to its existing level. As Esfir' Shub explained, 'critics have no right to say: "This is an important work of art, but it is a failure" . . . The task of a true critic is to create the climate for such "difficult" works. When an important achievement in the arts takes place, the critics' duty is to help it with their pens so that a temporarily incomprehensible work soon becomes comprehensible to everybody.'[9]

The 'leftists' did not form a homogeneous group, but one thing they did share was a passion for montage, or creative editing. This rested on the notion that the individual frames in a film meant nothing in themselves, they acquired meaning only when assembled in a certain order. In other words they were just raw material, building bricks out of which art could be constructed. Kuleshov first realized the potential of montage when he found that an expression on an actor's face could say very different things depending on what other images came before and after it. An expression of love turned into hunger when it was followed by the image of a bowl of soup, to grief when the soup was replaced by a child's coffin.[10]

It is questionable whether such creative editing is compatible with the notion of 'realism', to which the same film-makers were also pledged – especially since, as we shall see, it was often used as a vehicle for disseminating political messages. There was, however, some dispute over what realism actually meant. Eisenstein argued that 'absolute realism' was not always an accurate form of perception. He described a child's painting he had once seen depicting the lighting of a stove: 'Everything is represented in passably accurate relationship and with great care. Firewood. Stove. Chimney. But what are these zigzags in that huge central rectangle? They turn out to be – matches. Taking into account the crucial importance of these matches for the depicted process, the child provides a proper scale for them.'[11]

Lenin's more literal interpretation of realism found its reflection in the work of documentary-makers, the most celebrated of whom was Dziga Vertov. Vertov saw the fiction film as a bourgeois means of stupefying working-class people; the documentary, on the other hand, would wake them up to reality.[12] He called his productions *Kino-pravda*, or Cine-Truth; their aim was 'To see and show the world, in the name of the world proletarian revolution.'[13] His crew, the *kinoki* (Cine-eyes), took to the streets and filmed what they found there: street scenes, market scenes, Young Pioneers at camp,[14] students at an evening class, government officials at a meeting, workers eating lunch in a canteen. The *kinoki* and their cameras also appeared on screen, so that film-making was itself depicted as part of the great bustle of activity which was taking place in the new Soviet state.

Although the *kinoki* film-editor was a woman – Elizaveta Svilova, Vertov's wife – none of their early films focus on women. They could be said to reflect the general Bolshevik position, that women's emancipation was not an issue in itself but would come about as part of the emancipation of the working class as a whole. Women are not confined to traditional domestic functions in Vertov's films, but play a prominent role in a range of social activities portrayed on screen. All the same, Judith Mayne has suggested that the *kinoki* still do reproduce some traditional aspects of the representation of women. For example, as part of the kaleidoscope of daily city life depicted in their 1929 film *Man with a Movie Camera*, a woman is filmed getting up in the morning: 'That the projectionist is male, and the person whose waking rituals ... are witnessed is female, suggests the classic structure of the man who looks and the woman who is looked at ... the man who controls the image and the woman who *is* the image'.[15] As we shall see, in the 1930s, Vertov turned his attention more directly to women's role in society - and came up with some still more traditional images.

Esfir' Shub was one of very few female directors to achieve prominence in the 1920s, and was, like Vertov, committed to the documentary. Her impact on the film profession was considerable; indeed, she was described by the poet Vladimir Mayakovskii as 'The pride of our cinematography'.[16] She made more than a dozen films, wrote two books and was considered one of the supreme masters of film montage. Yet her work has received far less attention than that of Vertov. Perhaps this is because she blew few fanfares about it herself. As Selezneva puts it, unlike that of the more flamboyant *Kinoki*, 'her work was not attended by declarations'.[17]

Shub began her career as a film editor, which explains her unique contribution to Soviet cinema - the 'compilation' method. This involved re-editing existing material so that it told a new story; newsreel which was originally produced, as Jay Leyda puts it, 'with as little thought of permanent value as is put into a daily newspaper',[18] was transformed in Shub's hands into a testament of her times. Her first such film, and the best received, was *The Fall of the Romanov Dynasty* (1927). It charts the events leading up to the February Revolution against a backdrop of pre-revolutionary Russian life - the elegance of the Tsarist court, the religious rituals of the Orthodox church, the contrast between the wealth of the landowners and the poverty of the peasants. Shub described her work as 'ideological montage'; she reassembled old film sequences in such a way that 'counter-revolutionary material' was transformed into revolutionary statement.[19] For example, a scene showing members of the nobility dancing energetically on the Tsar's yacht is followed by that of peasants working hard on the land. The caption 'sweat' (*do poty*) appears on the screen between the two images, which serves both to link and contrast them. In this way, the audience is compelled to compare the sweat-inducing activities of the different classes, and reach its own political conclusions.

Shub's work of the 1920s does not explicitly address the position of women, but in the early 1930s she did start planning a film which would document the changes which the revolution had brought about in women's lives. She wrote the script for this film – simply entitled *Women* – but the film itself was never made. We will look at the reasons for this in the next chapter.

The work of Sergei Eisenstein could be seen as a compromise between the documentary and fiction film; he himself described it as 'a synthesis of art and documentary'.[20] His films were generally based on historical events, but since they were also replete with metaphor and symbolism, they were a long way from being objective documentary. (This did not stop later documentary-makers from using certain scenes from them, however – in particular, the storming of the Winter Palace in *October* – as if they were a faithful portrayal of events.) We will begin by looking at some of the most significant ideas inherent in his work, and then look at the images of women which they offered.

Eisenstein had worked with Esfir' Shub for a time and derived a number of editing ideas from her. However, he developed them into something that was distinctly his own. Whereas Shub made her political points by demonstrating the contrast between two events which were taking place simultaneously (such as the dancers and the peasants in the example given above), Eisenstein pioneered the use of the symbolic image. His first film, *Strike* (1924), offers a particularly clear example of this. It tells of the fate of pre-revolutionary factory workers who dared to organize a strike for better working conditions, but ended up being massacred by mounted Tsarist troops. The emotional impact of this final scene is heightened by the sudden introduction of the image of a bull being slaughtered in an abattoir.

The film *October* (1928), about the events leading up to the revolution, is literally saturated with such metaphors, though here they are more amusing than horrific. For example, Eisenstein makes clear his attitude towards Kerenskii, leader of the Provisional Government, by intercutting his image on one occasion with that of a preening peacock, on several others with a bust of Napoleon and throughout the film with a variety of Tsarist symbols. That he sees as absurd the last-minute pleas by the Mensheviks to compromise with the Provisional Government is indicated by the sudden ironic appearance of harps in the midst of the frenzied meeting hall where plans for the revolution are being worked out. Eisenstein also used such metaphors to convey his displeasure at women taking on certain roles; we shall look at this later.

Eisenstein rejected the notion that montage was 'a linkage of pieces. Into a chain . . . Bricks arranged in a series to expound an idea.'[21] For him it was a dialectical process, a collision of images which could produce an entirely new concept. It was, accordingly, intended to shock. This clash of images should have the effect of a controlled electric shock on the audience, forcing from it a certain emotional response.

If it sounds as though Eisenstein were attempting to manipulate his audience as if they were Pavlovian dogs, this is no accident. Eisenstein was, indeed, a great admirer of Pavlov, and, like him, saw both animal and human behaviour as the result of conditioned reflexes to external stimuli. If the cinema audience were the human equivalents of Pavlov's dogs, films should function as the electric shocks to which Pavlov subjected them. As Eisenstein put it, the content of a film 'is a series of connecting shocks arranged in a certain sequence and directed at the audience . . . All this material must be arranged and organized in relation to principles which should lead to the desired reaction in the correct proportion.'[22]

Eisenstein's films are celebrated in particular for their crowd scenes. Indeed, his earlier films had no individual heroes; that role went to 'the masses'. Rarely did the audience learn the names of any of the characters on screen; their collective action, not their individual attributes, was the focus of attention. When Lenin made an appearance in *October* (played by an unknown worker), he too functioned as little more than a cipher. As the poet Mayakovskii complained, although Lenin struck the right poses, 'behind this exterior you can feel complete emptiness, the complete absence of life'.[23]

The most famous crowd scene appears in *Battleship Potemkin* (1926), a film about the mutiny of sailors in Odessa during the 1905 uprising. A crowd has gathered on the Odessa Steps leading down to the docks, to show support for the sailors, but suddenly they become aware that a battalion of troops has amassed at the top of the steps and has begun moving towards them. The image of soldiers' legs marching in slow formation down the steps alternates with scenes of the terrified crowd scattering before them. Individual figures are picked out from the crowd but in the words of Soviet critic Adrian Pyotrovskii, 'they emerge only to dissolve once more into the mass'.[24]

Curiously, these individual figures are almost exclusively female. One woman walks in protest towards the troops cradling her dying child in her arms; another attempts to organize a small crowd around her to challenge the soldiers; a third stands frozen in terror beside her infant's pram. All are mowed down by the troops. The young woman with the pram provides the most memorable image in the sequence because of the way the camera records it. As she falls back from the force of the bullet she dislodges the pram, sending it bumping down the steps by itself. The camera, which until now has merely observed the surging crowd, suddenly moves with it, following the pram and focusing its gaze on the screaming face of the child. In this way, Eisenstein demands and directs the sympathy of the audience.

Women and children also figure prominently in the massacre scene in *Strike*. The soldiers cruelly thrash one woman, threaten another with violence and drop a small infant over a parapet to its death. In fact, women come into their own in Eisenstein's films in scenes depicting the brutality of the Tsarist regime. Evidently this is a way of highlighting the ruthlessness of the Tsarist troops.

It could also be argued that women are used to symbolize the Russian people, abused victims of an inhumane system.

At the same time, women are also depicted in Eisenstein's films as symbols of cruelty. In *October* these two different uses of the female figure - as the embodiments of purity and evil - appear side by side in early scenes depicting the suppression of a workers' demonstration. Forces loyal to the Provisional Government raise the drawbridges across the Neva river in order to cut off the workers' suburbs from the city centre, and a young woman in a horse-drawn cab is caught mid-way. As the horse begins to slither through the widening gap, the camera rests on the poignant image of the innocent victim's long blonde hair fanned out across the ground. The very next scene shows a group of bourgeois women brutally attacking a young Bolshevik, the delighted expressions on their hard faces showing how they relish his pain. How can we explain this seemingly contradictory use of woman to portray both innocence and cruelty? It could be argued that the woman functions not as the epitome of a certain kind of morality, but as a standard of morality in general. In the case of the proletariat and the Bolsheviks, this is positive; with the bourgeoisie it is horribly warped.

The image of the bourgeois woman is often imbued with distinctly sexual overtones. This is especially clear in *Strike*, where there are two principal images of womanhood - the wives of the striking workers, who are pictured in an entirely domestic setting and betray not a hint of sexuality, and the consorts of male capitalists, whose clothes and manners are clearly seductive. This, of course, is the classic dichotomy embedded in Western as well as Russian culture - woman as madonna, or woman as whore. Eisenstein had an evident fascination for the contrast. On holiday once in Mont St Michel, he is said to have been delighted by the discovery of two post-cards depicting the same woman; in one she was dressed up as a saint, in the other as a whore in the arms of a sailor.[25]

There is a clear contrast in *Strike* between the private domestic space of the woman and the public space peopled by men. The factory is pictured as a virtually all-male domain, which was hardly a true reflection of reality. Russia, like all industrializing countries, had seen a steady increase in its female workforce before the revolution: by 1901 women already formed 26.1 per cent of the total workforce, and the First World War pushed this figure up to 40 per cent.[26] Yet although Eisenstein shows women marching alongside their menfolk in demonstrations, there is scarcely a female face to be seen in the factory scenes. The one exception is that in which the workers discuss the demands they will put to their bosses. The male workers seek a shorter working week and more pay; a lone female worker demurely asks for 'courteous treatment' on the part of the management.

On the other hand, when the strike results in workers spending long periods at home, they find themselves thrust into an all-female environment which excludes them. The women wash the children and prepare the food, while the men have little to do but lie around and sleep. The extra time they now have does not facilitate their entry into the female world; indeed, as the strike continues, their wives becoming increasingly irked by their presence, or at least by the financial crisis which it brings about.

It is not the case, however, that Eisenstein's films depict only the familiar gender stereotypes. In *October*, he also offers what at first glance seems a very different view of womanhood – the female soldier, in the all-female Shock Battalion of Death which defends the Winter Palace against the Bolsheviks. While a female battalion certainly did exist during the rule of the Provisional Government, the journal *Novyi Lef (New Left)* noted, in the year of the film's release, that Eisenstein gave it far greater prominence than it had in reality.[27] As the images unfold, however, it quickly becomes clear that he disapproves of women in uniform: an empty wine bottle rests comically on the arm of a nearby statue, suggesting that they are drunk; a somewhat furtive clasping of hands hints at lesbianism; a statue of a woman teaching a child to walk is juxtaposed with, and then provides the backdrop for, female soldiers at bayonet practice – in this way a 'natural' female activity is contrasted with one which apparently defies nature. (The thrusting bayonets also hint at an aggressive, masculine sexuality; Freudian symbolism appears on a number of occasions throughout Eisenstein's films.) One female soldier catches sight of a Rodin sculpture depicting two lovers embracing, and tears spring to her eyes; the implication is that she is shocked at the comparison between her role and that of the woman in the statue. As *Novyi Lef* pointed out, Eisenstein was mocking the idea of women in the military: 'Carried away by his satirical portrayal of the woman soldier, he creates, instead of a satire on the women who defended the Provisional Government, a general satire on women who take up arms for any cause at all.'[28] In contrast, the Bolshevik women pictured in the film are all engaged in administrative tasks, helping the revolution by handing over arms and provisions to the male revolutionaries.

Eisenstein's 1929 film *The Old and the New*, about an early voluntary experiment in the collectivization of agriculture, breaks his usual mould in more than one way. Firstly, it offers an individual rather than a collective hero; secondly, that hero is female. In accordance with Eisenstein's general preference for 'real people' rather than trained actors, the heroine was herself a peasant woman, Marfa Lapkina. She had worked as a farm labourer since she was 9 years old, was uneducated and illiterate and had a small child whom she insisted on bringing with her to every shoot. She was pregnant again before the film was finished, and the last scenes had to be shot in such a way as to disguise her rapidly expanding body.[29] Yet although Eisenstein took great pains to find his unconventional 'star', audiences were not impressed. As Oksana Bulgakova explains in her chapter in this book, people went to the cinema halls for a taste of glamour, a respite from reality; they did not want reality leaping out at them from the screen.

Eisenstein began the film in 1926, but it was postponed when he was asked to make *October* for the tenth anniversary of the revolution. Ironically, this meant that *The Old and the New* was finally released the same year that Stalin's forced collectivization drive began - a process which met with determined resistance and resulted in countless deaths and deportations. Eisenstein's peasants, however, have pooled their land voluntarily, though with considerable persuasion from Lapkina and from the local Party representative. This entitles them to government credit, which enables them to invest in a bull, a milk separator and a tractor. By the end of the film they are set for a golden future as a milk co-operative.

The Old and the New is a celebration of the mechanization and collectivization of agriculture, not of a new image of womanhood. Lapkina could be said to function, once again, as a symbol; she is Russia, the land, the peasantry. Under the guidance of the Party, she - Lapkina/Russia - will embrace the new ways. Far from being a film about women's changing roles, Eisenstein is more concerned with portraying the relative *absence* of women from the work process which the mechanization of agriculture will bring about. As he explained himself, before mechanization, the fields were full of them:

> Rows of women raking,
> Women turning the hay.[30]

Once the machines have taken over, 'There are no women. The claws of the hay spreading machine lightly and loosely spread the hay that has been thrown to one side. There are no women . . .'[31]

In fact, the machines are the film's real heroes. The milk separator is depicted as a virtual god, promising the peasants heaven on earth; but unlike the one they worshipped in the past (and much attention is given to the worthlessness of religious ritual), this one will not let them down. The scene in which the milk separator performs its first miracle is an astonishing combination of religious and sexual imagery. The peasants' faces shine with the joy of requited faith as, after building up to its climax, the machine literally spurts its substance over them.

In conclusion, then, if Eisenstein's characters in general function for the most part as ciphers, this is especially the case with women. They represent above all a measuring stick of morality, the Russian people and the motherland. He was not the only director of the 1920s of whom this could be said.

In Vsevolod Pudovkin's celebrated *Mother* (1926), we find another clearly symbolic use of the female figure. Pudovkin's films have often been compared and contrasted to those of Eisenstein.[32] There are a number of reasons for this. Firstly, and most obviously, they depict the same or similar events. *Mother*, like *Battleship Potemkin*, is set in 1905, a year of great political unrest; Pudovkin's *The End of St Petersburg* (1927) and Eisenstein's *October* are both about the 1917 revolutions. Secondly, the two directors approached their subject matter from very different angles. To borrow Yurii Vorontsov and Igor Rachuk's description, Eisenstein painted revolutionary events 'on a large scale'; Pudovkin was more concerned with showing how individual lives were affected by them. Eisenstein's hero was 'the mass', while Pudovkin plucked individuals out of the mass and looked at the unfolding of history through their eyes.[33]

This personalized view of history made Pudovkin's films rather more accessible than those of Eisenstein. *October* in particular was singled out by critics as a difficult film which confused its audience; 'it does not arouse our feelings and it acts entirely upon our reason', one contemporary observer explained.[34] *Mother*, on the other hand, was one of the few films by a leftist director which met with untrammelled enthusiasm from all quarters. In fact, Pudovkin is said to have been somewhat put out by the scale of his success; as Vorontsov and Rachuk put it, 'he had tried to be innovative, and new methods in art do not always find acceptance with the mass of viewers. He began to wonder if he had given way to traditional tastes.'[35]

Mother was based, albeit very loosely, on Maksim Gorkii's novel of the same name. Though it deviates considerably from the original, both the book and the film could be said to have the same basic purpose. This is to portray the growing self-awareness and politicization of one poor, uneducated woman, who becomes converted to the revolutionary cause already embraced by her son, Pavel. This enables her to move beyond the boundaries of a purely domestic existence and take a place in the broader social world. As Judith Mayne puts it, 'she moves from an identity defined exclusively in patriarchal terms to an identity shaped by commitment to political struggle'.[36] However, as Mayne goes on to note, the film turns out to be not so much a challenge to patriarchy as a rewriting of it.

The mother's personality does not undergo any kind of profound development as a result of her political activity. In fact, the principal change she experiences is that her relationship with her son moves onto a new plane. Although she does come to understand the justice of the cause, her initial conversion stems not from this but from love and loyalty to her son, and the guilt she feels at her own inadvertent complicity in his arrest: he has stored weapons beneath the floorboards of their house and she gives him away to the police, naïvely convinced by their assurances that they will not detain him if they are told the truth. Her subsequent political activity consists of carrying on Pavel's work while he is in prison, so whereas she was once his domestic servant, she now becomes his political assistant.

Like *Strike*, the film sets up a clear contrast between private and public space. Initially, the mother's sole domain is the home. The world beyond it - the factory, and the bar where the workers head on leaving it in search of solace - are peopled exclusively by men. However, Pudovkin does not redefine the relationship between them once the mother's political activities propel her into the public realm. As Mayne points out, the private space is merely obliterated; after the mother's political awakening we see inside the home only once again, to find her using her son's old hiding place to store political leaflets.[37] Hence her relationship to the private space has become much the same as his - it is merely a background to public activity. Who will now do the cooking and the cleaning is left to the imagination. The scene in which we see the mother retrieving the leaflets from their hiding place so mirrors that in which Pavel hid the guns that it also serves to emphasize the mother's role not as an independent political actor, but as an extension of her son.

There is one other significant female character in the film, the only woman in Pavel's group of revolutionaries. She evidently does not work in the factory, and when she is pictured together with her comrades she is always physically at a small distance from them. From her facial expressions, it soon becomes apparent that she is in love with Pavel and we cannot even be sure that her involvement in politics is not just a way of getting close to him. Unlike in Gorkii's novel, there is no hint of a developing relationship between her and the mother. Again, then, she cannot be said to function as an autonomous individual. She, like the mother, is merely a support for Pavel.

We have noted already that Pudovkin, unlike Eisenstein, is credited with developing his characters as individuals rather than using them merely as symbols. However, this does not mean that his films function only on a simple narrative level. The principal characters in *Mother* have a clearly symbolic message as well. The father is a cruel drunkard who continually mistreats his wife. He represents the forces of reaction, or, as Richard Taylor puts it, 'the old ways: tyranny, brutality, autocracy'. The son, on the other hand, is the golden future, 'a world of freedom, equality and justice'.[38] What, then, does the mother symbolize? Once again, she is the land and the people: the mother is actually Mother Russia. At first, she is under the yoke of the old autocracy, but even when this proves mortal, she is held back by ignorance, naïveity and the inertia born of years of repression. Only under the enlightened influence of Pavel - Bolshevism, harbinger of the new order - does she embrace the revolution. The images of nature which recur throughout the film, and particularly the image of the unfolding of seasons, could be said to suggest the naturalness and inevitability of the revolution, as well as strengthening the mental link between the mother and the land she represents.

Both mother and son perish at the end of the film. However, in her final moments the mother is seen holding aloft the revolutionaries' banner and gazing, statuesque, towards the future - perhaps a Russian version of Marianne, the French symbol of the Republic and of civic virtue [39] - before she is trampled by mounted police. This is arguably the most crucial scene in the film. Indeed, Pudovkin himself said that it provided the starting point for the script-writer, Natan Zarkhi: 'When he began work . . . Zarkhi first of all clearly imagined - literally in visual terms - the image of the old mother lying on the bridge with the torn banner clutched to her breast'.[40] In the film's last scene the banner is flying above the Kremlin, signifying that the glorious future she envisaged has finally arrived.

In Pudovkin's next film, *The End of St Petersburg*, the protagonist is definitely male. In fact, there are few female figures in the film at all. One woman does play a significant role, however, even though she appears only briefly at intervals throughout the film. Once again, she is not a revolutionary in her own right but only becomes one through her relationship with a man - in this case her husband, the Bolshevik organizer in a Petersburg factory. The relationship between husband and wife is reminiscent in a number of ways of that between Pavel and his mother. Initially, the woman is resistant to the revolution; while her husband is organizing a strike at the factory, she can only think of the financial privation this will bring. However, his arrest serves to force her to rethink her position, just as Pavel's did in *Mother*. In contrast to *Mother*, it is not she herself who brings about her man's arrest, but a destitute young peasant who had come to the city looking for work. Yet she was inadvertently complicit: earlier, she had advised the new arrival to ignore the strike and find himself a job, so angry was she at the difficulties the strike had made for her. He had done so, and was persuaded by his new bosses to inform on the strike's organizer. Her husband's downfall convinces her of the need for solidarity. In the final scene, just after the revolution, she finds her husband inside the Winter Palace with the victorious Bolsheviks. He looks at her uncertainly, but she proclaims loudly: 'Long live the city of Lenin!' Again, the woman is the symbol of Russia, finally accepting the need for, and the inevitability of, the revolution.

It would seem that neither Eisenstein nor Pudovkin was concerned about creating a model of the 'new woman' *per se*. This was not the case with all of the directors of the 1920s, however. A veritable array of films appeared in that decade which either tackled the 'woman question' directly, or at least included unconventional images of womanhood in films about other subjects.

Aleksandra Khokhlova, wife of the director Lev Kuleshov and the leading actress in all of his films, provides the best example of the latter. She offers a complete contrast to the classical beauties of pre-revolutionary Russian cinema, the 'queens of the screen'. She is skinny and eccentric, a 'character actress' instead of a beauty. In a way, she can be seen as the post-revolutionary counterpart of Vera Kholodnaya. While Kholodnaya symbolized the passive female victim of the old era, Khokhlova's odd appearance hints at women's liberation from the conventions of that era. She could be described as the 'new woman' incarnate.

The long collaboration between Kuleshov and Khokhlova began in 1920 when Kuleshov founded his 'Workshop for Failed Actors'. This came about completely by chance, when he dropped into VGIK (The All-Union State Institute of Cinematography) one day and came across a group of despondent students who had just failed their first round of exams. He offered to help prepare them for the second attempt, and devised a new acting technique which became known as 'the Kuleshov method'; this replaced the old, slow style of theatre acting with one geared towards the cinema, placing stress on movement. When they were re-examined, the students gained top marks.

In contrast to Vertov and Shub, Kuleshov was an unabashed devotee of the fiction film. In contrast to Eisenstein and Pudovkin, he made films which were light-hearted to the point of flightiness. He did not reject the educational function of the Soviet cinema, but felt it could best be incorporated into a good yarn. Above all, the cinema's function was to entertain its audience, and instead of denouncing the bourgeois cinema of the West, Kuleshov felt that much could be learned from it. In fact he had, as he put it, 'Americanitis' – an infatuation with the energy and dynamism of the Hollywood movie. The most obvious example of this can be found in his 1924 film, *The Extraordinary Adventures of Mr West in the Land of the Bolsheviks*.

Mr West is a delightful, eccentric comedy which playfully parodies Soviet stereotypes about Americans and vice versa. A good-natured but thoroughly naïve New Yorker, 'Mr West', has come to the Soviet Union on a business trip. The anti-Soviet propaganda which fills the pages of the New York papers has convinced him that the Bolsheviks are evil, shaggy-haired primitives in animal skins. Accordingly, he brings along a bodyguard, a lasso-swinging cowboy called Jeddy. Jeddy can afford him little protection against these Soviet villains, however. Mr West immediately falls victim to a gang of crooks who discover and manipulate his fear of the Bolsheviks, extracting wads of dollars from him for the purpose of 'protection'. Jeddy, who has managed to lose his master, can do nothing but race round the city in futile pursuit, giving Kuleshov the opportunity to transpose Hollywood chase-scenes to the snowy streets of Moscow. Finally, Mr West is rescued by a real Bolshevik, and the film ends with his new friend giving him a rather more positive view of the city. He ends up a convert to Bolshevism: 'Burn the New York papers,' he cables his wife enthusiastically, 'and hang a portrait of Lenin in the study!' This is revolutionary propaganda at its most entertaining.

Aleksandra Khokhlova plays a member of the gang of criminals which kidnaps Mr West. She is a 'countess' according to the film's titles, though the inverted commas round the word leave it to us to decide whether she is a real dispossessed aristocrat or representative of the criminal element thrown up by the NEP. While the women of pre-revolutionary cinema were tempted and ultimately destroyed by charming but ruthless seducers, it is 'the countess' who does the seducing in *Mr West*. She is no victim of passion; instead she is portrayed as a woman totally in charge of her sexuality, using it to get what she wants from her own hapless victim. Mr West fares better than the female victims of the past; he manages to overcome temptation by avidly studying a portrait of his wife. His resolve is evidently slipping, however, and with a little more time – or if this had been a drama rather than a playful comedy – the countess may well have caught her quarry. Another noteworthy point about Khokhlova's heroine is that she gives no hint either of present or pending motherhood. In an ideological climate which stressed women's maternal duties as well as their equal rights, this is indeed a rare occurrence.

Yet Khokhlova ultimately proved unacceptable to critics, audiences and, finally, the film industry as a whole. This is an indication of how limited the change in women's status really was. As Kuleshov put it, the cinema was still in 'pursuit of beauties'; the prevailing attitude was that 'one must film only pretty girls'. Although Kuleshov dismissed this as 'hidden pornography or psycho-pathology, for which there is absolutely no place in Soviet cinematography', he was eventually forced to give in to it when it became clear that he would only be allowed to continue making films if he agreed not to use Khokhlova in them.[41]

Grigorii Kozintsev and Leonid Trauberg also explored images of 'new women' at their Factory of the Eccentric Actor (FEKS) in Leningrad. The odd title of their studio was coined in 1922 when, still teenagers, they arrived in the city from the provinces and sent out advertisements inviting young people to join them in putting on pantomimes and street performances. They were 'discovered' by the head of the city's film studio, and FEKS was propelled into film-making. Like Kuleshov, they took their inspiration from the Hollywood comedy, adapted to Soviet purposes. Their films were even more eccentric than his, an 'unrestrained collection of stunts', as one Soviet writer put it.[42]

Their first film, made in 1924, was a short comedy called *Adventures of Oktyabrina*. 'Oktyabrina' would translate roughly as 'woman of the October Revolution'. The heroine was an ardent member of the Komsomol (the

Communist Youth League), the manager of an apartment block and the proud bearer of a Red Army beret; her adventures included bringing to justice a tax-evading Nepman, and foiling an attempt by a foreign capitalist to recover his Tsarist debts. This foreign villain represented the United States, Britain and France, which had each sent troops to Russia during the Civil War to help the counter-revolutionary forces (to help audiences get the point, his name – Coolidge Curzonovich Poincaré – was an amalgamation of those of the president of the United States, the British foreign secretary and the French prime minister). It seems likely that Oktryabrina also functioned as a symbol – the embodiment of the new socialist society.

The FEKS film which produced the greatest controversy was *New Babylon*, made in 1929. Viktor Shklovskii described it as a cinematic version of a French impressionist painting,[43] meaning that it was way above the heads of the average audience. Like many other films of the 1920s it is set in the past, positing a continuity between the Russian revolution and earlier revolutionary upheavals. In this case, the setting is Paris in 1871, the time of the Commune.

New Babylon has such a profusion of symbols that they take some sorting out. The film's name refers to a Parisian department store-cum-nightclub in which the opening scenes are set, and which appears again and again at intervals throughout the film. It is a place of corruption and debauchery, of fat businessmen wooed by drunken prostitutes; it is full of luscious fabrics and twirling decorative parasols. It represents Paris under the old administration, before the establishment of the Commune. This bacchanalian Paris is also symbolized by a bawdy showgirl, a cigar in one hand and a glass of champagne in the other. France is not much better – another showgirl, surrounded by symbols of the country, grins seductively at the audience. The country has evidently sold itself to the Prussians: a caption reads, 'Paris the Gay, Paris the Replete, Paris the Carefree . . .'; the irony becomes clear when we suddenly learn that the French army has been crushed.

The same words are repeated, with even greater irony, when the camera shows us the city's poor. Impoverished, exhausted female workers are washing clothes in a laundry; a sick woman lies untended in bed; people sleep rough in the streets. It is these seemingly hopeless people, however, who form a militia to defend the city. When the Provisional Government orders them to surrender, they set up their own government, and the Paris Commune is born.

Once the city is governed by the Communards, the drudgery and misery abruptly ceases. The women are still washing clothes, but they are laughing happily as they work; seamstresses grin over their sewing machines. Parisians are working for themselves now, not for the bosses. They introduce new and enlightened laws to protect the rights of Paris citizens – the same laws which the Bolsheviks will later introduce in Russia.

It is not patriotism which leads the citizens to defend the city. When an army officer later appeals to them 'as fellow Frenchmen', they yell back, 'That's a lie. We're not Frenchmen - we're Communards!' Accordingly, the film's young heroine, Louise, represents not France, but the new order.

Louise, a shopgirl at New Babylon, is one of the founders of the Commune. Her moral conviction is contrasted with the weakness and uncertainty of Jean, a young soldier undergoing a crisis of conscience. He is tempted to throw in his lot with the Communards, but is exhausted and demoralized and cannot bring himself to do so. He just wants to return to his village and have done with the fighting. This, however, is not to be his destiny. On the narrative level, he falls in love with Louise, and becomes obsessed with her; on the symbolic level, he represents the old order teetering on the brink of capitulation to the new. The time, however, is not yet ripe for socialism in France.

The Communards are defeated and sentenced to death. The officer in charge is attracted to Louise, and offers her a reprieve if she pretends she was a prostitute rather than a committed Communard. She slaps his face, so signing her own death warrant. Jean, who has been desperately searching for Louise, arrives just in time to witness this exchange. He almost strikes the officer with the spade he is bearing but his moment of courage and potential conversion passes. Instead, he is forced to use the spade to dig Louise's grave. Yet despite the deaths of the heroes, the film finishes, like Pudovkin's *Mother*, on a note of optimism. Louise yells at Jean that they will meet again; her fellow Communards join her in declaring defiantly that they will be back. This could signify that Paris will one day be under communist rule. More likely, Kozintsev and Trauberg are implying that the Commune has now been reincarnated in Russia.

In *New Babylon*, we have a gender reversal of the symbolism in Pudovkin's *Mother*. Louise takes over Pavel's role as the embodiment of the new order; Jean is in the mother's place, representing a confused nation unsure about which way to turn. Although both Jean and the mother hover for some time on the brink of conversion, they end up going in different directions - the mother crosses the barrier and embraces the revolutionary cause, while Jean falls back and allows himself to become the instrument by which the revolution is buried. The implication is that Russia was ready for revolution; France, alas, was not.

New Babylon is one of the finest Soviet films of the 1920s, a mass of energy and innovation. It was not well received by either critics or audiences, however. This lack of enthusiasm had little to do with the characterization of its heroine. The film was simply too avant-garde for the average cinema-goer: the cinema's 'Rite of Spring', to borrow Denise Youngblood's analogy.[44] It was also unfortunate in its timing. By 1929, experimentation in the cinema was on its last gasp; so was the chance to produce a new art form for the screen. The new model for film-makers was 'proletarian cinema', which would become the hallmark of Stalin's Socialist Realism. Pavel Petrov-Bytov, writing in *Zhizn' Iskusstvo*, argued that *New Babylon* was virtually incomprehensible, a text written in a foreign language: 'We . . . do not have to be like the Frenchman explaining, in his own language, "art for art's sake" to a Russian. The Russian will spit and walk out, just as the public is walking out of *New Babylon*'.[45] He went on to say that instead of advocating 'art for art's sake', the cinema should be addressing the needs and concerns of ordinary people: 'What do we have to offer the peasant woman, thinking with her ponderous and sluggish brain about her husband who has gone to make a living in the town, about the cow that is sick in the dirty cow-shed with tuberculosis of the lungs, about the starving horse that has broken its leg, about the child that is stirring in her womb?'[46] Louise, shop-girl turned Communard, was apparently not an appropriate role model for Russian womanhood.

Abram Room's 1927 film *No. 3 Meshchanskaya Street* (better known abroad as *Bed and Sofa*) was also highly controversial, though for very different reasons. The film deals with a number of issues of topical concern at that time, such as the chronic housing situation in Moscow, the new sexual mores of the post-revolutionary era and the impact of the revolution on relationships between men and women. In short, it tackled the 'woman question' head on. Ultimately, it is an exploration of one woman's process of self-development. So, once again, although it is a much more light-hearted film, it begs some comparison with Pudovkin's *Mother*. This time, however, the woman develops successfully not through her relationship with a man, but when she breaks free of this relationship. This renders Room's portrait of womanhood far more revolutionary than that of Pudovkin, though his heroine's development is personal rather than political.

The film opens with a young man, Volodya, heading by train towards Moscow early one morning. The scene then switches to Meshchanskaya Street, where Lyuda and Kolya are waking up in their cluttered one-room apartment. The street's name gives the audience a clue about the type of people it is to meet: Meshchanskaya means 'petty-bourgeois'. Watching their morning ritual, we soon grasp the unrevolutionary nature of their relationship. It is based on entirely unreconstructed gender roles. Lyuda's life is confined to the private domestic sphere, a daily grind of housekeeping for a husband who takes her for granted. Kolya, on the other hand, moves between the private sphere of home and the public sphere of work. Lyuda is irritable and frustrated as another day of tedium stretches before her, while Kolya heads off to his job as a building supervisor with pleasure and optimism. Lyuda is buried within the oppressive confines of the basement flat, with only a window to give her limited access to the world above her head. Kolya is working on the roof of the Bolshoi theatre and is literally on top of the world, looking with delight at the city spread beneath him.

Volodya turns out to be an old friend of Kolya's. He has found a job in Moscow but, given the housing shortage, has nowhere to live. Lyuda and Kolya have only the one room, but Kolya insists that his friend move in and sleep on the sofa. At first Lyuda is furious, but her anger dissolves when Volodya turns out to be rather more attentive to her than her husband generally is. When Kolya goes away on a business trip, Volodya's attentions increase. He gives Lyuda some link with the outside world by bringing home a radio, a magazine. He takes her on an aeroplane ride, which gives her an even more commanding view of the city than Kolya had from the top of the Bolshoi theatre. He takes her to the cinema, the first time she has been to see a film for as long as she can remember, though we know it is a passion of hers since a cover of the magazine *Ekran* (*Screen*) hangs on the wall. When Kolya comes back from his trip he finds that Volodya is no longer sleeping on the sofa.

Kolya attempts to find somewhere else to live but has no more luck than Volodya did. Lyuda, feeling guilty, suggests he take over the sofa now. He and Volodya quickly re-establish their old friendship and spend their evenings playing checkers, while Lyuda finds herself keeping house for the two of them. One day, in a fit of exasperation, she prepares to leave the flat, but Volodya locks her in; her estwhile liberator has become her jailor. Volodya reclaims the sofa, and Kolya takes his old place in the bed.

Then Lyuda finds she is pregnant. Notwithstanding their friendship, neither of the men is happy at the prospect of taking responsibility for a child which the other may have fathered, so Lyuda is bullied into an abortion. As she is awaiting her turn at the clinic, she looks through the window – and the world outside seems suddenly replete with babies. She resolutely leaves the clinic, writes a curt note for the two men and sets off for an unknown destination to bring up her child alone. The film ends as it began, with a train speeding through a bright open landscape; but this time it is the woman who is surrounded by light and space, while the two men are left within the cramped confines of the room.

Despite the enormous differences between Pudovkin's *Mother* and Room's *Bed and Sofa*, they do have one obvious thing in common – they both depict motherhood as a source of liberation. In *Mother*, the heroine's political development stems from devotion to her son; in *Bed and Sofa*, the heroine's personal development stems from commitment to her unborn child. In both cases, motherhood is not what traps women in the private domestic sphere, but what releases them from it. However ironic this may seem from our vantage point, it is not a surprising position to find in the Soviet Union in the 1920s.

As we have noted, Bolshevik ideology placed considerable stress on women's maternal duty; it also made a strong link between women's equality and the right to have children without fear for the future. Aleksandra Kollontai claimed in 1914 that in a socialist society, when a woman gets pregnant, 'she does not have to worry about what will happen to her or the child. Society, that big happy family, will look after everything.'[47] Lyuda is not quite so confident; she assures herself, though with evident unease, that she will be able to find a job and support herself and the child. Given the high level of unemployment in the 1920s, and the limited resources which were allotted to domestic and maternal services, it would be interesting to learn what actually did happen to them. Alas, Room did not give us a sequel.

Bed and Sofa could also be interpreted on a more symbolic level, like so many of the films of this era. The train with which the film begins and ends could represent a transition to the new society; the apartment on Meshchanskaya Street, on the other hand, is the lazy, stagnant world of the petty-bourgeoisie, refusing to play its part in the building of socialism. When Volodya arrives in Moscow by train and installs himself at Meshchanskaya Street, he introduces aspects of the new society into the lives he finds there. The sharp division between private and public space begins to erode, and Lyuda begins - quite literally - to see wider horizons opening up before her. Rather than freeing Kolya and Lyuda from petty-bourgeois habits, however, Volodya begins to adopt them himself, and sinks into the inertia represented by the fussy apartment. Lyuda, on the other hand, succeeds in escaping from them. When she leaves Moscow by train, she - and, more significantly, the young life she carries inside her - are heading off not just towards a new personal future, but also towards a new society.

Bed and Sofa was not generally well received. Some critics admonished it mildly for not developing the heroine's self-awakening sufficiently. Others accused it of being 'psycho-pathological' and non-revolutionary, concerned with social misfits instead of people who were actively involved in the construction of a new society. One rural delegate to a Party conference on the cinema suggested that city film-makers should be more attuned to the impact their films would have on country audiences - 'the peasants come out spitting - "Ah, so that's how they behave in the city!".'[48] Just as the Bolsheviks eschewed political discussion on relations between the sexes, neither did they welcome their depiction on screen.

Yakov Protazanov offered a rather different version of the 'new woman' in The Forty First (1927), based on a short story by B. Lavrenev.[49] The film is set during the Civil War and the heroine, Maryutka, is a tough Bolshevik sharp-shooter trying to recapture Central Asia from counter-revolutionary forces. She takes great delight in counting her victims; she has already rid the revolution of forty of its enemies when she is entrusted with the task of escorting a captured White Army officer back to base. When the boat on which they are travelling is ship-wrecked, Maryutka and her prisoner find themselves castaways on a desert island. Forced into prolonged intimate contact, they begin to discover a humanity in each other which overrides their ideological differences. Maryutka's hard exterior conceals a girlish femininity, a maternal urge to nurture. The two eventually become lovers, and begin tentatively to discuss the possibility of a future life together. Then, one day, a ship appears on the horizon. Maryutka's elation turns to horror when she realizes that it is an enemy ship, and that her lover is enthusiastically flagging it down. Her sense of duty prevails, and her lover becomes her forty-first victim.

The Forty First can be seen as a Romeo and Juliet tale, adjusted to the circumstances of the Russian Revolution. It also provides a particularly clear example of the struggle between old and new images of womanhood. Soviet critic Miron Chernenko notes that Protazanov had a preoccupation with conflict which comes across in all of his films: the collision between the old society and the new, between feelings and duty, between the personal and the social. If the film had been made before the revolution, he continues (and Protazanov was one of the few directors of the 1920s whose career began in the Tsarist era), it might have taken the form of a romance between an aristocrat and a worker, and it could have been permitted a happy ending. In the 1920s, however, the couple could not be allowed to enjoy a future together. The new society, and revolutionary duty, had to be victorious.[50]

The film was generally well received. Maryutka's complex personality in particular was applauded; she was said to combine 'the poetics of femininity [and] . . . the strength and incorruptibility of the young partisan'; she had a normal, healthy desire for personal happiness, but would not allow this to get the better of her when it came to defending the Revolution.[51] However, Youngblood notes a sense of confusion on the part of some critics. They were not sure 'whether to regard the end [of the film] as the girl's victory as a Bolshevik or her defeat as a human being'.[52] Given the general resistance to new types of heroine, the woman's 'victory' in overcoming her feelings of love might have also been interpreted by viewers as her 'defeat' as a woman.

Peasant Women of Ryazan (1927), directed by Ol'ga Preobrazhenskaya and Ivan Pravov, placed the 'new woman' in a rural setting. Preobrazhenskaya began her career as an actress, but had moved into directing even before the revolution, in 1916. She went on to become the only woman director, apart from Esfir' Shub, to achieve any stature in the 1920s. In Peasant Women, she contrasts the new Soviet woman with the 'suffering victim' of those pre-revolutionary films. Anna is the victim, a young woman who marries into a wealthy peasant family during the time of the Civil War and is raped by her father-in-law while her husband is off fighting. She bears a child, her husband comes home and rejects her, and she drowns herself in the river. This tragic figure finds her antipode in the husband's tough-willed sister, Vasilisa, who defies her family, lives openly with her lover and even has a life outside of this relationship (she establishes a home for orphaned children).

Peasant Women of Ryazan was a great box office success, and generally had a favourable reception from critics. It was commended for its technical accomplishments, its rural setting (which would ensure a stronger appeal amongst peasants) and its exposure of pre-revolutionary rural traditions. [53] However, it was also criticized for not making enough positive references to Soviet power, nor being sufficiently clear about the positive changes which the revolution had brought. [54] On the whole, it seems to have been judged as much on its presentation of the revolution and rural life as on its images of modern and traditional women. Once again, women and relations between the sexes were apparently seen as fairly marginal.

What, then, can we say about the representation of women in Soviet films of the 1920s, and how this compared with their situation in real life? On cinema screens the image and behaviour of women did undergo considerable change. As we have stressed, however, symbolism was a strong feature of many films of this era, and this has to be borne in mind when looking both at their representation of women and at their exploration of male and female relationships. We have noted, for example, the frequent use of woman and man to represent the old and new orders (or, sometimes, vice versa); hence the relationship between them represents on one level the influence, and sometimes the victory, of one over the other. All the same, it is still the case that a number of directors allowed their female protagonists to leave the confines of domestic space and take up their places in the public arena, even if motherhood often lurked not far around the corner.

In real life, women were generally rather less successful. Little was done to secure their equality, despite proclamations and laws to the contrary. Although abortion was legal, it was frowned on, and motherhood was still promoted not as a choice but as an essential part of female existence. The 'woman question' was not seen as a priority, nor even as a political issue in itself. The high levels of unemployment made it impossible to draw women *en masse* into the public realm of work, and there was too little money to provide the services which would free them from the daily grind of domestic labour. A 'second revolution' was just around the corner, however, which would bring about a more decisive transformation in women's lives – though not one which was altogether welcome.

4 THE STALIN ERA

Lenin had died of a stroke in 1924. While film directors had continued to develop their editing techniques, a power struggle had taken place above them in the upper reaches of the Communist Party. By 1929 it was over: Josef Stalin had succeeded in outmanoeuvring his comrades and had emerged as the country's leader. The Soviet Union was poised on the brink of what has been described as a second revolution, which would arguably have a far greater impact than the first.

That year, Stalin launched a huge industrialization drive which led to the most rapid process of urbanization the world has ever seen. Whole cities sprang up almost overnight, and the urban population more than doubled in a decade.[1] The NEP was brought to an abrupt halt, and the small private businesses were replaced by huge, state-owned industrial enterprises. The production levels for each of them, throughout this vast, multi-national country, were to be decided by Five Year Plans drawn up in Moscow. This system of centralized economic planning would characterize the country for the next six decades. Stalin justified the speed of this venture by pointing to the threat posed by the capitalist West: 'We are fifty or a hundred years behind the advanced countries,' he asserted. 'We must make good this lag in ten years. Either we do it or they crush us.'[2]

There was considerable appeal in the prospect of turning the Soviet Union into an industrial power so rapidly. The Bolsheviks had not expected Russia to remain a socialist island in a hostile sea of capitalism for long. Their revolution, they thought, would be the first of many. Russia had been the 'weakest link' in the capitalist chain, and once the chain had been broken, capitalism as a whole would surely fall apart to be replaced by an international network of socialist countries, the richest holding out fraternal hands to the poor. As the 1920s drew to an end, however, it became increasingly obvious that this was not going to happen. When Stalin adopted as his rallying cry the slogan 'socialism in one country', it met a deep psychological need, a way out of the growing malaise in Soviet society.

If feeding the cities had always been a problem, the sudden swelling of the industrial workforce made it particularly acute. Stalin reverted to the old method of getting grain from the peasants by means of forced requisitioning. In order to reduce the number of collection points, as well as to make production more efficient, the small-scale family farmsteads were amalgamated into large collective farms. Some voluntary collectivization had already taken place, with peasants offered free agricultural machinery as an incentive to pool their land. This, as we have seen, was the subject of one of Eisenstein's films, *The Old and the New*. Yet few peasants had been tempted by the offer. By 1928 only 3 per cent of farmland was under collective control.[3] For Stalin, this process was impossibly slow; by 1936, he had forced 90 per cent of peasant households to collectivize.[4]

The peasants were far from enthusiastic. Many of them slaughtered animals, set fire to crops and even destroyed their own houses rather than have them fall into the hands of the state. Those who failed to co-operate were dismissed as *kulaks*, and were either killed outright or sent into exile to remote and inhospitable regions. (The term *kulak*, which literally means 'fist', had acquired the meaning of 'rich peasant' by the 1930s. Now, however, Stalin applied it to virtually anyone who did not support collectivization.) Estimates of how many peasants fell victim to 'dekulakization' vary, but some say the figure may be as high as 10 million.[5]

The speed of Stalin's social experiment led to gruelling living and working conditions. The mass migrations to the cities exacerbated the already acute housing problem, while the stress on rapid output meant that safety regulations went by the board. Those who expressed doubts about the speed of the venture were labelled 'saboteurs' or 'wreckers', and subject to an increasingly Kafkaesque judicial system. As historian Lionel Kochan puts it, 'The national effort was so comprehensive and inclusive that there could be no questioning of its aims or methods ... What mattered now was the urgency of building socialism – even though the precise meaning of the word might be conceived in practical terms without ideological content.'[6]

Methods of maintaining social control became increasingly brutal. In 1934, the period known as the 'Terror' began. It started with the arrests and show-trials of party and military elites, who were accused of plotting with foreign powers to destroy the Soviet Union. Most of the old revolutionaries were killed, and the party was decimated. Aleksandra Kollontai is one of the few who miraculously managed to survive; this can perhaps be partly explained by the fact that she was Ambassador to Sweden during the most violent years, and so out of Stalin's immediate reach. The officer corps of the Red Army suffered almost total extinction. The terror then spread into every layer of society, in the form of an apparently arbitrary wave of arrests, imprisonments and executions. With the exception of Stalin himself, no one was safe. The secret police might turn up at anyone's apartment, at any time. Since there was no apparent reason for an arrest, there was nothing one could do to avoid it. The Second World War brought a temporary respite from the horror, but it was resumed afterwards and continued up until Stalin's death.

There are no clear answers as to why this happened, nor how it could have continued for such a time. However, it is certain that the country was in a supreme state of social flux. The upheavals of the revolution and the Civil War, the suppression of religion and now the headlong dash towards industrialization and collectivization, had brought about a complete transformation of society. This would almost inevitably have plunged people were into a state of mass disorientation, making them highly susceptible, in the words of Moshe Lewin, to 'a miracle-worker with an appetite for ruling'.[7] With the Orthodox Church in tatters, Stalin was able to establish the communist party as the new church. He, as its head, became a virtual god.

This suggests that Stalin was a cynical manipulator of the popular consciousness. However, a number of scholars caution us against making this simple assumption. Notwithstanding the enormous personal power Stalin amassed, Yurii Bogomolov suggests that he too was in a state of disorientation; Soviet society as a whole was in trance, enveloping 'everyone, from the humblest cook to the General Secretary himself'.[8] As to how this situation came about, Bogomolov subscribes to the view which became prevalent in the Soviet Union in the Gorbachev era - that the origin of all social ills could be linked to the development of the concept of the 'mass' at the expense of the individual. Stalin, he argues, was the logical conclusion of melding the population into a single collective identity, which had the effect of destroying individual responsibility. He was 'the result of the mass, its ideal'; his dictatorship was 'the mask of the dictatorship of the masses'.[9]

Women's lives underwent a huge transformation in the Stalin era. The rapid industrialization brought to an end the unemployment of the NEP period, and women as well as men were recruited *en masse* into the growing ranks of industrial workers. Between 1928 and 1932, the number of women workers almost doubled.[10] Stalin had, then, brought about one of Lenin's prerequisites for women's emancipation - their mass participation in the public world of paid work. But although he made frequent reference to this fact, it was no more than happy coincidence. Ideological commitment to women's work happened to match the economic needs of the country.

Lenin's other demand - that women be liberated from the private world of the family - was quietly forgotten. The state provision of domestic services

would have diverted money away from heavy industry, which was out of the
question. Accordingly, women were saddled with what sociologists would later
dub the 'double-burden': obligatory participation in the paid workforce, in
addition to their old domestic functions. In fact, since much of the country's
strength was thought to rest on the sheer size of its population, there was even
a threatened increase to women's domestic workload – as well as entering the
workforce in their millions, they were being urged to provide millions of new
citizens for the Motherland. To encourage their compliance, abortion was
made illegal in 1936.

Even in the workplace, Stalin's claim that women stood alongside men 'in
every branch of the economy, culture, science and the arts' was not entirely
true.[11] Protective legislation and the establishment of quotas for women in
certain industries encouraged distinct areas of male and female employment.
These laws were often flouted by enterprise managers, but all the same, they
did result in a disproportionate number of women being employed in areas
which reflected their traditional domestic roles – the service industries,
clothing, health-care and so on.

What of the cinema in the Stalin era? Lenin, as we have seen, was well aware
of cinema's potential as an agent of socialization. It was Stalin, however, who
put it to use. He is said to have mused, 'If I could control the medium of motion
pictures, I would need nothing else in order to convert the entire world to
communism.'[12] In the Soviet Union he did control the medium. As Khrushchev
later made clear, it was the main vehicle through which he promoted his own
distinctive understanding of socialism, and his own glorified role in bringing
it about.

The experimentation of the 1920s was no longer acceptable. It was labelled
'formalism', which literally means a primary concern with form rather than
content. For Stalin, it meant anything which did not fit into the narrow
parameters of the new model of proletarian cinema, 'socialist realism'. Turning
the cinema into an art form was no longer a legitimate concern. Film-makers
were to concentrate all their efforts on 'educating workers in the spirit of
communism', which meant, in effect, propagandizing the party line. They had
to offer an unwaveringly positive image of the new society, and ensure that
it reached and galvanized the masses. This was to be done by means of simple
plots and 'positive' heroes – a gallery of celluloid role models for audiences
to pattern their lives on. Society and its citizens were meant to be in a state
of constant progress, which meant that films were suffused with a sense of
optimism. If the definition of realism had been stretched to the limits of
credibility in the past, then, this was still more the case under Stalin. Socialist
realism amounted to the presentation of an idealized image of life as if it were
reality: life as it should be, not as it really was.

This change in style was facilitated by the advent of sound, which arrived in the Soviet cinema at the start of the 1930s. By definition, sound was geared towards the narrative film; accordingly, it offered a far more appropriate medium than silent cinema for the simple plots and wholesome heroes which would form the basis of socialist realism. But it represented an enormous threat to the avant-garde film-makers. The absence of sound in silent cinema meant that it relied entirely on visual images. Early film theorists, particularly Eisenstein, believed that this gave it a strong resemblance to the thought process. As Peter Wollen writes, Eisenstein 'became increasingly interested in the idea that verbal speech is a kind of secondary process and that the primary, underlying level of thought is sensuous and imagistic'.[13] This 'inner speech' is more flexible, metaphoric and allusive than verbal speech, lending itself to the creative editing techniques of montage. The 'talkie' would replace the richness of inner speech by the more standardized process of 'everyday audible speech', to borrow Christie's description.[14] The relationship between the film and its audience would then be transformed. Watching a silent film involved people in an active, if unconscious, process of interpretation; the talkie, on the other hand, was 'a pre-formed, externalized address from the screen which would make the spectator little more than a passive eavesdropper'.[15] The creativity of montage would inevitably fall by the wayside, since it involved often rapid changes of image which need not always comply with any logically possible sequence of events. As Youngblood notes: 'Such cutting is impossible in the sound film because the ear understands more slowly than the eye sees.'[16] To film-makers committed to montage, sound threatened the complete destruction of cinema as an art form, turning it into nothing more than a filmed version of theatre.

Sound also threatened the international reputation which Soviet film-makers had earned in the second half of the 1920s. Firstly, it challenged the international nature of cinema as a whole, since it inevitably brought in its wake the problem of language barriers. Secondly, it gave Soviet film-makers a huge initial disadvantage, since it required new and expensive equipment which their impoverished country could ill afford.

As a result of both of these factors – resistance on the part of film-makers, and lack of equipment – production of the sound film did not begin in the Soviet Union until 1931, four years after its debut in the United States. For another five years it existed alongside the silent cinema. By the time it finally emerged as the sole form of Soviet cinema, the careers of many of the great directors of the silent era had already been destroyed – not so much by the advent of sound, however, as by the advent of Stalin.

The leftist directors of the 1920s generally had a hard time adjusting to the new demands of Stalinist cinema. Few of them met the brutal ends of intellectuals in other arts, however, since the cinema was too important to Stalin for him to destroy its practitioners. Accordingly, directors whose own careers were thwarted were still allowed to teach, thus nurturing the careers of the next generation of film-makers. Those who did continue making films themselves were placed in the position, as Ian Christie suggests, of 'latter-day court artists, subject to their patron's whims and dependent on his approval'.[17]

The documentary film-makers of the 1920s were particularly out of step with the new era, since fiction films were now seen as the only way to reach the masses. For Vertov, in particular, this was an acute blow. He had always categorically rejected the fiction film, and was the classic exponent of plotless cinema. His first production of the Stalin period, *The Donbass Symphony* (1931), was a great failure; it was dismissed as leftist abstruseness and 'documentarism', which was itself a word of abuse in this new ideological climate.[18] In his next effort, *Three Songs of Lenin* (1934), he tried to achieve a compromise between the documentary and narrative which would satisfy both himself and his critics. Yet although it received great praise outside the Soviet Union and took a prize at the 1935 Venice Film Festival, its reception was rather less enthusiastic at home.[19] At first glance it is hard to understand why; indeed, by the 1960s it was being described as an 'outstanding production of socialist realism'.[20] Vertov's error, however, was his failure to include a few songs of praise to Stalin as well as to Lenin. As Marshall puts it, 'Stalin didn't forget that kind of omission.'[21]

The film was a three-part celebration of the life and work of Lenin. The first part looked at the positive changes which the revolution had brought to Soviet Central Asia, particularly to its women, who had been released from darkness of both a real and metaphoric nature - horse-hair veils on the one hand, illiteracy on the other. The second part explored the path the Soviet Union had begun to tread under Lenin's leadership, and the nation's horrified reaction to his death. The third charted the legacy Lenin left behind in the form of the continuing development of socialism. Even if the film did not focus on Stalin himself, it clearly made a contribution to his attempted deification of the Soviet leadership. Lines such as this have a clearly religious tone: 'We never heard his voice . . . but he was as close to us all as a father. Even closer - no father did for his children as much as Lenin did for us.'[22] But if Lenin was God, Stalin clearly should have appeared as Christ, or at least as Lenin's foremost disciple. Vertov's omission was later rectified by Stalin himself. A second version of the film was released three years later with a number of additional shots linking Stalin with Lenin, and with a new sequence at the end showing how Stalin was continuing Lenin's work.[23]

Vertov did make one more feature film, *Lullaby*, in 1937. This was received even less favourably than *Three Songs of Lenin*, and signalled the end of his career as a film director; he was thereafter confined to newsreel. From our point of view, however, this film is perhaps his most interesting since he focused his attention for the first time primarily on women – and once again, they served a symbolic function. Ostensibly the film is about, as N.P. Abramov puts it in his brief biography of Vertov, 'the happy Soviet woman', for whom all paths are open, and who is certain of the future security of her child.[24] Scenes of Soviet mothers cuddling their infants and dancing joyfully at public festivals are contrasted with race riots and religious wars in capitalist countries. These are no ordinary mothers, however. Vertov wanted to convey with these images 'not just a mother but The Mother'.[25] Hence the series of mothers on screen 'crystallised into the idea of mother as Motherland'.[26] The contented, gurgling infants presumably symbolized the glorious Stalinist future.

Like Vertov, Esfir' Shub did not find it easy to enter this Stalinist future. Her style did change since she moved to contemporary themes and so she began shooting material herself rather than using her old compilation method. However, it remained firmly lodged in the documentary mould. *Today*, released in 1930 and shown abroad under the name of *Cannons or Tractors*, provoked immediate controversy. The plan was to present a battle between the world's old and new social and economic orders, and to predict the victory of the new order. Shub did this by means of contrasting images of the Soviet Union with the United States and Germany. Later, in the more liberal climate of the 1960s, the film would be described as 'one of the sharpest, most political, most topical works of Soviet documentary cinema', portraying the United States as 'a country of scandalous social contradictions, exploitation and slave labour'.[27] The American authorities evidently agreed, for in 1932 they seized the film just as it was about to be shown there.[28] Contemporary Soviet critics did not get the message, however. The Leningrad newspaper *Kinofront* (*Cinema Front*) perceived in the film a 'relish and admiration for life in foreign countries', an 'openly bourgeois orientation . . . [which] . . . protrudes insolently from each frame. How this anti-Soviet rubbish got onto the screen,' it continued, 'is beyond comprehension.'[29]

Shub survived this attack and went on to make her first sound film, *KShE*, in 1932. The initials stand for The Komsomol – Leader of Electrification, and the film was a celebration both of the development of power during the First Five Year Plan, and the Komsomol's (Young Communist League) role in the process. It could also be seen as a celebration of the arrival of sound in the cinema, since it begins with the setting up of a movie camera and the filming of a classical music concert. The film goes on to explore images of factories and power plants, a mass of machinery and new technology which gives it a visual similarity to Fritz Lang's *Metropolis* (1926). In Shub's film, however, the machines are a benign force, working with people instead of against them. In fact, the workers seem as happy at their factory posts as they evidently are when they are dancing at a picnic on the beach. The film also provides an interesting illustration of the distinct sexual division of labour which had already been established in the early 1930s. In scenes of heavy industry, the workers are all male; when the camera runs along a light-bulb conveyor belt, they are exclusively female.

In 1933, Shub started work on the script for a film to be called *Women*. She planned to explore the revolution's impact on women and to look at the social and psychological changes they had gone through from the time of the First World War until the beginning of the 1930s. She wanted to contrast the limited understanding of women's potential which existed before the revolution, and which was reflected in the art and the films of the day – the madonna, the noble lady, the nude, the prostitute – with the more diverse possibilities which faced the new Soviet woman. Bowing to growing pressure, Shub intended this film to be a virtual marriage between the fiction film and the documentary; it would have a clear narrative, but would continue to use real people and real events instead of actors and stage sets. [30] *Women* was never filmed, however. As Turovskaya notes in Chapter 10, the complex issues Shub wanted to tackle were not consistent with the simple plots and simple heroes of the Stalin era. The script can, then, almost be seen as an epitaph to the 1920s. Despite such setbacks, Shub continued to make films until the late 1940s. Yet she, like Vertov, never regained the prominence she had enjoyed in the 1920s.

Eisenstein occupied a more ambiguous position in the Stalinist world. In 1930, his *Battleship Potemkin* was hailed as one of the 'signposts' on the path to a genuine proletarian Soviet cinema. [31] Yet most of his subsequent films were subject to long delays, and several were ultimately banned. *Que Viva Mexico!*, begun in 1931 during his extended stay in the Americas, was never completed, though it is unclear how much responsibility Stalin bears for this one. The collapse of the project is generally attributed to disagreements between Eisenstein and his American producer, Upton Sinclair. However, Herbert Marshall, a close associate of Eisenstein, blames the Soviet authorities for refusing to provide the necessary funding for Eisenstein to bring the film back to the Soviet Union for editing. [32]

Marie Seton, Eisenstein's friend and biographer, later located much of the original footage in Hollywood and attempted to edit it in accordance with his original plans for the film. The result was *Time in the Sun* (1940). If this does truly reflect Eisenstein's original intention, it shows an interesting evolution in his attitude towards women. There is much reference to the matriarchal culture of the Indians of southern Mexico; in some regions so many men have been killed in battle that women have taken over all social and political functions, and 'do not consider it a pitiful fate for a woman to assume responsibility and independence'. The images which correspond to this text are of strong, independent women taking on a full range of social and civic duties, with the evident approval of the film's director. This is a far cry from the representations of women in *Strike* and *October.*

In 1934 Eisenstein started work on *Bezhin Meadow,* his second film about the collectivization of agriculture. This was based on the true story of Pavlik Morozov, a young martyr of the Stalinist era who was killed by relatives when he reported his parents to the authorities for helping some dispossessed kulaks. Yet despite the ideological correctness of his subject matter, Eisenstein had no more success with this film than the one before. He had to completely remake it once on Stalin's orders, and then the second version was banned and destroyed. In 1968, an attempt was made to reconstruct the film from individual frames Eisenstein had stored in his files;[33] this gives us some idea of what it might have been, and provides the basis for the following description.

Morozov's story underwent some important changes in Eisenstein's film. The hero, renamed Stenok, is a young pioneer living on a collective farm and proudly sporting his red kerchief. His father is a vicious kulak, determined to sabotage the collectivization drive by setting fire to the farm's grain harvest. When Stenok thwarts his attempts he murders him, claiming God's sanction for his actions: 'God said be fruitful and multiply,' he intones to the terrified boy, 'but if a son betrays his own father . . . kill him!' As with many films of the previous decade, the protagonists function at least in part as symbols of the new and old orders. The father, once again, represents the old autocratic and patriarchal order: not only does he kill his son, but he has already beaten his wife to death for daring to side with the boy; Stenok, on the other hand, represents the young socialist ideals. The link between the old order and the Orthodox Church is made clear when the father uses the Bible to justify his violence, and when he and the other kulaks seek refuge in the church when the peasants are pursuing them after the attack on the harvest. The peasants, who are almost all female, succeed in banishing the kulaks; could they represent the Russian people again? They decide to turn the church into a club and set about stripping it of all its icons, implying that they turn their backs on religion. As Marshall notes, as well as indicating the 'liquidation of the Kulaks as a class', the film was portraying the 'liquidation of the Church as an institution'.[34]

Yet despite this apparent anti-religious flavour, the film was criticized above all for making its heroes seem like religious icons rather than real people. The young hero in particular was said to be depicted in 'pale and luminous tones and given the face of a saintly youth'.[35] This criticism is perhaps not quite as ironic as it seems. There is a curious hint of ambivalence in Eisenstein's portrayal of religion, which is especially clear in Seton's reconstruction of *Que*

Viva Mexico!; even though Christianity was imposed on the Indians by their Spanish captors, it is still shown to provide them with a source of strength and solace.

After a number of other abortive projects, Eisenstein was allowed to bring a film to term – *Aleksandr Nevskii* (1938). This was about the thirteenth-century Russian monarch who saved the country from Teutonic invaders and was later sanctified by the Orthodox Church. Stalin evidently wanted the audience to associate himself with the hero. He was clearly pleased with the result, and Eisenstein was awarded the coveted Order of Lenin in 1939. However, these were volatile times; the film was withdrawn later that same year after the declaration of the pact between Hitler and Stalin made anti-German works inappropriate. [36]

Eisenstein's last film, *Ivan the Terrible* (1944-6), was to have been be a trilogy. Only two parts were ever made, however, and the second was banned until 1958, five years after Stalin's death. This was too late for Eisenstein, who died himself in 1948. In this case, the reason for Stalin's displeasure is not hard to find. Ivan, the ruler of Russia in the sixteenth century, is generally seen as an absolute tyrant, a power-hungry despot who destroyed anyone who stood in his way. Stalin, however, saw him as a man of integrity committed to creating a strong and united Russia out of the fragmented mess left by feudalism. If this required the merciless destruction of enemies, it was done for good cause. The boyars, the old feudal aristocracy, were determined at all cost to preserve their own power and wealth; they would happily give Russian land away if this served their own ends. Ivan, on the other hand, had only the future of Russia at heart. His goal was to rid Russia of all threat of foreign occupation, and extend its borders to the Baltic Sea. Since this inevitably brought him into conflict with the boyars, he established a band of body-guards, the Oprichnina, who would form an 'iron ring' between him and his enemies. This too was done for the good of Russia.

The reasons for Stalin's promotion of this version of history are obvious. He too had just rid the country of enemies and saboteurs by ruthless and merciless means. He went on to defeat the Nazi occupiers, though at enormous cost to the population. He also added the Baltic republics to Soviet territory, thus securing access to the sea. Last but not least, he too was surrounded by an 'iron ring', the *apparatchiki* of the KGB. The film was, then, to be a justification of Stalinism.

Eisenstein seemed to comply with Stalin's wishes for the first part of the trilogy, delighting his patron enough to win the highest accolade of the times, the Stalin Prize. In the second part, however, he paints a rather different picture. Ivan's vigilance has become paranoia; his strength has become cruelty; his forcefulness has melted away into uncertainty and self-pity. The Oprichniki have turned into black-caped, bloodthirsty thugs employing increasingly senseless and arbitrary violence. As their boorish leader mutters of one intended victim, 'We'll start off with some of his distant relatives', an obvious reference to the punishment of the families of Stalin's victims. In this film, like the first, there are strong parallels between Stalin's rule and that of Ivan - but not the ones which Stalin intended. The Central Committee of the Communist Party gave the following verdict of *Ivan* Part II, which sealed its fate: 'Eisenstein displayed his ignorance of historic facts by showing Ivan the Terrible's progressive army of Oprichniki as a band of degenerates in the style of the American Ku-Klux-Klan; and Ivan the Terrible, a man of great will-power and strong character, as a weak and feeble being, a sort of Hamlet.'[37]

Since Parts I and II of *Ivan* are both dominated by male characters, it may seem a pointless task to ponder on the images of women which they contain. However, we do not have to look far to find the familiar dichotomy we noted in Eisenstein's earlier films - woman as the embodiment of both good and evil. In Part I, Ivan is a not unsympathetic character, but this is still more the case with his wife, Anastasiya. She is loyal, virtuous and faithful, clearly innocent of the crimes which her husband will later commit and which she does not live to see. The only other prominent female character is Ivan's aunt Efrosiniya, who murders Anastasiya and later tries unsuccessfully to have Ivan killed. She wants a Tsar on the throne who will rule on behalf of the boyars, and intends that her own son, the mentally retarded Vladimir, shall take the crown. Clearly, Efrosiniya is a representative of the old, threatened order, although this is a role more usually given to men - the father, for example, both in Pudovkin's *Mother* and in Eisenstein's *Bezhin Meadow*. Anastasiya, similarly, could be said to represent the possibility of a new and gentler future, which is destroyed before it has the chance to begin. In other words, the tragedy begins when Ivan (and, by extension, Stalin) adopts the brutal, autocratic methods of the old regime to achieve his new society.

It is widely held that Eisenstein always intended to produce two versions of Ivan's story, the official one in Part I and his own in Part II.[38] If this is so, he must surely have known what the fate of the second film would be. Unless he merely underestimated the observational abilities of Stalin and his henchmen - which seems highly unlikely, given the blatancy of the parallels - making the film must have been an act of sheer defiance, a fist to shake in Stalin's face.[39] As Marshall notes, Eisenstein was well aware that he had a bad heart and would not live much longer, and so perhaps he felt he had little to lose in taking a final stand.[40] Others, however, suggest that Eisenstein did not begin with the intention of offering two different images of Ivan, but was not clear what his attitude towards Ivan was at the outset. He was able to work this out only in the course of making the films.[41] Given the continuing paucity of reliable information about the Stalin period, this is a debate which will no doubt continue.

Ironically, falling foul of Stalin has not saved Eisenstein from later charges of acting as his tool. Some Soviet critics of the present day find an indication of totalitarian leanings even in his films of the 1920s, in his use of 'collective heroes' and his passion for crowd scenes. In Yurii Bogomolov's rather over-blown words, the Odessa steps in *Battleship Potemkin* functioned as a cross on which the 'innocent crowd (was) crucified', to be resurrected as 'the spirit of the human mass'.[42] Eisenstein's films of the Stalin era have come under still stronger attack, with *Aleksandr Nevskii* in particular denounced as a celebration of Stalinism.[43] It is, however, too easy now to condemn those who had to live through that period. The Eisenstein of the 1920s may have made errors of judgement, but he had no idea what was around the corner. Once he did know, he - like other directors - was surely only doing what had to be done in order to stay alive.

Of the directors who found fame in the 1920s, Kozintsev and Trauberg, the founders of FEKS, made the most successful transition to the Stalin era. Their first film of the 1930s, *Alone* (1931), had a mixed response, however. (This is sometimes described as the Soviet Union's first sound film, though it was made as a silent film and had sound added later.) It was about the experiences of Kuz'mina, a female teacher from Leningrad, who is sent to work in the Altai region of Siberia. At first she is devastated. The village is a primitive backwater, ruled over by a 'shamin' (a medicine man), a local kulak and a corrupt Party official. Each of these men has a vested interest in preserving the status quo, and sees Kuz'mina as a threat to his own position. Attempts to shatter her nerves are followed by an attempt on her life, when she is lured to the snowy wastes near Lake Baikal and abandoned. She is rescued by a passing aircraft and, as she is taken off to hospital, she pledges to return to the village. In the end, it seems that the village will succumb to the enlightened ideas of the Soviet state. Again, the female hero could be said to represent the new society.

Critics expressed misgivings about lingering formalist pretensions. I. Vaisfel'd, for example, pointed to the idealized images of Leningrad at the start of the film, which were meant to convey Kuz'mina's frame of mind before she knows she has to leave: the streets are too startlingly white, he complained, and the trams too resplendently red. He was particularly irritated by the use of a shadow falling across the building in which Kuz'mina gets her job assignment, while sun pours down on the opposite side of the street. He also felt that the images of the Altai were unnaturally severe, from the dead horse's head at the entrance to the village to the harsh, ascetic shots of the landscape. They contrived to give a negative, pessimistic view of the future.[44] Kozintsev and Trauberg themselves later acknowledged their 'misguided understanding' of the epoch, and their tendency to focus attention on an individual hero pitted against the odds, which they agreed produced a feeling of pessimism about the future.[45] Yet they earned the praise of Boris Shumyatskii, head of the Soviet film industry throughout the 1930s (until he became an 'enemy of the people' and was executed in 1938). To him, Kuz'mina was one of the new 'positive heroes' of the Stalin era.[46] She was, incidentally, the only woman to appear on his list.

Kozintsev and Trauberg's next 'positive hero' received a wholly positive reception. This was Maksim, protagonist of the celebrated Maksim trilogy – *The Youth of Maksim* (1934), *The Return of Maksim* (1937) and *The Vyborg Side* (1938). In the first film, Maksim is a simple young worker in Tsarist St Petersburg (the film spans the years 1907-10), who reluctantly parts from his girlfriend, Natasha, to join the Bolsheviks. The second film, set in 1914, charts the development both of the party and of Maksim, who is transformed into 'a fully-formed revolutionary Bolshevik'.[47] The third film takes place during the Civil War and Maksim, now Finance Minister in the new Bolshevik government, has the task of apprehending a gang of counter-revolutionaries. The working class, of course, is ultimately victorious.

The success of the Maksim trilogy was enormous. Indeed, Maksim spawned a virtual generation of real-life namesakes, including the son of composer Shostakovich (who wrote the music for the film).[48] Maksim's popularity stemmed from the fact that he was 'one of the people', entirely on their level and devoid of any intellectual pretensions. By undergoing his development before the audience's eyes, he provided them with a vibrant role model, someone who could inspire them to similar feats. Yet despite the enhanced pledge to realism in the 1930s, there was evidently still room for symbolism. Zorkaya makes the point that in the course of three films, Maksim is never referred to by his family name; this gives him a 'symbolic and generalized nature'.[49] B. Aganov, in his review of *The Vyborg Side*, suggests that Maksim is not an individual but represents the working class as a whole.[50]

Maksim was one of two major 'positive heroes' to burst onto Soviet screens in 1934. The other was Chapaev, a Civil War hero brought back to life by the 'Vasiliev brothers' in a film of the same name. (Georgii and Sergei Vasiliev, despite sharing a surname, were not actually related.) The films have much in common. Most obviously, both are rousing adventure stories set in the past, aimed at giving the younger generation an idealized version of a history of which it had no personal experience. As an editorial in *Pravda* said of *Chapaev*, it offered audiences 'a magical return to those heroic days when the Revolution had only just won the chance to build a new life on earth'.[51] In addition, both heroes were simple, likeable chaps the audience could easily identify with.

Chapaev was based on the memoirs of Dmitrii Furmanov, a commissar who was assigned for a time to the regiment in which Chapaev was the commander of a troop division. The film intentionally defied any expectations one might have of a classic battle hero; in fact, the hero was much smaller in the film than he was in real life. The directors explained that if they had offered the audience a huge man with abundant qualities, the response would have been, 'Yes, this is really a hero, but I could never be like him.'[52] Instead, they gave them someone who could have been plucked from their midst. Chapaev is scarcely literate, he tells Furmanov that he learned to read only two years before. He knows nothing of Marxist theory, and little more about the revolution he is fighting for. This is made clear when a peasant asks him which he supports, the Bolsheviks or the Communists - he is plunged into confusion, not realizing they are the same thing. After a pause he finds a way to save face: 'I support the International!' he declares triumphantly. But Furmanov will not give up his game so easily. 'Which one, the second or the third!?' he asks playfully. Chapaev, clearly confounded, demands, 'Which one does Lenin support?' 'The third,' says Furmanov with a smile – 'he set it up!' 'Then I support the third as well,' says our hero, considering the matter closed. It is hard to understand why he is risking his life for something he knows so little about. One contemporary commentator explains that he has an 'innate' inclination towards communism;[53] alternatively it could be seen as blind faith, a substitute for religion. His ignorance has an obvious function, however. It is a way of telling the spectators that they need not feel guilty about their own lack of knowledge; it is enough, as Youngblood says of Chapaev, to see communism as 'some sort of vaguely good cause'.[54]

At the start of the film, Chapaev is a man of many foibles. He is scruffy, immodest, quick-tempered and inclined towards hasty decisions. Yet as the film develops he turns into a real hero, no less brave but rather more considered. Much of his progress is due to Furmanov, an educated man of much greater intellectual capacity. Although Chapaev is at first highly suspicious of him, this gradually gives way to respect and affection. Once again, there is a symbolic aspect to the two central figures. Furmanov, who has been sent by the Party, represents its guiding hand; Chapaev represents the 'ordinary man' and makes it clear what heights he can reach under the Party's gentle tutelage. Following his progress on the screen, the spectators are inspired to make similar improvements in themselves.

Chapaev could be seen as the incarnation of the New Soviet Man. What of the New Soviet Woman? In this film she appears in the form of Anna, a machine-gun operator who appears to be the only woman in the detachment. Yet although the directors were applauded for exploring the role of women in the Red Army,[55] in many ways Anna reaffirms rather than challenges traditional femininity. Firstly, one of her main functions is to soften the film by adding some romance; she is wooed and, after a brief resistance, won over by Pet'ka, a fellow machine-gunner. Secondly, although she becomes good at her job, it is Pet'ka who makes her so - she knows nothing about guns before he begins teaching her. This allows writers such as Dolinskii to credit Pet'ka for her bravery, pointing out that only with his help does she have 'the possibility ... of becoming level with men even in the most trying conditions'.[56] There are also clear hints that women's involvement in such masculine pursuits is unnatural, and will only be necessary in times of crisis. In one amusing but absurd scene, Anna is lovingly and painstakingly polishing her machine gun as if it is a piece of household furniture. The implication is that this is what she should - and, one day, will - be doing. Anna, and her relationship with Pet'ka, could also be seen to represent the promise of the communist future, although Pet'ka dies before it can be realized; this is suggested by Chapaev's wistful prophesies about the life ahead as he observes the couple's pleasure in each other.

If Anna represents the New Soviet Woman, then, this is clearly not meant to be a female version of Chapaev or Maksim. The closest we do come to their equivalent is the character of Aleksandra Sokolova in *Member of the Government* (1939), by A. Zarkhi and I. Kheifits'.[57] The directors were both male, but the screenplay was written by a woman, Katerina Vinogradskaya. The film is, again, about the process of development of a simple person, this time a poor, uneducated female farm-worker. At the start of the film, she is miserable and down-trodden, the victim of her husband's casual cruelty. (In one scene, after slapping her for some trifle, he turns round and cheerfully plays with a pet bird, while another man in the room yawns unconcernedly.) By the end she is the head of her collective farm, and a delegate to the Supreme Soviet.

In his short biography of the actress who played Sokolova, Vera Maretskaya, O. Yakubovich suggests that the film 'gave an answer to the question "what is socialism?"'.[58] It meant that people - women no less than men - would become the masters of their own fate. Sokolova was the incarnation of Lenin's dictum, that every cook could learn to govern.

Alternatively, one could see in the film a version of Cinderella, adapted for the Stalinist audience. Stalin is himself the prince, and his palace is the Kremlin. This is where the transformed Cinderella finally arrives in the final scene, joyfully addressing the Supreme Soviet in the presence of Stalin himself.

Sokolova was not the only Stalinist Cinderella. In *Circus* (1936), directed by Grigorii Aleksandrov, this role falls to 'Marion Dickson', an American circus performer on tour in the Soviet Union. When she meets her Soviet 'prince' and decides not to return to America, her manager is furious and threatens to expose her terrible secret - that she has an illegitimate Black child. She decides to stay anyway, and he carries out his threat before a packed circus audience, producing the child as shaming evidence. To his astonishment, he is greeted with an ironic laugh; the child is passed from person to person, and is exposed to a deluge of lullabies sung in the different languages of the Soviet republics. Racist America thus constitutes the wicked step-sisters, while the Soviet Union, in the words of one critic, proves itself 'the mother of all workers, of all nationalities and skin colours'.[59] Oksana Bulgakova gives examples of other Cinderella tales in her chapter in this book.

One prominent female function in films of the 1930s is to serve as the 'prize' over which two men compete. One of the men is a 'positive hero', while the other is distinctly flawed. After leaning dangerously towards the wrong man, the heroine eventually comes to her senses and the 'positive hero' receives his due reward. One such film was Yulii Raizman's *Pilots*, made in 1935. The 'positive hero' is Rogachev, the head of a flying school; his competitor is a pilot called Belyaev; the woman they both love, also a pilot, is called Galya. Rogachev is a restrained and self-disciplined character, committed to socialism, who always places the good of the collective above his personal desires. Belyaev is dashing and impulsive, an individualist of distinctly bourgeois mould. Both men find great satisfaction in their work, but for rather different reasons; for Belyaev it is something to be enjoyed simply in itself, whereas for Rogachev its significance lies in its social function, in its contribution to the new society.[60] Shumyatskii described *Pilots* as a struggle between 'two different concepts of the hero and the heroic', one belonging to the bourgeois past and the other the communist present.[61] Of course, the latter eventually wins the woman.

The effort to place collectivization in a positive light concentrated particular effort on films with rural themes, and as Bulgakova makes clear elsewhere in this book, many of the plots were based on similar 'triangular' relationships. Some of these films – particularly those by Ivan Pyr'ev, such as *The Rich Bride* and *Tractor Drivers* – were among the most popular of the 1930s. In an attempt to propagate the myth that collectivization resulted in great prosperity and happiness, there was always an abundance of everything. Vast oceans of corn swayed under blue, cloudless skies, fruit hung heavy from trees and the tables laid out for village celebrations sagged under the weight of their treasures. Zorkaya notes that in one film fruits which grow in different countries and at different times of the year were depicted happily sprouting side-by-side in the magical Soviet summer, 'bananas next to strawberries and water-melons next to mangoes'.[62]

From the middle of the 1930s, the stakhanovite, or shock-worker, became the principal 'positive hero'. Aleksei Stakhanov was a miner in the Donbass region, who, in 1935, managed (apparently with much behind-the-scenes help) to vastly over-fulfil the usual level of coal production. Thereafter, Stakhanov was the nation's role model. The screen stakhanovite was soon joined by the screen saboteur, who was determined to destroy the communist achievement. He would try to explode the mine shaft, put glass in the oats of the collective farm horses, mix poison with the seeds which were about to be sown or commit any number of other such treacherous acts.[63] The film generally consisted of a battle between the two, with the stakhanovite always the winner.

Bulgakova, in her chapter in this book, gives a number of examples of female stakhanovites on screen. They took the form of extraordinarily accomplished tractor drivers, pig keepers, cow milkers, and so on. In real life, however, breaking production records at work did not fit too comfortably with the demands of running a home. Those women who dedicated themselves to over-producing at work were notably less accomplished at reproducing the workforce.[64] Accordingly, women were generally encouraged to support their stakhanovite husbands rather than try to break records themselves. In 1936, there was even a conference for the wives of shock workers at which delegates related the heroic feats of their husbands and discussed what they had done to help. This generally amounted to relieving them of all domestic duties.[65] Yet in the films of the Stalin era, it was taken for granted that the heroines were generally mothers as well as successful workers. The real-life difficulties they faced in combining these roles were not addressed.

The vast majority of 'positive heroes' were male in the years before the 'Great Patriotic War' (as the Soviets term the period of their direct involvement in World War II). However, in films either made during the war or that look back to the war years, women suddenly came into their own. The film industry was evacuated to Central Asia, where it was harnessed to the production of tragic but inspiring tales of Soviet resistance. A large number of the protagonists were women and teenage girls. In Friedrich Ermler's 1943 film *She Defends the Motherland*, the collective farmworker Praskov'ya Luk'yanova becomes a partisan leader to avenge the deaths of her family: her husband had been shot by the Germans, her son crushed by a German tank. The heroine of *Zoya* (1944), directed by Lev Arnshtam, is an 18-year-old girl who is captured and tortured by the Nazis. *Prisoner No. 217* (1944), by Mikhail Romm, is about a young girl who is taken off to Germany and forced to work in a state of virtual slavery for a German family. *Marite* (1947), by Vera Stroeva, is about a Lithanian girl (with the innocent and well-groomed appearance of a Soviet Deanna Durbin), who becomes the organizer of the republic's partisans in their struggle against Nazi occupation. (Stroeva was one of the very few women directors of the Stalin era, though she generally worked together with her husband, Grigorii Roshal'. *Marite* is one of the few films she made by herself.)

This use of female heroines in war films could be said to serve a number of symbolic functions. We have already seen that women were often used as a standard of morality in films of the 1920s. The female war heroine takes this still further; she is a veritable icon of morality. Though she may perish at the end of the film, she retains her spiritual strength to the final gasp, and in this way represents her country's great moral fortitude. She also symbolizes the country itself. We have seen a number of examples of this use of the female figure in the cinema of the 1920s. We have also noted Vertov's unambiguous portrayal of the motherland through images of motherhood in *Lullaby*. In films about the war, the young girl fulfils this function better because she represents the youth and innocence of the socialist order, which the Nazis are attempting to destroy.

Zoya provides a particularly good example. While she is in captivity and undergoing torture, the heroine relives her childhood and youth, and these reminiscences form the basis of the film. She was born in the year of Lenin's death and so was a true child of the Stalin era. As O. Leonidov put it in his review for *Moskovskii bol'shevik* (*The Moscow Bolshevik*): 'the nature and character of *Zoya* was formed under the influence of the Soviet environment, was formed in the Stalinist epoch . . . The film-makers showed how her homeland reared her, gave her courage and strengthened her.'[66] Accordingly, images of her own life are interspersed with those of events in which she did not directly participate but which 'moved the nation',[67] and so became part of her life. Stalin was apparently no less important to her than the members of her own family. One contemporary writer describes her rapture when, participating in a sports parade on Red Square, 'her eyes, together with millions of others, bright with love and joy', were directed towards Lenin's mausoleum, from which Stalin himself surveyed the spectacle.[68] This historical portrait of the Stalin epoch, this interweaving of news events with scenes from Zoya's own life, this stress on the social construction of her identity, suggests that the character was not offered merely as a product of her country. Rather, she was her country.

Despite the stress on 'realism', symbols and myths are a strong feature of films of the Stalin era. This is true not just of those about the war. They are also evident in the use of mythologized Russian leaders to symbolize Stalin, in the tales about down-trodden Cinderellas who finally enter the 'prince's palace', and in the simple division of characters into heroes and villains, communists and capitalists, positive heroes and saboteurs.

Symbols and myths were also present in cinema of the 1920s, as we have seen. However, in the 1930s they ceased to be confined to movie screens; the fairy tale dichotomy of heroes and villains stepped down from the screen to become the basis of state policy. Zorkaya notes that the monumental parades and the joyful songs which typified the Stalin era combined with the positive heroes appearing on cinema screens to produce an image of perpetual holiday.[69] This was heaven being created on earth – but evil enemies were out to destroy it.

They had to be rooted out and annihilated. This, then, justified the show trials, the executions and the incarcerations in labour camps. Cinema and real life became intertwined.

Bogomolov suggests that Soviet society began to take on the form of a Greek myth. Mount Olympus was the Kremlin and Stalin and his chosen ones were gods. 'The heroes', who play such a prominent role in Greek mythology, were played by stakhanovites, by certain select writers such as Gorkii and Mayakovskii and by film characters such as Chapaev and Maksim, who almost became real people to their loving audiences. Beneath them were 'the mortals', the anonymous masses, whose primary function was to 'bear witness to the immortality of the first, and the valour of the second'. There was even a Tartarus, the inner reaches of the mythological hell; this took the form of 'the immense wastes of the Gulag Archipelago'. [70]

Given the enormous role the cinema played in promoting Stalin's view of society, it seems unfair to single out Eisenstein for special attack as a contributor to the totalitarian ethos. All film-makers of the Stalin era were helping to promote the Stalinist vision of society. Whether this was conscious or not is scarcely relevant. As Zorkaya notes, the phenomenon of 'double-think' affected artists as much as anyone else: 'This was not falsity, it was not a lie, it was not deception; it was a surprising manifestation of the strategy of psychological division . . . These people were treading an extremely difficult path; they knew what they 'had to do' to avoid death.' [71]

As the Stalin era came to an end, what situation did Soviet women find themselves in? One of Lenin's prerequisites for women's equality had, unarguably, been achieved. They had been drawn *en masse* into the public sphere of work. However, this did not mean that they enjoyed equality with men, despite the official proclamations to that effect. From the outset, distinct types of male and female work had emerged, with women over-represented in the least well-paid and least prestigious areas of the workforce. They were also largely absent from the political arena. After the middle of the 1930s, there was no more discussion about the state taking over their domestic burden, nor was there any attempt to reconstruct male and female domestic roles in order to divide the load more fairly between them. There were some female stakhanovites, but women's contribution to the movement was seen primarily in terms of freeing their husbands from housework so that the men could devote themselves more fully to productive work. The one sphere in which women were actively encouraged to become over-producers was that of reproduction. The pro-natal drive urged them to make more and more babies for the motherland.

This rather dismal reality stopped at the threshold of cinema halls. The women who smiled from the screen were the heads of collective farms, they served on the highest political bodies and won prizes for their own work efforts. When the Soviet Union entered the war, they were the country's finest heroes. Once the war was over they returned to work and family life with cheerful equanimity, juggling children and employment with apparent ease. The myth of women's equality was propagated in films of the Stalin era as ably and glibly as the myth of the Soviet paradise.

5 KHRUSHCHEV AND THE 'THAW'

Stalin died of a stroke in 1953. Three years later, Khrushchev, who had emerged as the country's new leader, delivered his 'secret speech' at a closed session of the 20th Communist Party Congress. He told the party faithful that they had been following a false god for the past two decades.

Khrushchev's speech evoked an image of a man so vain-glorious he was swept away by his own rhetoric. He had come to believe in his own idealized vision of society. The cinema had played a particularly powerful role in this process. '[Stalin] knew the country and agriculture only from films,' Khrushchev claimed. 'And these films had dressed up and beautified the existing situation . . . Many films so pictured collective farm life that the tables groaned beneath the tables of turkeys and geese. Evidently Stalin thought that it was actually so . . .'[1]

Yet Khruschev's rejection of Stalinism was far from complete. He applauded the rapid industrialization drive and the collectivization of agriculture, arguing that these had lain the foundations on which communism could be built. The tragedy had begun in 1934, when Stalin's craving for power and increasing paranoia had reached such proportions that they exploded into the Terror. The clock, in effect, had to be put back. 'Now that we possess a powerful heavy industry developed in every respect,' Khrushchev declared, 'we are in a position to promote rapidly the production of both the means of production and of consumer goods.'[2] Without Stalin's abuse of power, the country would forge ahead and abundance would become a reality, not just a myth in Stalinist films. The Soviet Union would overtake the productive capacity of the United States by the 1970s; it would achieve full communism by 1980.

Thus began the period known as 'the Thaw'. The rule of law was reasserted, so that citizens no longer had to live in fear of being arrested in the middle of the night for something they had not done, or had done in perfect innocence. Writers who had long languished in prisons or camps were released or, if it was too late for that, were posthumously rehabilitated. Books were published which exposed the realities of Stalinism. They told of factory managers who destroyed their workers' health for the sake of plan fulfilment, of wartime army officers who sacrificed their soldiers' lives in hopeless manoeuvres, of the idiocy of accusations which led to hordes of innocent people being incarcerated in labour camps. Painters rediscovered abstract art; the cinema rediscovered real people and ordinary concerns.

Soviet cities also began to take on a new appearance. Stalin had left a particularly vivid stamp on Moscow's architecture and the capital brimmed with grandiose monuments to his glory. These included a metro system whose spacious stations looked like stately homes, replete with marble statues, mosaics and chandeliers. They provided a stark contrast to the cramped 'communal' apartments in which people actually lived. (The euphemistic name conceals the fact that several families have to live together in one apartment, sharing cooking and washing facilities.)[3] Now, blocks of flats suddenly sprouted around the edges of cities, providing people with the previously unknown luxury of privacy. Ugly and of dubious quality, they at least attempted to tackle a very real human need.

In industry, there was an attempt to diversify, to move some of the country's resources away from Stalin's heavy industry and into consumer goods. In agriculture, the Virgin Lands project was launched; armies of young people set off for Kazakhstan to plant crops on previously unsown land.

Khrushchev also attempted to introduce some far-reaching educational reforms. He came from a peasant background and felt little empathy with the educational élite. In any case, the country had a need for skilled manual workers. In an attempt to reduce the burgeoning white collar intelligentsia, Khrushchev cut the period of compulsory education from ten to eight years. He also expanded the provision of evening classes, correspondence courses and part-time courses, so that further education could be combined with work. This was one reform which faltered from the beginning, however. In a society with minimal private property, education was one of the few ways in which the intelligentsia could pass on their privileged status to their offspring. Khrushchev found himself leaning against a wall of opposition.

A more flamboyant innovation was the space programme. In 1961 Yurii Gargarin was the first man to be launched into space, to be followed two years later by the first woman, Valentina Tereshkova. The West was sent into a state of alarm. Khrushchev's enthusiastic pledge that the USSR would 'catch up and overtake the USA by 1970' began to look feasible.

It was an exciting if confusing time to be in the Soviet Union. This was particularly the case for the young, whose generation had not known the worst of the Terror, nor had they been decimated by the war. They were eager to move more quickly along the road to liberalization and democratization, and when they found themselves blocked by persistent elements of the old bureaucratic apparatus, they merely stepped outside it.[4] An unofficial youth subculture came into being. It formed around political discussion groups, independent theatre companies, unofficial folk concerts and poetry gatherings. Evgenii Evtushchenko became the Mayakovskii of the Khrushchev era, railing against the vestiges of Stalinism which lingered on in the new society.

Young people did not, for the most part, reject socialism, even though their only experience of it came in the distorted Stalinist form. What they wanted was to reclaim it from the abuses of the past. This autonomous youth activity was relatively mild and idealistic, then. Still, the authorities were alarmed by it and made attempts to draw the young back into the fold of the official youth organizations. They were largely unsuccessful, and an independent youth culture has existed in the Soviet Union from that time on.

What of the position of women in the Khrushchev era? A somewhat contradictory assessment of women's gains in Soviet society began to emerge. The press continued to publish articles asserting that socialism had granted them equal rights with men. Yet these were effectively debunked when Khrushchev drew attention to women's complete absence from the country's higher political bodies, and mention was finally made of their 'double-burden' – their full-time work in and outside the home – and the effect this had on their chances of political and professional advancement.[5] Some attempts were made to improve the situation. A woman, Ekaterina Furtseva, was appointed to the Politburo, the apex of political power. The pro-natal drive was relaxed, and abortion legalized in 1955. There was also talk of the need to provide more labour-saving devices in order to ease women's domestic burden. However, these innovations had little long-term effect on women's position in society. Furtseva lasted only three years in office, and until recently was the only woman ever to serve at that level. (In July 1990 another woman, Galina Semenova, Editor-in-Chief of the journal *Krestyanka* [*The Peasant Woman*], was made a member of the Politburo. It is ironic that this female ascension to the top of the Party ladder came at a time when the power of the Party was already in sharp decline.) While men were called on to help their wives more at home, there was no discussion about redefining male and female roles so that housework would be considered equally their duty.

In fact, few of Khrushchev's reforms were ultimately successful. He proved rather better at identifying problems than finding solutions to them. The housing programme had slowed down by 1964, and the cheaply-built apartment blocks were already crumbling. Heavy industry continued to consume the lion's share of resources. The Virgin Lands project, which was initially very successful, suffered the effects of over-enthusiasm; the land was worked too extensively, with the result that some of it was rendered infertile.

The renaissance of the arts also proved rather limited. Censorship began to reassert itself in literature, and the new flowering of modern art was abruptly stifled. (Khrushchev's ferocious attack on 'formalism' after attending an exhibition of abstract art in Moscow would have done credit to his predecessor.)[6] Film-makers also found that they still had distinct boundaries within which to work.

Despite Khrushchev's tirade against Stalin's misuse of the cinema, he did not eschew using films himself as an agent of mass education. From the beginning, film-makers found themselves with less freedom than writers, because their product was geared towards the population as a whole rather than just the intelligentsia. 'When a book appears,' Khrushchev explained, 'not everybody reads it. Some books are within reach of only the advanced reader, and besides, it takes a good deal of time to read them and to grasp their meaning. Films are easier to understand.'[7]

All the same, film-makers were able to shed some of the absurdities of the past. A commitment to socialism no longer required the idealization of life. Directors did not have to devote themselves to the record-breaking feats of stakhanovites, or the fake prosperity of collective farms. Ordinary people could now take the place of 'positive heroes', living their ordinary lives in the overcrowded apartments of shabby Soviet cities. Even the weather was allowed to conform to reality, with the perpetually sunny skies of Stalinist films finally clouding over.[8] Film-makers discovered psychology and began to explore the emotional lives of their heroes. Instead of a simple commitment to the golden future, they brought to the screen a mass of uncertainties and confusions.

A new generation of young film-makers had been nurtured within the belly of the Stalinist beast. The great Soviet directors had turned to teaching when their own creative endeavours were stifled, especially in Stalin's final paranoid years. They passed on their skills to their young protégés. The diploma films produced in the last years of Stalinism, the final stage in a student director's assessment process, were, to borrow Westwood's observation, 'a far cry from the turgid studio productions made for public screening'.[9] Now these young directors were able to make their debuts on the nation's screens.

The attention of film-makers in the Khrushchev era was focused to a large extent on young people. This was not only the case with the new arrivals to the profession; some of the older film-makers who had established their careers in the Stalin years now turned with apparent relief in this new, more humanist direction. Marlen Khutsiev's *Spring on Zarechnaya Street* (1956), *I am 20* (1964) and *July Rain* (1966) all addressed the problems of the young. So did Yulii Raizman's *But What if This is Love* (1962), Otar Ioseliani's *Falling Leaves* (1967) and Stanislav Rostotskii's *We'll Get By Till Monday* (1968). Their young heroes went to school, started their first jobs, coped with a combination of full-time work and evening classes, asserted their independence from the previous generation and tried to come to terms with their new adulthood in the new social conditions which surrounded them. They also fell in love, as film heroes always do, not amongst the rippling cornfields of Stalin's fake collective farms like their predecessors, but against the drab reality of Khrushchev's urban housing projects.

Marlen Khutsiev was the most notable of the new film-makers to emerge in the Khrushchev era. *I am 20*, in particular, could be said to sum up the feelings of his generation. Khutsiev intended to call it Zastava Il'icha, the name of the new residential district in Moscow where the film was set. The film incurred Khrushchev's wrath – possibly it was seen as insufficiently optimistic – and, with a number of scenes removed, it was released under the new name. It was finally restored to its original length in 1987 and shown in cinemas under the intended title.

I am 20 is a slice of life, a meander through the daily experiences of three ordinary young Soviet men. Sergei, Kolya and Slava are close friends, reunited at the start of the film when Sergei returns from his military service. Sergei and Kolya spend much of their time with the mass of youth hanging around the courtyards of the new apartment blocks; Slava is married with a small child, and finds himself pulled in different directions by the domestic demands of his wife and the social demands of his friends. Sergei, the film's principal hero, lives with his mother and sister. The camera observes him dealing with the pleasures and frustrations of family life, of work, of evening classes and of his budding sexuality. He experiments with one-night stands, but believes that somewhere there is 'the one' for him. Much of the film is concerned with his pursuit of, and developing relationship with, Anya, a young woman he spies on a bus and who he thinks might just be the one.

Khutsiev's three protagonists lack the simple assurance of the 'positive heroes' of the past, of the Chapaevs or Maksims of the Stalinist cinema. They are confused characters, trying to work out what life is about and what direction they should take through it. Yet they have not abandoned socialism. In fact, the film could be said to convey a rediscovered faith in the original ideals of the revolution. This is indicated by the portrait of Mayakovskii, spokesman of the 1920s, hanging in Sergei's apartment. A May Day parade, formerly a contrived way of showing popular support for the state, is now depicted as a genuine celebration. An older man at work attempts to get Kolya to inform on a colleague, and he responds with fury: Stalinist tactics and hypocrisy have no place in this new society.

Although Anya's relationship with her father is somewhat strained, in general Khutsiev's youth have great respect for their parents' generation. Sergei's mother finds some wartime ration coupons which she recalls hunting for once in desperation; this prompts her into reminiscences about the horror of those years which give Sergei a sudden stab of empathy. When potatoes are later sent rolling on the floor during the frenzied dancing at a party, Sergei rescues them and a flippant exchange conceals one of the most important lines in the film: asked if he takes anything seriously, he says, 'I'm very serious about the revolution and I like the Internationale. I'm serious about the fact that very few of us have fathers and I respect potatoes which helped us survive in those hungry years . . .'[10] Later, in a scene which Khrushchev originally had deleted, Sergei has a fantasy meeting with his father, who was killed in the war when he was not even Sergei's age. The father can give his son no guidance in this new world. He can merely entrust the future into his hands. Through the affectionate analysis of the emotions and confusions of his heroes, Khutsiev assures his audience that socialism is not lost, but nor does it have to mean the suffocation of the individual against the bosom of the mass.

Women weave in and out of the heroes' lives, but Anya is the only one who is developed in any way as a character. Even so, we observe her only through Sergei's eyes. She is a classic example of what Oksana Bulgakova describes as a 'nymph' elsewhere in this book; although sex would not be portrayed on Soviet screens for some time to come, the young heroines of the Khrushchev era offer a hint of eroticism that had not existed since the 1920s. This is still a young man's world, however. As Sergei leaves the flat of one young woman early in the morning – a coy indication that he has stayed the night – she says sadly, 'You won't respect me now.' Sergei's subsequent indifference suggests that she was right.

The excellent photography in Khutsiev's film was the work of a woman, Margarita Pilikhina. As we shall see later in this book, she became the inspiration of a later generation of women camera-operators.[11] A number of women directors had also begun to emerge by the end of the Khrushchev era. Larisa Shepit'ko, Kira Muratova and Lana Gogoberidze were working on their diploma films as the clock ticked towards the close of the Khrushchev era. Their careers would not take off until the Thaw had come to an end, however. We will look at their work in the next chapter.

As the 1960s progressed, Khrushchev was becoming increasingly unpopular amongst his party colleagues. Many owed their own privileged positions to the Stalinist system for if they had not all been active supporters of Stalin, they were at least tacit collaborators. They were nervous about how far the changes would go, and what the effects would be on their own positions. Khrushchev's optimistic slogans also began to look increasingly absurd as his projects faltered. At worst, he began to be seen as a dangerous meddler, at best, an embarrassing buffoon. In October 1964, the Central Committee summoned him back to Moscow from his holiday in the Crimea, read him a list of his failings and removed him from office. Thus began another new era in Soviet history.

Khrushchev's de-Stalinization of Soviet society was obviously far from complete. If there were distinct limits to the extent of reform permitted on the domestic front, this was still more the case with the country's 'buffer zone'. The brutal suppression of the Hungarian revolution in 1956 made it clear that Khrushchev intended to set both the parameters and the speed of reform for the Eastern bloc as a whole. Nonetheless, the very fact that he could be so easily dethroned is evidence of the enormity of his reforms. As a British journalist commented at the time, 'Ten years earlier no one would have imagined that Stalin's successor would be removed by so simple and gentle a process as a vote.'[12] Whether they wanted to or not, his successors had no way of turning the clock right back to the Stalinist era.

6 LEONID BREZHNEV: THE 'ERA OF STAGNATION'

The two decades in which Leonid Brezhnev ruled the Soviet Union are now known as 'the era of stagnation'. At the time, however, they went under a rather different name - 'developed socialism'. This was a way of defusing Khrushchev's impossible promise of communism by 1980, while still conveying a sense of progress. It signified that the Soviet Union had reached a qualitatively new level of development, that its productive capacity was now sufficiently high for more resources to be poured into consumer goods and services, and hence for improvements in its citizens' quality of life to be a top priority.

In reality, little had changed. The economy still operated according to the old centrally-planned system established in the 1930s, and geared, as always, towards heavy industry and munitions. Iron, steel, coke and coal continued to forge ahead. Of a working population of around 100 million, one Soviet economist has estimated that 30 to 40 million were involved in weaponry and defence.[1] Inevitably, any resources left over for consumer goods, housing, the service industry and agriculture were bound to be inadequate.

There were attempts to restore some of the old Stalinist control mechanisms. The Party tried to re-establish Stalin's 'Cult of Personality', for example - the virtual deification of the leader - around Brezhnev. These could not work so well the second time round, however.[2] Ideology had lost much of its potency during the Thaw, particularly amongst the intelligentsia. The old Stalinist mythology had been exploded, and the more open debates of the Khrushchev era had produced a new breed of people, the *shestidesyatniki,* or 'those of the sixties'. A new psychological atmosphere prevailed which could not easily be reversed. When the authorities attempted to idealize society once again, people now responded with a mixture of hypocrisy and cynicism. In public, they supported the system; in private, they either attacked or ignored it.

Many aspects of daily life began to take place outside the official Soviet institutions. As the economy failed to produce even what was essential for everyday life, a burgeoning black market took over. As the Komsomol continued to ignore young people's need for autonomy, they turned increasingly to unofficial youth groups. As the Party press reverted to an artificial view of life, it was challenged by underground publications. A 'second economy' and a 'second culture' took their places alongside the official Soviet versions.[3]

The dissident movement represented the most open challenge to the authorities. This came into being almost at the start of the Brezhnev era. In 1965, the writers Yulii Daniel and Andrei Sinyavskii were arrested on the charge of 'slandering the Soviet state' when their collection of satirical short stories, banned in the Soviet Union, was published in the West. To serve as an example to others, they were subjected to a show trial reminiscent of the Stalin years. In the less compliant atmosphere of the 1960s, however, this action met with organized protest. Supporters bombarded the official press with angry letters. When these were ignored, samizdat (literally, 'self-publication') came into being.

The dissident movement represented a significant new development in Soviet society. However, its influence was limited. With access to photocopiers severely constrained, samizdat took the form of individually typed manuscripts which were passed from person to person. Inevitably, it reached only a tiny constituency, made up exclusively of the intelligentsia. Manual workers for the most part were still loyal to the Soviet system, even if they adopted a more critical stance to aspects of it than they had in the Stalin years. As Alix Holt notes, they found their country's postwar super-power status something to be proud of. They were also inclined to see dissidents as traitors, pandering to the West for their own personal gain.[4] Certainly Western governments were able to make political capital out of Soviet dissent and to use it to detract attention from injustices in their own countries or spheres of influence.

Dissidents applied themselves to a range of human rights issues, but women's equality was not on the agenda. This changed briefly in 1979, when a group of Leningrad women produced a samizdat journal called The Almanac: Women and Russia. The group was short-lived, however. The KGB responded by intimidating, arresting and finally sending into exile most of the contributors.[5] Many of the articles had a stridently anti-Soviet tone, and it is likely that the women were persecuted more as dissidents than as feminists.

Amongst the population as a whole, feminism found little resonance. The Soviet press portrayed the Western women's movement in wholly negative terms, as an hysterical middle-class phenomenon which had no relevance in the Soviet Union. This notion seeped into the minds of the population. The predominant image of the feminist was of a woman, dressed in overalls, who both hated men and yet wanted to be like them.[6]

At the same time, some aspects of the 'woman question' found their way onto the official agenda. In 1969, a remarkable short story by Natalya Baranskaya, 'A Week Like Any Other', appeared in the literary journal *Novyi Mir* (*New World*). The heroine, Ol'ga, receives a government questionnaire which is aimed at determining how women divide their time between work, family and leisure in a typical week. The reader follows Ol'ga through her own week, an hilarious but gruelling gallop between the never-ending demands of work, husband and children. 'Leisure pursuits?' asks our heroine when she finds a moment to fill in the form. 'Me, I'm addicted to sport: running! I'm always running: to work, from work, to the shops, from the shops . . .' Meanwhile, her 'sympathetic' husband sits and watches this frenzy of activity, bemoaning the fact that he has so little of Ol'ga's time.[7]

Baranskaya's story turned out to be the precursor of a glut of writings on women's roles. In the 1970s the Soviet press was suddenly replete with articles with titles such as 'Where are the 'real' man and woman?' and 'The Bitter Fruits of Emancipation'. It turned out that sexual equality was a more complex issue than had hitherto been supposed. Women had been forced into two virtually full-time jobs and their inability to deal with them had saddled society with a range of disturbing social problems. The divorce rate had reached alarming proportions, the birth-rate had collapsed and neglected children had grown into teenage delinquents.

These later articles had a rather different approach to both the origins of, and solutions to, the crisis. Baransakaya had pointed her finger above all at men and the dismal contribution they make to housework. Now the focus shifted to women. The answer was not for men and women to take on a more equal share of household duties. It was for equality to be to 'redefined', so that it was not incompatible with women putting work in second place and devoting more time to the family. 'Equal but different' was the new motto.

The reason for these articles was, above all, growing concern about the birth-rate. The so-called 'demographic crisis' hit the headlines of the Soviet press in the middle of the 1970s. There was said to be an alarming drop in the birth-rate in the country as a whole; but, still worse, there was an increasingly sharp imbalance in the rates for different parts of the country. In the towns and cities of the European republics, the one-child family had become the norm. In Soviet Central Asia, the average couple was still producing six to ten children.

The ostensible cause for concern was that there would soon be an acute labour shortage in the European republics, where most of the country's industry was located. The high birth-rate in Central Asia would not help because Central Asians were notoriously unwilling to move to where the work was. Indeed, while there was already a shortage of workers in the industrial areas, rural Central Asia was experiencing the first signs of unemployment.

There were, in addition, a few less publicized concerns. The Soviet government had never been kindly disposed towards Islam. It was seen both as a mass of backward, barbaric traditions and as a challenge to the Soviet authorities. If there was ever a major clash of interests between Islam and communism, where would the loyalty of Central Asians lie? After 1979, when the country found itself at war in Afghanistan, this was a particularly worrying question. The relative growth of the Central Asian population meant that an increasing proportion of the Red Army was made up of Moslems. It also meant that Russian numerical supremacy in the country as a whole was under threat.

Accordingly, a campaign was launched in the European republics to persuade women to have more children. The sudden gush of articles in the press about women's roles formed its cornerstone. In addition, a new school course on 'The Ethics and Psychology of Family Life' was introduced, aimed at socializing children into more 'appropriate' gender roles. Laws were also passed which (at least in theory) enabled women with small children to work part-time, or even to work from home. This new-found concern about the negative consequences of women's emancipation was to find its reflection in the films of the day.

The Brezhnev era was, on the whole, a 'Period of Stagnation' for the film industry no less than other areas of society.[8] Yet not all of the gains of the Khrushchev era were lost. Film-makers could not openly challenge the Soviet leadership, but they were not forced back into the sycophantic homilies which characterized the Stalin era. Nor did they have to produce a completely artificial image of society. The shabby realism of the urban landscape portrayed in films of the Thaw did transmute into something more glossy and prosperous, but responsible analysis of certain social problems was permitted. There were boundaries, however, around what was acceptable. Since these were ill-defined, censors tended to err on the side of caution.

As Zorkaya notes, a split occurred within the film industry. Some directors continued to 'serve the regime', making bland but uncontentious films which earned them Party Awards and trips abroad. Others now tried to assert their independence as film-makers. They no longer risked their lives in doing so, but they did jeopardize their careers.[9] Many films were refused general release and sat gathering dust for decades. At best, they might get a few private showings in film clubs.

Despite the general lack of experimentation in the Brezhnev years, one prominent new genre did emerge. This was based on an exploration of women's lives in Soviet society. Names like *Sweet Woman, Strange Woman, Young Wife* and *The Wife Has Left*, appeared one after the other on cinema bill-boards. Others, such as *Wings, Brief Encounters, Long Farewells* and *Some Interviews on Personal Questions* addressed the same themes, if under less obvious titles. In the centre of such films, as Elena Stishova puts it, 'stands the modern business woman – emancipated, independent, equal, but all the same, for some reason not very happy'.[10] These films can be seen, at least in part, as an outgrowth of the pro-family campaign in the European republics, exploring the role-conflict experienced by contemporary woman and its effect both on family relations and family functions.

This is not to say that film-makers were willing or even conscious participants in the pro-family campaign. The fact that this subject was of topical concern would have made it an obvious choice for cinematic treatment in any country. In the Soviet context there was an added enticement: the media attention meant that this was an area in which a critical stance was welcome, where film-makers could engage in a more complex analysis of a social problem than was usually permitted.

There is another reason for film-makers' sudden interest in women's roles. The psychological explorations which began in the Khrushchev era had survived the change in leadership, and women's combination of professional and domestic roles provided a classic example of psychological conflict. Men were not so interesting, since they did not have to juggle with these different areas of life, they were more firmly rooted in the public sphere and hence in the bureaucratic state system. As script-writer Natal'ya Ryazantseva jibes, 'listen to how [the Soviet man] speaks. He talks in professional jargon, with the stamp of the newspaper. He is indescribable in any realistic way; he imposes a ban on himself . . .'[11]

Yet even if film-makers were not conscripted into the pro-family campaign, they did remain immune from it. Many of these films, like the articles in the press, betray nostalgia for a mythical epoch in which men were supposedly knights and women were 'ladies'. As Stishova notes, there is a concern in films of this era that women have taken on inappropriate masculine characteristics, while the 'strong half of humanity' is losing them.[12] On the whole, however, film-makers, unlike journalists, were not in the business of offering simple solutions to such problems; they were more concerned merely with analysing them.

Some of the more interesting analyses came, not surprisingly, from the new women directors who began to enter the profession in the Khrushchev era. Larisa Shepit'ko, Kira Muratova and Lana Gogoberidze each explored the 'Woman Question' in at least one of their films. Dinara Asanova also analysed family relations, though from the standpoint of the adolescent offspring rather than the overworked mother.

Larisa Shepit'ko was one of the most celebrated Soviet directors of the 1970s, until her career was brought to an abrupt and tragic halt by a fatal car crash in 1979. Yet she had almost been denied admission to the profession. Zorkaya tells us that when she first applied to the directing faculty at VGIK, the recruitment committee told her that directing was too masculine a profession for a woman, and 'since she was extremely good looking, they advised her to try the acting department'![13] She refused, and the Ukrainian director Aleksandr Dovzhenko agreed to take her into his workshop. She is invariably described by Soviet film critics as a director who transcends gender, and whose films cannot be described as 'women's cinema'. Nonetheless, *Wings* (1966), based on a screen play by Natal'ya Ryazantseva, is a classic study of the female situation in postwar Soviet society.

The protagonist is a former wartime bomber pilot, Nadezhda Petrukhina, who is now the principal of a technical school for difficult teenagers. She is also the mother of an adopted daughter who is little older than her pupils. In neither role is she successful. She is not a cruel woman, but she is strict and authoritarian in her attempt to get the best performance out of those around her, and society no longer values this in a woman. Her pupils hate her; her daughter withdraws from her, even marrying to get away from her. Nadezhda is a museum exhibit in both a literal and a metaphorical sense. Not only do her wartime feats get a mention in the local museum but she is a relic herself of an era which has passed, in which different demands were placed on women and different characters bred in them. She is haunted by the memory of her wartime love affair with a fellow pilot, which was based on equality and respect. Now women occupy more traditional female roles, both at work and at home. One of the school's sillier female pupils asks a boy she has taken a liking to, 'Which do you prefer, smart girls or stupid ones?' 'Idiots like you,' he tells her – he could be speaking on behalf of his generation.

Throughout the film, Nadezhda gazes longingly at the sky where she once flew. She torments herself by going back to the airfield where she trained, meeting male colleagues who are still able to fly. In the final scene they allow her, as a joke, to sit once more in the cockpit. Their amusement turns to horror when she suddenly roars off. At last Nedezhda Petrukhina is back, literally and figuratively, in her element.

Curiously, Soviet critics have tended to see the film as a rejection of the role-reversal which the war brought about. Neya Zorkaya holds that although 'we are sorry for the woman who had suffered so much . . . her anachronistic personality is not appealing'. She describes Nadezhda as 'the tragic product of a certain period of Russian history' which promoted a false notion of female heroism.[14] Oksana Bulgakova, in her chapter in this book, describes Petukhina as 'shrivelled' and 'old-fashioned', 'a non-modern woman who has blundered into modern life'.

Western audiences might react rather differently, however. I found in the film an implicit criticism of the partial nature of women's emancipation. Nadezhda was applauded for her strength and bravery when this was what her country needed. It cannot now expect her to meekly return to a traditionally 'feminine' role. That she is portrayed as a sad and unhappy woman is beyond dispute, but the tragedy is not that she is unable to adjust to her new life - it is that she is forced to try and do so.

It is interesting to note that while Soviet critics do not appreciate the lack of feminine graces of Shepit'ko's heroine, they applaud the 'manly' touch of the director herself. M. Zak, for example, praises Shepit'ko for her powerful depiction of the horrors of war in *The Ascent*, with these words: 'The director was severe, in a non-womanly way; she did not back away from the portrayal of suffering; she left nothing off the screen. The audience experienced, together with the hero, the weight of his martyred journey: from the icy wind which blows under his greatcoat, from the injury he receives when his foot is burned in a fire.'[15] In a society in which women are consistently undervalued, the greatest professional praise a woman can get is, evidently, to be disassociated from her gender.

Muratova has been more directly associated than Shepit'ko with the exploration of the 'Woman Question'. She too began her career in the Khrushchev era, studying at Sergei Gerasimov's workshop at VGIK. On graduation, she began directing together with her husband, Aleksandr Muratov, but branched out alone when they divorced. *Brief Encounters* and *Long Farewells* both deal primarily with the female personality, and the effect that a career has on a woman's personal life.

Brief Encounters, made in 1968, is a study of contrasts, of different personalities and different life-styles. Muratova herself appears in the role of Valya, an independent urban woman committed to her work; she is a prominent member of the city council and her particular concern is the water provision in new apartment blocks. Maksim, played by the singer Vladimir Vysotskii (who became a virtual cult figure in the 1970s), is her 'gypsy' of a husband, a geologist who spends most of his time working away from home. Nadya is a young rural woman with whom he had an affair on one of these trips. The two women are brought together when Nadya, not knowing Maksim is married, follows him to the city and finds herself on Valya's doorstep. Maksim is away again, and Valya mistakes Nadya for the home help she has been expecting. It soon becomes clear this is not the case. Yet despite Nadya's rather odd demeanour and her failure to explain why she has come, Valya still persuades her to stay. Beneath her aura of independence, she is evidently very lonely. The two women settle into a domestic routine, and Muratova explores their characters both through their interaction with each other and through flashbacks about their separate relationships with Maksim.

The two women could not be more different. Nadya is sweet, simple and traditionally feminine; she has had little education, has no professional ambition and lives in a world of emotion and feelings rather than intellect and reason. In Maksim's absence, she nurtures Valya; they settle into something not unlike a traditional marriage, with Valya going out to work and Nadya feeding her and fussing over her on her return.

Valya is intelligent, practical and dedicated to her work. Yet despite her educational and professional advantages, she does not turn out to be the better off of the two. She is an unhappily divided character, torn between work and personal life, between rationality and spontaneity. Maksim is light-hearted and flippant, he neither understands nor respects the importance Valya's work holds for her, and his refusal to take life seriously both attracts and irritates her: 'You've grown quite wild again,' she reproaches him on one of his visits home. If she were to succeed in 'taming' him, however, she would not like the result.

As the story unfolds, it becomes clear that Valya's dedication to her job is an obsession rather than a source of satisfaction. The corruption, inefficiency and complacency of the system give her little scope to make constructive improvements. Nor are her efforts appreciated by those around her. Her hairdresser, discussing this high-powered client with her colleagues, says scathingly, 'She's just a woman, just an ordinary "baba".' ('Baba' originally meant simply a peasant woman, but has now acquired a derogatory sense; it would be the equivalent of something like 'mare' or 'dame' in English.) Valya's own clients are no more generous. The future tenants of a new housing block, who cannot move in until she gives the building an official stamp of approval, blame the delay on the fact that she is a woman. 'That's no woman,' one man jokingly corrects the others, 'that's "a responsible worker"!' To hold such a position is clearly perceived as inappropriate for a woman.

Valya has one admirer, a sad young woman called Zina. Zina is trying to put a brave face on her inability to find a husband. To some extent this is Valya's doing, Zina declares one day. She used to be attracted to loud young men who stood out in a crowd, but under Valya's influence she now likes only the intelligent ones – and they do not like her since she is not smart enough herself. This means she has no chance of getting her own home (an impossibility for a single woman), but she has friends at the hostel where she lives, and they manage well enough together. While Zina differs enormously in educational and professional level, in some ways she is a mirror image of Valya. Both display a combination of independence and vulnerability; both have paid a high price for their unattainable ideals.

Valya does not lose her husband, though she comes close to doing so. Realizing the strength of her competitor's feelings for Maksim, Nadya finally abandons her own claims on him. She lays the table for a celebratory dinner in honour of his homecoming, then packs her bag and sets off home. The conflicts between Valya and Maksim will undoubtedly continue, however, and Nadya will not be the last woman to tempt him into a more feminine embrace. The ultimate message is that women who develop intellectually and professionally will find that this comes at the cost of personal happiness.

Muratova's next film, *Long Farewells*, was completed in 1971. Based on a script by Natal'ya Ryazantseva, it explores the relationship between a mother and her teenage child. Evgeniya is a translator, divorced and middle-aged, living alone with her son, Sasha. Stishova describes the heroine as the archetypical liberated woman, who has chosen a life of independence: 'her femininity is a cloud, a subconscious trace of genetic memory'.[16] I found in her an exaggerated femininity, however, an irritating coquettishness. As V. Bozhovich puts it, she has the affected manner of a teenage girl who has somehow failed to notice that time has passed and turned her into a middle-aged woman.[17] All the same, she is warm and outgoing, and happy enough about her status as a single, independent woman. Or so it seems. As the film unwinds, her mask of contentment begins to come apart. It turns out that Evgeniya's emotional equilibrium is based solely on her relationship with her son, Sasha. She is desperately trying to keep him in a state of dependency in order to have someone to look after, and hence some reason to exist. At the same time, Sasha is determined to assert himself as an adult.

When Evgeniya discovers that he is planning to leave her and join his father in a distant Siberian city, she falls apart. In the final scene, at a party at her workplace, she has what is almost a breakdown and reveals herself for what she is: a deeply unhappy woman, terrified of being left alone. Sasha is shocked and horrified, but promises to stay with her. The film ends here, with Evgeniya's crisis temporarily averted, just as Valya's was in *Brief Encounters*; in both cases it is obvious, however, that this is merely a postponement, not a solution. The lingering message is, again, that education and career do not in themselves bring happiness for women. Love and family remain their real priorities.

Muratova is now hailed as one of the pioneers of psychological and humanitarian cinema, concerned above all with the individual rather than the 'social type'.[18] She had to wait a long time for such praise, however. Both *Brief Encounters* and *Long Farewells* fell foul of the censor and were shelved for some two decades. In the case of *Brief Encounters*, reasons for official displeasure are not hard to find. Indications of inefficiency and corruption abound. The widespread lack of running water in the city's apartment blocks is presented as a ludicrous failing of state communism; as Valya points out to Maksim, even the ancient Romans were better provided for. There are also frequent references to the privileges which come with local government jobs. One of Valya's clients, for example, complains that the water supply had stopped abruptly in his flat not long before and Valya works out that this coincided with the death of a government official who lived on the same floor – the apartment block had water only because this one privileged man lived there. Vysotskii's appearance in the role of Maksim might also have been a black mark against the film, since by the time of its completion he was already developing a reputation as a figure of dissent.

With *Long Farewells*, the reasons for the ban are less obvious. The film seems to have upset the authorities primarily for its inappropriate choice of heroes, for focusing on the everyday trifles and traumas of inconsequential people. 'This is not socialist, but petty-bourgeois realism,' was the censor's verdict.[19] In any case, Muratova's career was placed in abeyance until the Gorbachev era.

The Georgian director Lana Gogoberidze offers a more clearly sympathetic portrait of an independent woman in *Some Interviews on Personal Questions* (1979). Gogoberidze acknowledges that it has not been easy for women to combine career and family, but is adamant that retreating back into the family is no solution. 'The process of female independence is irreversible,' she has declared, 'rivers cannot run backwards.' Without naming names, she expresses regret that so many film-makers have produced films which 'grieve over the misfortunes of emancipation, as if it were responsible for all female adversities'.[20] In *Some Interviews*, she points to a different culprit.

Sofiko, the heroine, is a journalist who works in the letters section of a local newspaper. She is currently conducting a series of interviews with local women who have written to the paper about their family problems. The stories which emerge from these interviews form the backdrop to Sofiko's own domestic crisis.

Sofiko loves her job, her husband and her two children, but never seems to have enough time for all of them. Her husband, Archil, feels increasingly neglected and suggests that she transfer to a less demanding job. She is appalled at the idea. So Archil finds himself another woman, many years his junior, who is more willing than Sofiko to place him in the centre of her life.

When Sofiko realizes what is happening, she makes a desperate attempt to keep hold of her husband. She dons an absurd wig to make herself look younger, and takes an obsessive interest in the family matters she has previously neglected. But it is too late, and sadly she accepts the inevitability of divorce. In any case, it is obvious that Sofiko would not be able to keep up this charade indefinitely; she would not be able to accept the sacrifices Archil demands.

Some Soviet critics have held Sofiko to blame for her husband's affair. L. Mamatova, for example, criticizes her for being so absorbed in her professional life that she fails to notice how tired Archil has become of her continual absences from home, how irritated he is by her enthusiasm for her work. When he asks her to sew a button on his shirt, she even has the audacity to refuse! It is only when she learns that Archil has a lover that she begins, for the first time, to doubt the correctness of her behaviour.[21] If this were an ideal world, Mamatova continues, Sofiko might be able to live the life she wanted, for her personal happiness and her social duty should not come into conflict: 'But in real life contradictions often arise, and then one has to make a choice.'[22] Clearly it is only the woman who needs to make these choices, however. A man is apparently entitled to everything, including a wife who ministers to his every need; if she fails to do so, it is within his rights to find another.

Anna Lawton suggests that the film intentionally allows the audience to decide where to lay reproach. She explains: 'The admirers of "manly" films would have no trouble pointing a finger at Sofiko. The script allows this presumptuous interpretation. But the camera does not. Throughout the film it conveys Sofiko's point of view . . .'[23] In answer to the question 'who is to blame?', she continues, Gogoberidze's film quietly suggests that it is 'the habits and conventions of a society which places on the woman too many demands and expects too much from her'.[24]

Gogoberidze never reduces her heroine to a state of self-humiliation, as Muratova does with Evgeniya in *Long Farewells*. Even when Sofiko parades coquettishly before Archil in her foolish wig, her underlying strength is never in question. In fact, as Elena Stishova suggests, it is the very fact of her dignity that makes the charade seem so inappropriate.[25] Stishova sees Sofiko as a typical Georgian woman, tough and straightforward; the kind who 'look[s] fate straight in the eye while it reads [her] sentence'.[26]

Throughout the break-up of her marriage, Sofiko continues to conduct interviews with other women. She finds her own story reflected again and again in theirs. In this way, she comes to understand that her personal experience of repression is, in fact, a social phenomenon. This articulation of a collective female experience makes the film oddly reminiscent of the 'consciousness raising' of the early years of the Western feminist movement. Perhaps we can see in it the early glimmerings of Soviet feminism?

It was not only female directors who ventured into an exploration of women's roles. Gleb Panfilov is particularly well known for his attention to female characters. His wife, the actress Inna Churikova, takes the lead role in all of his films. She has offered a range of strong, intelligent and often artistic characters who symbolize the 'new Soviet woman'. Sometimes they rise to professional success from humble origins, and so are faintly reminiscent of the 'Cinderellas' of the 1930s. For example, in *No Ford Through the Fire* (1968), Churikova appears as Tanya Tetkina, a peasant woman who became a great painter during the Civil War. In *Debut* (1970), she is a simple worker who turns out to be a talented actress. The similarity goes no further, however. Unlike the film-makers of the Stalin era, Panfilov is less concerned with what his characters do than with the psychological consequences of their actions. These are no simple stakhanovites; they have a psychological complexity absent from their predecessors.

The most notable example of this is the character of Elizaveta Uvarova in *I wish to Speak* (1976). She is the mayor of a provincial Russian city and on the surface could seem to be an Aleksandra Sokolova, protagonist of the 1930 film *Member of the Government*, transposed to the 1970s. Sokolova's ascension to power was unproblematic, however. This is far from the case with Uvarova.

Uvarova is a fine and intelligent person, dedicated to the improvement of her city and the lives of its citizens. But her civic duties so dominate her life that they virtually obliterate her family concerns. She has a husband, Sergei, and two teenage children, but at times seems scarcely aware of their existence. This fact is emphasized by details, such as her response to a colleague's request that she give his greetings to Sergei: 'Sergei whom?' she asks absently.

This time, the heroine does not pay for her professional success by losing her husband. She loses her son instead. He is killed in a fatal shooting accident, and although it was his own finger which pulled the trigger, the film hints that Uvarova's neglect is the real cause of his death. Her own hobby is rifle shooting, which provides the audience with a mental link between her and the accident. Her culpability is compounded when, despite her grief, she goes straight from the funeral to the office.

Panfilov's attitude towards his heroine is not as negative as this implies, however. He is concerned about the adverse effects of her success on the lives of herself and her family, but he also respects her dedication and achievements. This ambiguity lies at the centre of his character study. He neither applauds nor condemns his characters, he merely explores them. This is what distinguishes his films from those of the 1930s. As he puts it, 'today . . . we need much more to study the strong character, its inner problems and complexity, i.e. the dialectics of character. I want not just to share its experiences, but to understand and analyse it.'[27] Yet at the same time, the now-familiar message comes across once more - that for a woman, there is a high price to pay for professional success.

Despite his undoubted interest in developing the psychology of his characters, it is interesting to note that Panfilov's heroines sometimes also assume a symbolic function. As we have seen, it has long been a Russian tradition to use women both as an icon of morality, and of the motherland. In *The Theme*, Panfilov could be said to do both. The film was made in 1979 but shelved until 1986. This may have been because one of its minor characters was a Jew who was planning to emigrate, a sensitive subject at that time. Alternatively, it could be due to its subtle indictment of the state of the arts in the Brezhnev era.

Churikova does not play the central character in *The Theme*, though her role is vital. The protagonist is instead a man, a famous playwright called Esenin, who goes to the ancient town of Suzdal to gain inspiration for his latest work. There he meets Sasha Nikolaeva, played by Churikova. Sasha is a guide at the local museum and the author of a book on a local poet. In a quite literal way therefore, she is responsible for preserving and promoting the country's cultural treasures. Yet she is also the symbol of Russia's heritage on a deeper, metaphorical level. Sasha is immune to Esenin's supposed brilliance, and because of her he comes to see himself as he really is - a fraud and a fawner, whose fame has been won by serving a false morality. Sasha represents the true morality; indeed, she is the very soul of Russia. [28]

There are no such ambiguities and complexities in Vladimir Menshov's *Moscow Doesn't Believe in Tears* (1981). By the late 1970s, the cinema's key role in the Soviet entertainment field was increasingly being challenged by television, and film-makers had to woo prospective audiences from their apartments to the film theatres. *Moscow Doesn't Believe in Tears* was a frank attempt to do this, capitalizing on popular interest in the 'Woman Question' and presenting it in a glossy 'Hollywood' style. It succeeded. The film attracted 80 million domestic viewers (the most popular films in the Soviet Union normally draw between 40 and 70 million). It also won an American Oscar. [29]

The film begins in Moscow in the time of Khrushchev's Thaw, and explores the fates of three very different young women. They have recently arrived from the provinces and find themselves sharing a room in a workers' hostel. One is quiet with limited ambitions, who soon marries an unremarkable man and settles down into uneventful family life. The second is her opposite, a lively and spirited woman who is determined to succeed in life; the easiest way of doing so, she decides, is to ensnare a successful husband. The third is in some ways a combination of the other two. She is generally serious and thoughtful but has an adventurous streak which almost proves to be her downfall. She allows herself to be drawn into her room-mate's adventurism, is seduced by a young sports star and then abandoned when she gets pregnant. It is this woman, Katya, who proves the true heroine of the film.

The film leaps to the present day, and we find that Katya, against all odds, has become the manager of a large factory. She is independent, confident and self-assured, and enjoys a good relationship with her teenaged daughter. Yet her happiness is marred by the fact that she does not have a man. When Gosha arrives on the scene, he seems like a gift from heaven - except for the fact that he is a manual worker, and Katya is worried that he will reject her if he finds out how far above him she is professionally. She hides the truth and lets Gosha show off his 'real man' credentials by rescuing her daughter from local thugs, installing himself as the head of the family and generally taking over Katya's apartment and her life. This turns out to be exactly what she wanted. The manly Gosha is contrasted with his 'feminized' counterpart, Katya's former lover, who is now a pitiful alcoholic pleading for her help.

When Gosha finds out the truth about Katya's position, his pride at first seems fatally wounded. However, when he realizes that he can still enjoy supremacy in the family, he forgives her for her professional success. The film's ultimate message is that it is right and proper for the man to be the head of the family. Neya Zorkaya's words suggests that this found universal acceptance amongst Soviet audiences: 'When Katya realized that, she shut up like an ordinary housewife, and the audience greeted her with laughter and cheers'.[30]

Moscow Doesn't Believe in Tears is a 1970s version of the Cinderella tale. Against the real-life backdrop of rising divorce and broken families, a 'real man' becomes the prince and a Moscow apartment the palace. Happiness is conjugal life organized along the lines of traditional gender stereotypes. As V. Kichin and N. Savitskii note, the ultra-masculine Gosha is presented as a man 'with an absolute lack of inadequacies'.[31] Whether or not this was the director's intention, the film is a clear reflection of the pro-family campaign, with its call for the resurrection of more traditional male and female roles.

This is still more the case with *One Day 20 Years Later* (1980), directed by Yurii Egorov. The film tells of the reunion of a group of women who were class-mates twenty years before. All of them have become successful professionals except for one, Nadya Kruglova. She is the mother of ten children and a full-time housewife. 'At first glance she has nothing to boast about', wrote I. Langueva in *Komsomol'skaya Pravda*, but when they meet her children, 'her classmates realize that hers, Nadya's, is the highest prize after all'.[32] In another article in the same newspaper, O. Dmitrieva applauds the film for 'rehabilitating' the full-time housewife and showing that her contribution to society is as great as that of any professional woman.[33] *Komsomol'skaya Pravda* subsequently organized a round-table discussion on how to boost the nation's birth-rate, and invited the film's script-writer, Arkadii Inin, to give his views. He talked of his own efforts to put the large family in a positive light, and called on other film-makers to help create a 'thirst for fatherhood and motherhood' in the country's citizens.[34] I met Inin at the Moscow Film Festival in 1989 and asked about the role he had played in the pro-family campaign. He insisted that it had not been his intention to contribute to any pro-natal propaganda. In view of his comments quoted in *Komsomol'skaya Pravda*, this claim sounds rather weak.

Another film that is central to our discussion of women's roles is Aleksandr Askoldov's *The Commissar*. Elena Stishova discusses the film at length in Chapter 12, but since Klavdia Vavilova has now become one of the best known Soviet portraits of womanhood to appear on international screens, she deserves at least a brief mention here. The film was made in 1967, but released only in 1988. It is set in the Civil War and Klavdia is faced with a rather different role-conflict to that of the other characters we have been discussing. She is torn not between work and family, but between motherhood and the military. She is the commissar of a Red Army regiment, who is forced to retire from battle to bear a child she does not want. Yet the birth summons up a host of latent maternal instincts - Klavdia will have to give up one of her passions, the child or the army, which will it be? The army eventually wins.

Despite the difference in subject matter, Askoldov's message is much the same. He is sympathetic towards his heroine and does not judge her harshly for her choice, but he evidently sees it as unnatural. Like Egorov and Inin in *One Day 20 Years Later*, Askoldov contrasts two distinct types of woman and makes it clear where his own inclinations lie. Klavdia, the 'new woman', is counterpoised with an exaggerated maternal image in the form of Maria, the woman in whose home she is billeted while she awaits the birth of her child. Maria (the name is surely not accidental, even though the character is Jewish) is the mother of six children, and despite the harshness of her life, she is beautiful, cheerful and vivacious. She is free of the psychological trauma which afflicts Klavdia because she knows where a woman's place is: it is not, Askoldov argues, on the battlefield.

Askoldov's film provides a particularly appropriate conclusion to this chapter, since its historical setting, the immediate aftermath of the revolution, gives us a clear reminder of the original ideas about women's equality. As we have seen, equality was thought to require two basic processes: women had to be drawn into the public realm of work, and be freed from the private realm of the household. Only the first of these had ever been achieved. In the Brezhnev era, the wisdom of having done even this was being questioned.

Klavdia is an extreme example of a figure who appears again and again in the films of the Brezhnev years - the masculinized woman. Her feminine qualities have been suppressed but not destroyed; they lurk just beneath her army uniform. When the birth of her child allows them to struggle briefly to the surface she manages to beat them down again. However, we are made to understand that this victory over her nature does not make her happy. Askoldov is suggesting that the old understanding of women's equality was false. It amounted to women denying their true selves, trying to become men.

It could be argued that there is a similar message, albeit in a more subtle form, in most of the films of this era. Gogoberidze's film *Some Interviews on Personal Questions* is one of the few to depict a woman who can be strong without losing her femininity, and whose problems stem not from the fact that she is defying nature but from the lack of support she gets from her self-centred husband. The solution to Sofiko's problems, and to those of the women she interviews, is not for them to go back home and devote themselves to their families, but for men and women to establish more equitable domestic relationships. More often, however, we find in films of this era an echo of the simple solution offered in the press – that women might be happier if they were to revert to their true destinies.

Although this is the ostensible message in most of the films we have discussed, in some cases we can discern a second, more covert meaning. The reader will have noticed that in a number of these films the heroine's job, to which she is committed, roots her firmly in Soviet officialdom. Muratova's Valya (in *Brief Encounters*) holds an important position in the local city council, for example, while Panfilov's Elizaveta (*I Wish to Speak*) is a city mayor. Both are evidently representatives of the Soviet system in a literal sense, but it could be argued that they also symbolize it on a more metaphorical level. The fact that their dedication to work has resulted in unhappiness in their personal lives is a negative comment on the Soviet Union's insistence that the social good always has to be placed above personal interests. Askoldov's Klavdia (*The Commissar*) takes this sacrifice to the ultimate extreme when she abandons her child in order to return to the revolutionary struggle. Askoldov contrasts her behaviour with that of Maria, for whom the family and personal life is everything; he quietly invites the audience to make their own decisions about the value of Klavdia's hard idealism against Maria's warmth and humanity. These women, then, could be said to symbolize the Soviet Union itself, and the distortion it has wrought on human values.

Why were women used to portray the Soviet Union, with its bureaucracy, its officialdom and its negation of human values? Surely, men would have been more appropriate, since they were less involved in family life and so less 'softened' by this web of personal relationships? There are two probable reasons. One is simply that it would shock the audience more to see a woman in this kind of role. This is especially the case in the Soviet Union, where people's sense of what is gender-appropriate behaviour is much stronger than in the West. The second reason is that this is a continuation of the symbolic representation of women which we have charted throughout the history of Soviet cinema, but adapted to the new social conditions. In the past, women were used as symbols of Russia and its eternal values. Now, some of the more daring directors of the Brezhnev era were using them to represent the Soviet state and its distorted values.

There is one more film we should discuss before we end this chapter of Soviet history, though like *The Commissar,* it was not shown until *glasnost'* began emptying the censors' shelves. This is *Stolen Meeting,* by the Estonian director Leyda Lajus, made in 1981 but released only in 1988. It is a departure from the pattern we have seen in so many films of this era; in fact, in many ways it can be seen as a precursor of the Gorbachev era. The heroine has just been released from prison after serving time for black marketeering. Her small son was placed in an orphanage when she was arrested, and she is determined to find him. She learns that he has been adopted and eventually tracks him down to his spacious new home and his wealthy professional family. She manages to kidnap him from his nursery school and they spend a pleasant day together, but he is devastated when she tells him he is never to go home. Finally, she realizes that the pain of separation from his new family cannot be justified, and that in any case he will have the chance of a better life with them. She reluctantly returns him.

The film was based on a script by Maria Zvereva, who believes it was banned because of its sympathetic portrayal of a woman who at that time would have been considered a complete reprobate.[35] Women who demanded the audience's sympathy had to be upright citizens and loving mothers, society's moral flag-bearers. If women with dubious morals were depicted, they had to be placed in a wholly negative light. Yet the heroine of *Stolen Meeting* is both an ex-convict and a sexual profligate (the film starts with her having a casual one-night affair), and the film-makers refuse to condemn her.

The film was also ahead of its time in its treatment of ethnic relations. Throughout Soviet history two versions were made of most non-Russian films, one in Russian and the other in the language of the republic. There was just one version of *Stolen Meeting*, however, which used both Russian and Estonian in accordance with the speaker and the situation. The Russian had Estonian sub-titles, and vice versa. This bilingualism gave a more realistic feel to the film, since switching continually from one language to the other was an inevitable part of life outside the Russian republic. It also helped to convey something of the ethnic tension which was developing around language long before *glasnost'*. The Estonian characters in the film speak their own language amongst friends and family, but whenever they are in an official situation they switch to Russian. The audience gets an inescapable feeling that this is a country under foreign occupation.

7 1982–5: THE INTERIM PERIOD

Brezhnev died in November 1982, at the age of 76. In the absence of competitive elections and fixed terms of office, the country was by now in the hands of a gerontocracy. Brezhnev's successor had, inevitably, to be drawn from this collection of infirm old men. Yurii Andropov was the chosen one. At 69 he was one of the youngest members of the upper echelons of the Party, and despite a kidney problem, he seemed to be in reasonably good health. The demands of office evidently proved too much for him, however, and only thirteen months after taking office, he was dead. Yet during his brief year in power, he had a decisive impact on the future direction of the country. He was, firstly, a friend and benefactor of Mikhail Gorbachev and during his year in office did much to promote his younger comrade. He also set in motion an anti-corruption campaign which proved to be a precursor of Gorbachev's later reforms.

Andropov seems to have been a genuine believer in the Soviet system, although he must have been far from happy at the way it had turned out.[1] By the later years of the Brezhnev regime, the party élite was up to its neck in a trough of corruption. The taking of bribes was commonplace, and there was a network of special shops, hospitals and holiday homes for privileged Party members. There was even involvement in organized crime. Of course, little of this found its way into the pages of the official press. All the same, it was fairly open knowledge. Information has a way of travelling, and in the Soviet Union the informal information networks have been particularly effective. It is not surprising, therefore, that confidence in the government and public morale were at an all-time low. If the country's leaders were living this way, ordinary people saw no reason to support them.

In Andropov's view, society was in need of total moral regeneration. His first move on taking office was to fight corruption at the government level, and the inertia and lack of work discipline down at the grass roots. But in order to deal effectively with social problems, it was necessary first to identify them: 'We are a society which does not know itself', Andropov asserted in the journal *Kommunist*. [2] In an attempt to help it to know itself, the limited range of topics open to public discussion in the Brezhnev era was suddenly expanded. This was reflected in the films of the day.

As we have noted, some directors had persisted in taking a candid look at Soviet society throughout the Brezhnev era, though this generally meant that their films ended up languishing in darkness. Occasionally, however, such a film did manage to slip through the cracks, to the astonished delight of cinema audiences. This began to happen with increasing frequency towards the end of the Brezhnev era, suggesting that the tight system of strictures was beginning to loosen up even before Brezhnev's death.

On a trip to Moscow in the spring of 1980, I found the city buzzing with amazement over El'dar Ryazanov's *Garage*. The film is ostensibly about a battle amongst the local élite in a city blighted by a housing shortage, over which of them will have to do without a garage; Ryazanov uses this story as a springboard for a satirical look at the privileged and corrupt lives of the Soviet élite in general. Two years later, Vadim Abdrashitov used the police investigation into a train crash in *The Train Has Stopped* (1982) as an excuse to probe into bureaucratic obstruction and corruption. With the Brezhnev era at an end, such negative aspects of society, which everyone knew existed but had always pretended did not, began to pour onto cinema screens.

The black market now entered the artificially prosperous world depicted in films. It made its first appearance in Sergei Mikaelyan's 1982 comedy *Love By Request*, about an ill-matched but ultimately successful relationship between a drunken ex-sportsman and a prim librarian. Mikaelyan merely takes an amusing sidelong glance at the strange workings of this 'second economy' when the heroine, Vera, buys a foreign blouse in a shady backstreet deal, only to find when she gets it home that it has somehow turned into a jumble of rags.

A year later, El'dar Ryazanov made the black market one of the central themes in his comic satire *Station for Two*. In the film, a man misses his train connection and, because of a series of bizarre mishaps, is forced to spend two days at the station. Drawn into a strange relationship with the waitress in the station restaurant, he finds himself plunged into a black market netherworld; it turns out that the station staff supplement their meagre wages with rather more profitable alternative businesses. The station, with its second economy and miscellany of ulterior functions, stands as a metaphor for Soviet society.

Human relations were also open to more honest scrutiny, and were found to be sadly lacking. In the Brezhnev era, a number of directors looked at the psychological consequences which women faced as they were torn between the public sphere of work and the private sphere of the family. In his acclaimed

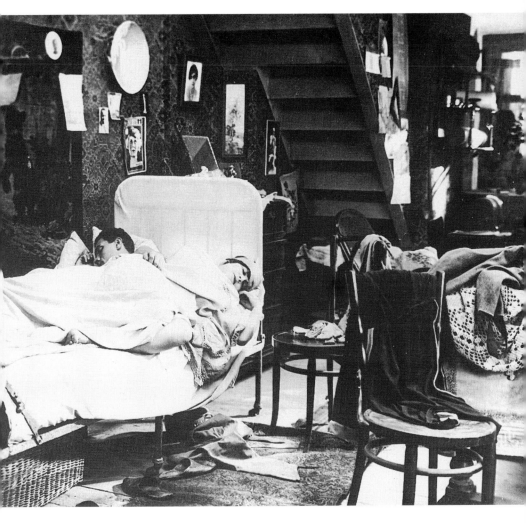

Nikolai Batalov and Lyudmila Semenova in *Bed and Sofa*
(Abram Room, 1927).

Sovexportfilm and National Film Archive, London

Sergei Stolyarov, Lyubov' Orlova and Jimmy Patterson in
Circus (Grigorii Aleksandrov, 1936). *Sovexportfilm*

Lyubov' Orlova in *Circus* (Grigorii Aleksandrov, 1936).

Sovexportfilm

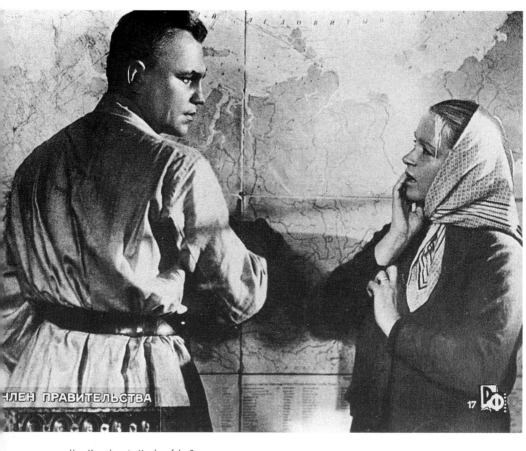

Vera Maretskaya in *Member of the Government*
(A. Zarkhi and I. Kheifitis, 1939). *Sovexportfilm*

Vera Maretskaya in *Member of Government*
(A. Zarkhi and I. Kheifits, 1939).

Sovexportfilm

ABOVE AND BELOW: Tat'yana Samoilova in *The Cranes are Flying* (Mikhail Kalatozov, 1957). *Sovexportfilm*

Sovexportfilm and National Film Archive, London

ABOVE AND BELOW: Maya Bulgakova in *Wings*
(Larisa Shepit'ko, 1966).

Sovexportfilm and National Film Archive, London

Nina Ruslanova and Vladimir Vysotskii in
Brief Encounters (Kira Muratova, 1968/1988).
Sovexportfilm

film *Private Life* (1983), Yulii Raizman flipped over the coin; he explored the psychological effects which virtual confinement to the public sphere had on men. The hero is the manager of a large industrial plant, whose life falls apart when he retires. So immersed was he in his work that, without even noticing it, he had lost all contact with the world outside it. He observes the shambolic life of his extended family like an outsider, a guest in a hotel. It is only when he is finally able to express his sense of isolation that the women in his family gently draw him back in.

In *A Time of Desires* (1984), Raizman shifts the focus back to a female protagonist. She is a cool, calculating fortune-hunter, hoping to improve her social standing by finding a materially well-endowed husband. As Ian Christie observes, Raizman portrays Soviet society as 'materialistic and corrupt . . . ravaged by war and deformed by years of repression'. Its citizens bear no trace of the old idealism; it is simple opportunism which guides their actions.[3]

Dinara Asanova also depicts a moral world in increasing disarray in *Dear, Dearest, Beloved . . .* (1984), completed shortly before her death. Her teenage heroine has kidnapped a baby with the intention of luring her ex-boyfriend back by pretending it is theirs. With the babe in her arms, she latches onto a stranger, telling him she has been abandoned by her 'dear, dearest, beloved'. When he sees through her garbled story he hands her over to the police. He is startled by her lack of interest in society's norms: '[D]o you understand anything about these . . . kids?' he ponders in confusion. 'Before, when there was famine around, they engaged in theft, vandalism . . . this can be understood, justified. But now, what do they want?'[4]

Rolan Bykov offers another portrait of youth alienation in his 1984 film *Scarecrow*. A 12-year-old girl, Lena, has recently moved with her family to a new town and enrols at the local school. Yet although her new class-mates look perfectly normal, there are some alarming personality traits lurking behind their pleasant young faces. When these children reject her for some minor misdemeanour, Lena finds herself the butt of their cruelty, and what begins with taunts and intimidation moves on to torture and almost ends with death.[5]

The film generated intense concern amongst parents and educators. The author of one letter to the Soviet press was evidently as confused as Asanova's hero in *Dear, Dearest, Beloved . . .*: 'Where does such cruelty come from among Soviet children, brought up in a humane society, reading humane books? To this the film gives no clear answer.'[6] Anna Lawton does find an answer, however. Echoing a view which, as we noted earlier, has become prevalent amongst Soviet writers, she places blame squarely on the promotion of 'the collective' at the expense of the individual. As a central feature of Soviet ideology, the idea of the collective also played a prominent role in the education and upbringing of Soviet children. But the collective can become a tyrant, overriding any sense of individual responsibility. In Lawton's own words: 'In this teenager microcosm one can observe familiar patterns of denunciation, purge, demagoguery, lack of moral stamina, and loss of individual integrity,' which were especially characteristic of the Stalin years, but which did not altogether die with him.[7] On one level, the school is a metaphor for Soviet society.

Meanwhile, if unprecedented change was taking place in cinema halls, this would soon be still more the case in the world beyond. Andropov died of kidney failure in February 1984, and was succeeded by Konstantin Chernenko. At 72, he was already seriously ill when he took over and made it through little more than a year in office. There was obviously a limit to how long this parade of old politicians could be allowed to stagger through leadership on their way to their graves. It came to an end in March 1985, when Mikhail Gorbachev came to power.

8 *PERESTROIKA, GLASNOST'* AND THE CINEMA

Gorbachev's comparative youth – he was 54 when he took office – placed him in a different generation from his predecessors, both in a literal and a figurative sense. Those who came before him had established their careers in the Stalin era. Gorbachev, however, was of the Khrushchev school, and his formative political experiences were of the Thaw rather than the Terror. He had joined the Party while Stalin was still alive, in 1950; but he was only 25 years old when Khrushchev delivered his Secret Speech. According to his own testimony, he was aware even before then that much was not right in the country;[1] Khrushchev's denouncement of Stalin merely confirmed this belief. He became a quiet dissident, determined to reform the system from within.

Gorbachev had been Yurii Andropov's protégé, and he shared many of his concerns. At the top of the list was the moral degeneration of Soviet society, manifested in the corruption of the leadership and the apathy and drunkenness of its citizens. Gorbachev saw these social ills as symptoms of a much deeper crisis, stemming from the complete failure of the economy to meet even basic needs. Within a year of taking office, he had introduced two new words to the world's dictionaries – *perestroika*, or 'restructuring', and *glasnost'*, or 'openness'.

Perestroika was initially directed at the economy. Its original aim was to devolve economic responsibility, making managers look after the cost-effectiveness of their own enterprises. State factories which persistently ran at a loss would no longer be bailed out by the government, but would be allowed to go under. Private businesses were also introduced, under the somewhat euphemistic name of 'co-operatives'. They were supposed to be jointly owned by all their workers, with none of the hiring and firing of staff which characterized the exploitative world of capitalism.

In the early years of *perestroika*, party ideologists turned their attention to an earlier period in Soviet history, the New Economic Policy of the 1920s, which also saw the introduction of a limited marketization. In the past, the NEP had been portrayed as a temporary deviation from the true path of socialism, a postponement of radical reform until the country was back on its feet. Now, this view was exposed as a Stalinist distortion of reality. It turned out that Lenin had changed his mind not long before his death and decided that the NEP represented not a sidestep away from socialism but a legitimate path towards it. In some respects, *perestroika* was to pick up where the NEP had left off. There was, accordingly, much discussion about the positive effects that the NEP had had on the economy, while its negative aspects were studiously ignored.

It soon became apparent that the economy was not an isolated segment of society that could be reformed by itself. If *perestroika* were to succeed, it had to enter the political system, the education system and all other areas of life. People had to be encouraged to believe in the system again, and to put to its service the skills they had previously been using to circumvent it. The only way to get their support was to give them a genuine political role, and the information they needed in order to effectively play it. As a result, *glasnost'* was launched.

The intelligentsia embraced *glasnost'* with a vengeance. Books which had been banned for years were published, and films which had long been shelved were screened. Hidden areas of history began to resurface, and the Soviet media provided news which in the past could only be had from illicit foreign radio stations. *Glasnost'* was, in effect, a gesture of conciliation, an assurance that the people were no longer seen as children in need of protection but as mature adults who could be trusted with the truth.[2]

Perestroika and *glasnost'* both proved to have their own momentum. The scale of the changes which took place in the Soviet Union was not anticipated by the Soviet leadership any more than it was by the world at large. Although *glasnost'* was intended to introduce more open discussion and a wider range of opinions, it was thought that these could be contained under the umbrella of the Communist Party. However, they stimulated demands for political pluralism, and increasingly bitter conflicts within the political élite. Popular elections and the creation of a new parliament (the Congress of People's Deputies) were not enough; ultimately, and inevitably, the Communist Party's monopoly on power had to be challenged.

Ironically, the Soviet economy, with which everything began, proved the most resistant to change. The failure of this Stalinist cadaver to come back to life led to more and more radical proposals, with the later versions of *perestroika* bearing little resemblance to the first, and increasingly less resemblance to anything that could genuinely be called socialist. Although Gorbachev still clung to the term as if to a ideological lifebelt, the main dispute between him and most of his political colleagues became the speed of the journey away from socialism.

The 'Shatalin plan' was commissioned by Boris Yeltsin, President of the Russian Republic, in the summer of 1990. Yeltsin was by then Gorbachev's major opponent on the 'left', as the radical reformers were termed both by the Western and the Soviet press – a somewhat confusing use of the term since what they envisaged was the end of communism and its replacement with a market economy. The Shatalin plan amounted to a 500-day dash to capitalism, a massive programme of privatization and the break up the centralized economic structure. It would also have destroyed much of the old imperial power base, since it envisaged a much looser federal system in which republics negotiated between themselves for resources. Gorbachev seemed at first to be in agreement with the plan, but by the autumn he had begun to shelve most of it under pressure from the conservative communists, the supporters of the old centralized system.

Whether Gorbachev actually agreed with their position or was merely attempting to act as power broker between the country's increasingly acrimonious political extremes is the subject of continuing dispute amongst political analysts. So too is his role in the brutal military suppression of nationalists in Lithuania and Latvia in January 1991. At the very least, his response to this act was seen as totally inadequate. His popular support within the country continued to plummet; at worst he was seen as a self-server determined to preserve his own power at all cost, and at best as a vacillator, unsure which way to turn.

By the summer of 1991 Gorbachev had turned back in the direction of radical economic reform. In July, he presented the so-called 'Grand Bargain', approved by both him and Yeltsin, to the heads of the world's most industrialized nations at the G7 Conference in London. Worked out jointly by Soviet and American economists, the Grand Bargain amounted to a Marshall Plan for the Soviet Union, in which aid would be tied to specific economic and political reforms. The country would, then, be transformed in accordance with the West's specifications. Amongst the Soviet Union's pledges was a radical reduction in power at the centre, enshrined in the Union Treaty, which was to be signed in Moscow on 20 August. This would have rendered the Soviet Union a federation of virtually independent countries. At the G7 meeting, Gorbachev was met with cautious interest but no cash; he returned to a country in economic crisis and political turmoil. On the eve of the signing of the Union Treaty, the conservatives launched a coup in a last attempt to prevent what they saw as the otherwise inevitable break-up of the Soviet Union as a unitary power. It failed, and ironically pushed the country into even more rapid disintegration.

The eruption of nationalism, which brought about the end of the Soviet Union, was the least anticipated change spawned by Gorbachev's reforms. He had failed to consider the effect *perestroika* would have on relations between Russia and the other republics, and it evidently took him by surprise. In the early days of his leadership, his interest in the non-Russian parts of the country was confined to their potential role in promoting or hindering economic change. There was no discussion of decentralization until this forced itself onto the agenda. *Perestroika* was a Russian phenomenon, as an Uzbek man told me in the summer of 1987; it was never intended for the 'periphery', the republics outside the Slavic heartland. Yet it arrived there anyway, confronting Gorbachev with declarations of independence from the north and blood-drenched inter-ethnic battles in the south.

Glasnost' and *perestroika* were interpreted in a distinctly nationalist form in the other republics. There were demands for an end to linguistic imperialism and the resurrection of local languages for all purposes. (Russian had, until then, been the official language in all the republics.) There was a painful re-analysis of history from the local perspective and the discovery of brutal truths behind old protestations of voluntary union. In the past, people had been encouraged to see themselves primarily as Soviet, their national identity (be it Georgian, Armenian, Uzbek and so on) was meant to be of secondary importance. Now, national identification became a mass phenomenon. Anger was directed from all sides at the Russians, who were seen as the great colonizers; at the same time, submerged hostilities between other nationalities swam back to the surface. These were exacerbated by the worsening economic situation. With the republics so ethnically mixed, and nationalist feeling running so high, competition for increasingly scarce resources and commodities, especially urban housing, inevitably took on a national flavour.

The Soviet authorities were now confronted with a succession of ethnic uprisings and feuds, and no longer knew how to deal with them. The Party had ceased to be the only political force in the country, which had inevitably eroded its power, but in any case, in the new climate of openness, grievances could no longer be dealt with by the old, heavy-handed methods. The political apparatus that once had only to command was now having to try persuasion instead. This turned out to be rather harder.

The changes introduced by Gorbachev produced a range of traumas within individual republics as well as between them. *Glasnost'* shone a torch on a range of hitherto unacknowledged social problems; *perestroika*, in the meantime, was busy creating new ones. One of the immediate concerns of the new era was the alarming behaviour of the country's youth. Youth subcultures had existed in the Soviet Union in one form or other since the late 1960s, but they received the same treatment as other 'social problems' - publicly their existence was disavowed, while privately their followers were subject to harassment and arrest. All the same, small groups of hippies had roved the country throughout the 'period of stagnation', moving from the north to the south in accordance with the seasons, and hanging out in crash-pads known as *flety* (from the English word 'flat').[3] They were joined in the 1970s by an underground movement of rock musicians and their fans, while unofficial discos also sprang into being in workers' hostels and college dormitories. Mild as this may sound, it was sharply at odds with the official image of idealistic youth marching purposefully along the golden road to socialism, untrammelled by the vices of their capitalist counterparts. Rock music was seen at that time as a corrupting influence, something the bourgeois countries were consciously using to lure young Soviets away from their mission.

Try as they might, the authorities proved unable to divert the young into more wholesome pursuits. By the mid-1980s, various other subcultures had sprung into being, borrowing music traditions from the West: *mettalisti* (heavy metal fans), *punky* (punks), *breikery* (breakdancers). In 1986 motor-bike gangs made their first appearance in Moscow, haring round the city's ring roads on summer evenings with the traffic police in hot but fruitless pursuit. Still more alarming was the arrival of marauding gangs of young males, roaming the city streets looking for trouble. Some of these targeted their violence on young people imitating Western fashions. These self-styled vigilantes claimed to embrace the traditional Soviet values and to be cleaning up the streets for socialism. Here, then, was a direct backlash against *perestroika*.

The loose sexual morality of young people became another cause for concern. In the past, Soviet society presented a staunchly moralistic view of sex. It took place only between adults of the opposite sex, in multiples of two and within the parameters of marriage. Once *glasnost'* had freed journalists' pens from the old restraints, they revealed that promiscuity was in fact rampant amongst teenagers. In the absence of alternative forms of entertainment, many young girls sought excitement in bars and restaurants, using their bodies to pay the otherwise prohibitive price of such evenings.[4] Still more alarming was a novel new game called 'daisy'.[5] A group of teenagers would get together, take off their clothes and the girls would lie on the floor with their heads together and their legs radiating outwards like the petals of a daisy; the boys would then go from one to the other like bumble bees.

We should bear in mind that the media's virtual starvation in the past resulted in an initial over-gorging, and there was a considerable amount of exaggeration and sensationalization in its analysis of the warts and blemishes of society. All the same, even if youth alienation was not as widespread as journalists made out, it certainly existed. Various attempts have been made to explain why this should be and one consistent factor stands out. This is that young people were the main victims of the social hypocrisy of the past: '[T]he endless eulogising of our achievements . . . eternal incantations about the boundless worthiness of Soviet man. All this falsity and exaggeration, these back-slapping lies . . . have simply cultivated an atmosphere of cynicism, an almost open trampling underfoot of all moral laws'.[6]

If youth had stepped onto centre stage in the early years of *perestroika*, women were moving further away from it. As one Yugoslavian feminist said of Eastern Europe, what was emerging was a collection of 'male democracies';[7] this was no less true in the Soviet Union. The pro-family campaign which began in the 1970s was not discontinued with the onset of *perestroika*, rather it was adapted to a new purpose. It became a way of dealing with the mass unemployment which, it was soon apparent, would be an inevitable consequence of the switch to a market economy. Sociologists talked positively about women at last having the chance to stay home and devote themselves to their families.[8] New laws were passed making it easier for them to work part-time or from home. Three eminent female social scientists – Natal'ya Zakharova, Anastasiya Posadskaya and Natal'ya Rimashevskaya – wrote in the journal *Kommunist* that this was the first step towards preparing the population for a mass 'female "exodus" from social production'.[9] Managers who were now responsible for the profitability of their enterprises were increasingly reluctant to take on women, who were seen as the least productive workers because of their extra domestic and childcare responsibilities.[10]

Gorbachev himself gave out mixed messages about women's role in his new society. On the one hand, he expressed concern at their poor showing in the upper reaches of the professional and political hierarchies. On the other, he suggested that their past over-emphasis on work led to neglect of their families, and that steps should be taken 'to make it possible for women to return to their purely womanly mission'.[11] Despite her own much-lauded professional activities, Raisa Gorbacheva's status as the Soviet Union's first 'First Lady' reinforced the traditional Western gender stereotype of a wife acting above all as a support to her husband. Her functions also seemed to include an inordinate number of visits to schools and childcare facilities, a significant fact in itself; still more so was the comment she reportedly made at one Ukrainian kindergarten, that mothers would do better to bring up their children themselves.[12]

If staying at home did not threaten a financial crisis, many Soviet women would have welcomed it as a way of reducing their workload. Doing two virtually full-time jobs, one in the home and one at the workplace, had taken its toll on their commitment to professional equality. However, there was a small but vociferous opposition to this movement 'back to the kitchen'. Articles began appearing in the Soviet press from the start of the Gorbachev era calling for a 'defence of women's careers', and urging women to get more involved in the country's decision-making process in order to protect the gains of the revolution.[13] There was growing interest in Western feminism, and the beginnings of a home-grown version. The lifting of the old ban on autonomous organizations made it possible now for women to organize, and the new-found freedom of the press gave them a forum in which to challenge the authorities. A vast array of independent women's groups leapt into being, concerned with a range of disparate political and social issues, from the effects of unemployment on women to the brutal treatment of their young sons in the army to the preservation of folk culture. In 1990, a feminist research centre was established in Moscow, the Centre for Gender Studies, under the leadership of Natal'ya Rimashevskaya and Anastasiya Posadskaya. The Independent Women's Democratic Initiative followed fast on its heels, known by an abbreviated form of its name, NE ZHDI, which means 'Don't Wait'. In February 1991, this association held the first ever independent feminist conference the Soviet Union had ever seen.

The changes taking place in society at large were inevitably reflected in the cinema. Both the organization of the film industry, and the images appearing on screen, underwent a transformation. In May 1986, the Union of Cinematographers ousted most of its old conservative leadership, and elected as its new president Elim Klimov, former husband of Larisa Shepit'ko and a director respected for his independence and integrity. Films which had fallen foul of the censor and banned for up to two decades finally appeared on screen. In 1989, the union dropped the clause from its charter which demanded adherence to 'Socialist Realism' and pledged its commitment to a cinema which was fully independent of state control. Independent studios and film co-operatives came into being, demanding the right to make films in partnership with foreign companies and distribute them without recourse to official state channels. In 1990, after only four years in office, Klimov was replaced by Davlat Khudonazarov, a Tadzhik;[14] and as if that was not change enough, the union made the unprecedented move of electing a woman as one of its Vice-Presidents, the script-writer Maria Zvereva. (An interview with her appears later in this volume, in Chapter 16.) The other Vice-President was Andrei Razumovskii, President of the new Association of Independent Cinema, and a staunch adherent of privatization.

Women in the industry also created their own association. In 1987, with colleagues from various other countries, both East and West, they formed an international organization called KIWI (Kino Women International), aimed at promoting women film-makers. Its development was constrained by funding problems, but it was an important first step in asserting women's right to be part of the film industry, and a sign of a new willingness to protect that right through collective organization. However, the conflicts between the different republics had an inevitable impact on the cohesion of this multi-national union, and by the summer of 1991 it was in abeyance.[15]

If *perestroika* had transformed the organization of the film world, *glasnost'* had a profound effect on the films it produced. In many areas, film-makers anticipated discussions which were only later to emerge in the press. Not surprisingly, one of the first new tasks they tackled was an honest reappraisal of the country's history. This began with the Stalin era. As we have seen, Khrushchev's de-Stalinization process was only partial, and the cinema suffered tighter restrictions than those imposed on the other arts. Now, it could do as it liked. One of the most celebrated new films on this theme was Aleksei German's *My Friend Ivan Lapshin,* made in 1983 but released only in 1985. It was set in a provincial Russian town in the early 1930s, and showed the harshness of everyday life behind the official Stalinist slogans. German did not deny that there was genuine enthusiasm for the Stalinist vision; indeed, some Western critics suggested that the film betrayed almost a nostalgia for those years.[16] As Lawton points out, however, the nostalgia was for the lost idealism of that era, not for Stalinism.[17] German contrasted the illusion of the Stalinist dream with the reality behind it – of overcrowded communal apartments, poverty, theft, prostitution and growing state brutality.

A very different approach to the Stalin era was offered by Georgian director Tengis Abuladze in *Repentance*, made in 1984 and shown in 1986. Abuladze painted a portrait of a generic dictator, a cross between Stalin and Hitler, in an unspecified historical and geographical setting. The film moved back and forth between dream and reality, with scenes of surrealist fantasy interspersed with poignant episodes taken from real life. One of the most painful scenes has almost a documentary feel, with women in a timber yard hunting amongst logs which were cut by inmates at a forced labour camp, hoping to find messages carved by their loved ones.

Evgenii Tsimbal, historian turned director, made two successive films about Stalinism.[18] The first, *Defence Council Sedov* (1988), scripted by Maria Zvereva, was about a defence lawyer who risked his own life by attempting to save three innocent men from a Stalinist show-trial. He is successful – but finds, to his horror, that many more innocent heads roll as a result of this verdict, as the state looks for scapegoats. The second film, *Tale of the Unextinguished Moon* (1991), is set in 1925, long before Stalin was officially in control. However, Tsimbal suggests that the future leader already had much more power then than is commonly supposed. The film describes the fate of the charismatic defence minister Mikhail Frunze, who died on the operating table during a minor operation. Tsimbal asks if there may be more to this death than meets the eye – if Frunze may well have been the first political victim of the ambitious Stalin, who felt threatened by his popularity.

Kamara Kamalova, the only female feature film director in Uzbekistan, showed how Stalinism functioned in a Central Asian setting. *The Savage* (1989) tells the story of two Russian teenagers evacuated to Uzbekistan during the war, who began an innocent and happy romance which came to an abrupt end after the boy challenged the actions of a local corrupt official, and was sent to a labour camp for this audacity. His new neighbours merely averted their eyes and got on with their own lives. Their only hope for personal survival was to ignore the injustices and tragedies taking place around them.

Marina Goldovskaya, camerawoman turned director, used the documentary form for her analysis of Stalinism. The documentary experienced a rebirth in the early *glasnost'* era; as in the 1920s, it was seen by many directors as the most literal and powerful means of representing reality. *Solovki Power* (1989), which was directed and filmed by Goldovskaya, is one of the finest. It documents the history of the first Soviet labour camp - on the Solovki island in the White Sea - which was established in 1923 but reached its apotheosis in the Stalin era. In Russian the film's name is *Vlast' Solovetskaya*, which for Russian speakers instantly evokes the slogan *Vlast' Sovetskaya*, Soviet power, that adorned so many posters throughout the country's history. Officers used the pun as a cruel joke with which to greet new prisoners: 'There is no Soviet power here, there is only Solovki power.' In other words, 'do not expect to be saved by any higher authority - it is *our* rules which hold sway'. This was no exaggeration.

By the late 1920s Solovki had come to function as a state within a state, a separate totalitarian country with its own government, emblems, ministries, hierarchies of command, crude justice and crippling work regime. It therefore anticipated the system which would soon be established in the country as a whole. Against images of cheerful citizens taking part in the huge holiday parades in Red Square, the film's narrator muses that if they had been asked to describe what happened at Solovki, they would probably have said that criminals and counter-revolutionaries were being re-educated in order to return to more appropriate lives in the free society. In fact, it was the other way round: free citizens were being prepared for a society run along the lines of Solovki. The film documents the growing obsession with work which characterized the Stalinist order, the increasingly brutal and arbitrary system of justice manifested in crude newspaper headlines screaming for blood ('Execute the Traitors!' 'A Dog's Death for the Dogs!'). As the narrator puts it, 'the dividing line between Solovki and society as a whole was getting thinner and more obscure'. Prisoners included women as well as men, and we are told how eagerly the camp commanders waited for the train loads of female conscripts who could provide them with sexual services. This gruelling film is Goldovskaya's counterbalance to *Repentance*; it is an attempt to show the naked truth about Stalin, without recourse to metaphors and allusions.

A number of excellent documentaries came from the 'periphery'. The Latvian director Laima Zurgina broke from her usual type of film - lyrical portraits of ballerinas, painters, poets - and plunged into political cinema. Her promotion material still states that she 'does not belong to the emancipated and politicized women who readily discourse on international affairs'.[19] However, she came to feel increasingly that refraining from politics was a luxury no one in the Soviet Union could afford. *Categorical Imperative* (1989) explored the origins and legacies of Stalinism, focusing in particular on the annexation of the Baltic republics in World War II, and their later struggle for independence. Zurgina suggested - though this, alas, seems increasingly over-optimistic - that the common experience of the suppression of national identity could be a source of unity between peoples of different republics, and could override enormous cultural differences. As well as interviews with prominent public figures in Georgia, she included footage of the fateful demonstration in Tbilisi earlier that year, which the Soviet army dispersed with poison gas and which left twenty-five people dead.

Her next film, *These Are My Sons Too* (1990), looked at the actions of the army from a rather different angle. More than 20,000 soldiers were killed in the four years following the Soviet withdrawal from Afghanistan. These deaths are due to horrific initiation ceremonies, rivalry between different ethnic groups, brutal treatment on the part of officers or just simple insensitivity - for example, forcing young conscripts from the north of the country to march for hours in the Central Asian heat. From interviews with parents of the dead, Zurgina pieces together a chilling story of young boys being used as pawns in a military game.

The plight of women in Central Asia has provided material for a number of documentaries. Margarita Kazymova, the only female director in Tadzhikistan, produced a film called *The Scream* (1988), which explored the tightly circumscribed lives of rural women in her republic. From the age of 13 they begin working in the cotton fields, at first in their free time after school, then on daily eleven-hour shifts. This pattern is interrupted only by childbirth. Women have large families in Central Asia, but since their health has been damaged by a combination of heavy work, poor nutrition and constant contact with chemical fertilizers, they produce a succession of sickly children. Kazymova does not blame the Soviet government alone for the appalling lives of her compatriots, she also points to deep-rooted religious traditions in rural Central Asia which have kept women in a state of subservience throughout Soviet history. This, then, is the reality behind Dziga Vertov's fantasy of Central Asian life under Soviet control in *Three Songs of Lenin*.

Shuhrat Mahmudor, an Uzbek director, continued this theme in *Hudium*

(1988). The name is the Uzbek word for 'offensive', and referred to the Soviet fight against female oppression in Central Asia in the 1920s. Women threw off their veils and fought for their rights, even though hundreds were murdered by their husbands and brothers for disgracing the family. Seventy years later, equality seems no closer; women have even begun killing themselves, out of total despair. The film examines the phenomenon of self-immolations amongst Central Asian women which has been growing to alarming proportions in recent years. Yet some of the women interviewed by the film-makers claimed they did not want equality. They have been brought up believing themselves inferior, the narrator concluded, they have grown used to their oppression. A second *hudium* was needed – to unveil their minds, not their faces.

One of the major topics of cinema in the early *perestroika* period was youth alienation. Some directors again adopted a documentary format, and one of the best films of this type was *Is it Easy to Be Young?* (1987), by Latvian director Yuris Podnieks (former cameraman to Laima Zurgina). Podnieks' let young people talk for themselves, outlining their own frustrations and their reasons for them. The influence of the West was more than evident in their clothes and their musical affiliations, but the causes of their anger were entirely indigenous – the atmosphere of lies and hypocrisy in which they were reared, the distinctly Soviet double-think passed on to them by the previous generation. As one of them tells the audience, 'We are *your* children – you made us this way, with your dual morality, your self-righteous words and slogans . . .'

G. Gavrilov's *Confession: A Chronicle of Alienation* (1989) looked at one particular aspect of youth alienation, drug addiction. The film documents two sad years in the life of a Soviet 'hippy', Aleksei, in the early 1980s. He and his girlfriend, Sveta, live in a communal apartment in Moscow, but manage to keep up their heroin addiction despite the proximity of neighbours. They have a child, which inspires them to try to cure themselves; they call her 'Vera', meaning faith. But the attempt is short-lived. In any case, the drug treatment centres in which they are placed are Dickensian horrors more likely to encourage drug use than to cure people of it. Sveta gives in first, and Aleksei leaves her and takes the child to the countryside, where he finds a new girlfriend called Anyuta and feels he is finally on the right track. The film, much of which is shot in black and white, suddenly leaps into colour to convey Aleksei's new sense of hope. But then the authorities take Vera away from him, and his resolve collapses. By the end of the film, the future seems hopeless.

The film was descriptive rather than analytic, although there were some quiet suggestions that society bore a measure of responsibility for Aleksei's fate. The interviews with his family hint at the confusion of values with which Aleksei was reared, and one of the doctors who tries to cure him suggests that drug addiction is a response to social problems in the Soviet Union no less than in the West, even if the problems are different. Yet this viewer was left wondering about the point of the film. Was it really an exercise in social responsibility, as the director claimed? Or was it an attempt to feed public curiosity for simple commercial reasons?

The latter is obviously the case with some of the fiction films about youth alienation. This was, perhaps, a sad inevitability in the new economic climate, in which the film industry, like everything else, had been put on a system of self-accounting, and the earnings of film-makers were now directly linked to the commercial success of their product. As Soviet critic Yurii Gladil'shchikov complained: 'Every third movie in our country now is about young people, and all of them offer "truth": dark disillusionment with life, drug addiction, and "Satanic" rock music . . . The characters race around on motorcycles, cut each other up with knives, take their own lives, and so forth. There is much, much more of this "truth" on the screen than there is in real life.'[20] T. Khloplyankina made a similar observation: 'For a long time we . . . planted in [the audience's] consciousness the myth of some kind of special Soviet character. We showed it a luscious fake lawn and said, "this is your life". Now we are leading it to a rubbish dump . . . and replacing one illusion for another'.[21]

Probably such films had a combination of motives. The prohibitions of the past had left a huge void in what could be filmed, and now that they had been lifted, directors were understandably eager to jump in. Exploring youth alienation provided a perfect opportunity to delve into subjects which were long taboo and to pull apart some of the formerly sacrosanct Soviet icons. Because of the public concern about the subject, directors were able to do this under the rubric of responsible social comment. At the same time, the films were expected to achieve commercial success both because of public curiosity and because they were aimed primarily at the young themselves, the largest ticket-buying section of the population.

The glut of sex scenes in youth films reflected this variety of goals. On one level they represented nothing more than 'the rehabilitation of flesh' (to borrow Irina Levi's description), 'a reaction against the asceticism of the still recent past'.[22] This accounts for the inappropriateness of many of them; as Khlopyankina wrote, 'It is as if someone calls out the command "undress!" and the hero obediently strips off in every second or third frame, even if this has nothing to do with the action on screen.'[23] A film which included abundant sex seemed to be a sure way of attracting a Soviet audience, if only for its novelty value. At the Moscow Film Festival of 1989, the theatres showing films in a series called 'Sex in the American Cinema' were besieged by crowds.

Yet the very pointlessness of the sex could be said to be its point. As we have seen, there was much concern about the sexual profligacy of the young.

Sex had become a pastime, a way of alleviating boredom, an act of rebellion. In the cinema, the portrayal of pointless sex was another way of expressing youth alienation.

The family received much attention in films of the youth genre. In the Brezhnev era it had been proclaimed 'the basic cell of Soviet society'; it was the ultimate source of love, support and morality.[24] Now it was depicted as a mass of tensions and conflicts. If the parents had not yet divorced, they were so wrapped up in their own concerns that they had little time for their children.

A still more blatant example of iconoclasm was the ridicule of old communist slogans. The young hero of Karen Shakhnazarov's 1987 film *The Courier* observes grandly, 'I dream of communism one day being victorious in the entire world!' In Vasilii Pichul's 1988 film *Little Vera*, the heroine sprawls over her new lover, on a grotesque beach littered with abandoned industrial machinery, and tells him with mock seriousness, 'Our common aim is communism!' Cinema audiences dutifully erupted into laughter.

There are a number of distinct patterns to be found in films of the youth genre. One is based on inter-generational conflict. The protagonist is in his or her late teens and a student at a 'PTU', a trade school (literally, a vocational-technical institute). The standard of such institutes is notoriously low, and they developed a reputation as a dumping ground for the least able and least disciplined students. Our hero is one of these. He/she is from an average or low-income background, and often from a broken home. If the parents are still together things are not much better, since they turn out to be drunks or egoists who are indifferent to the needs of the child. The hero's relationships with the family and with society at large are marked by tension and conflict.

Accordingly, the peer group became the main support. The family has been replaced by the *tusovka*, the youth hang-out. This is a subcultural community in which an alternative set of values and norms prevail. Love has no place in this teenage world, but sex is rampant. It is a pastime, a diversion from the boring monotony of life, a way of getting back at the adult world.

Our hero finds that breaking away from society is not that easy, however. Instead of evading its norms, the *tusovka* embraces a distorted version of them. Ultimately, the protagonist can escape only into a narcotic haze or death. Many of the films ended with the heroes dying, or nearly dying, and often by their own hands.[25]

Little Vera, released in the Soviet Union in 1988, was the prototype of this pattern, and is still one of the most celebrated films of the youth genre. Directed by Vasilii Pichul, from a script written by his wife, Maria Khmelik, it was the biggest hit of the year at domestic box offices. It went on to achieve almost equal fame in the West, where audiences were lured to cinemas with the promise of the first Soviet sex scene in history - an assurance which the film's star, Natal'ya Negoda, obligingly underlined by posing semi-nude for *Playboy*.

The film is a tragic-comedy set in an industrial town in the south of Russia, where Vera and her friends are dragging themselves through a drunken and pointless summer. Vera's father is an alcoholic lorry driver, her mother works in a factory, and she is about to start a course as a telephonist at a PTU. This prospect does not inspire the slightest interest in her. Her one enjoyment is her new affair with Sergei, a newcomer to town. Sex is the main point about this relationship. Love does crop up in the conversation, but, as Irina Levi points out, in a wholly ironic way; Vera asks Sergei, 'Do you love me?' as if this is a password; his indifferent reply, 'it goes without saying', proves sufficient to gain him entrance.[26]

Vera moves Sergei into the family apartment, seemingly just to rile her father. She succeeds, and he stabs Sergei in a drunken fury. Later, in an equally drunken depression, Vera tries to kill herself. At the very end, her father dies of a heart attack. Thus ends the tale, the name of which in Russian serves as a *double entendre*, since *vera* means faith. The young people in the film have turned their backs on the old values but have nothing to replace them with; they have little faith, it seems, in anything.

Little Vera turned many of the old Soviet values upside-down. The family, that 'basic cell of Soviet society', was portrayed as a spiritually oppressive institution trapped in a physically oppressive space. Motherhood, which in official Soviet texts was woman's greatest joy and supreme social mission, now took on a materialistic form; Vera's parents admitted they only had her in the hope of being assigned to a bigger apartment. Sex, which was once hailed as an expression of true love between married partners, was now a casual act performed out of boredom, or in a futile attempt to connect with other people in whatever way possible.

If Western audiences were surprised at this unexpected image of Soviet society, those at home were devastated. Film journals, the film-makers' union, the director and script-writer, the actors and various legal and administrative bodies received an 'avalanche of letters' about the film.[27] The explicit portrayal of sex generated particular outrage. The Soviet Union was accused of emulating the debauchery of the West, married couples complained that they could no longer look each other in the eye and women wrote that they had lost their pride in themselves.[28] For all their prurient interest in sex, the film-makers were accused of not even understanding the sex act, since in several scenes they placed the woman on top![29]

Yet, according to Andrei Zorkii, of the journal *Sovetskii Ekran* (*Soviet Screen*), most people applauded Pichul and Khmelik for having the nerve to show reality on the screen. The claustrophobic apartment, the torn dress Vera always wore at home, the one good outfit she saved for going out, the boredom of young people with nowhere to go, was a far cry from the distorted, fairy-tale image of Soviet life which had been projected on screen in the past.[30] T. Khlopyankina, whose task it was to go through the *Iskusstvo Kino* mailbag, found readers less certain. One wrote, 'Of course, there are many negative aspects to life; but why do we have to drag it all onto the screen?' The old hypocrisies have left an indelible mark, Khlopyankina concluded: 'the majority of film-goers do not want to be confronted with this new cruel reality'. As *glasnost'* proceeded, they were left with increasingly less choice.[31]

There was another clear pattern in films of the youth genre of the early *perestroika* era. The hero was now exclusively male, and was pitted not against his parents' generation but against a 'mafia'. This term became a popular element in the new Soviet lexicon, applied to any organized crime circle. The hero was an 'informal', a member of an underground subculture which lived as far as possible outside the official Soviet structures. All the same, he had own sense of justice, and it was this which impelled him to take on the mafia. He generally had a girlfriend who was in some way connected with the mafia and she inadvertently caused his downfall. Often, at the end of the film, he was killed.[32]

The Needle (1989) was a clear example of this type of film. Directed by the newly-graduated Kazakh director Rashid Nugmanov, it was billed in the Soviet Union as 'the first Soviet feature film about drug addiction'.[33] It was set in Alma Ata, the capital of Kazakhstan, and told the tale of the hero's battle against a local drug mafia. Moro has just returned to Alma Ata after a long absence and looks up his ex-girlfriend, Dina. At first she seems a refreshingly independent female character, but it soon becomes apparent that all is not well. She works at a local hospital, and has been seduced into addiction by a crooked doctor. He steals drugs from the hospital supplies and stores them in Dina's apartment until his dealers distribute them. Moro takes on this gang in an attempt to save Dina, and much of the action in the film is centred around this all-male criminal underworld. However, there is also a long, surreal scene in the Kazakh desert, where Moro takes Dina in an attempt to cure her. Ultimately he fails, and in the end is stabbed (presumably to death) by one of the gang members.

In contrast to *Little Vera*, the generation conflict was not an important feature of this film. Indeed, as Elena Stishova pointed out, this was a mono-generational world, 'without parents or grandparents'. This would not be unusual in a Western film on this theme, but in the Soviet Union it was extremely unrealistic; the housing shortage made it virtually impossible for young people to leave their parental homes. Stishova suggested that this improbability was intentional, a symbolic statement about the spiritual alienation of youth – in her words, 'we lived in parallel worlds, my generation and the outsiders of Moro's type'. This is a film about Moro's world, and so the older generation are seen merely as shadowy figures in street scenes.[34]

Moro does not use drugs himself and the film certainly takes a negative view of addiction. However, the moral message, such as it is, is secondary to the film's need to entertain. This fact is underscored by the casting of well-known Soviet rock stars in two of the most important roles. The drug-dealing doctor was played by Petr Mamonov, lead-singer of *Zvuki Mu*; Moro was played by Viktor Tsoi, who was then the lead singer of the band *Kino*, and the action took place against a soundtrack of his music. (Tsoi died in a car crash the following summer, and immediately took on the status of a Soviet James Dean.)

Rock music was a strong feature of most of these films, regardless of plot. Setting the story against the background of a rock soundtrack could be said to serve two functions. On the one hand it was a way of enticing young audiences to the cinema. On the other, it could be seen as an expression of young people's desire for autonomy. For example, Anna Lawton suggested that in Karen Shakhnazarov's *The Courier* (1987), about a withdrawn teenager who only came to life when he was break-dancing, the 'bold spontaneity' of the dancing was a metaphor for young people's rejection of the rigidity of the past, of the false values of the older generation.[35]

There was a third type of youth film which was still more iconclastic. Whereas the first two were about disaffected young people who had withdrawn from the system, the third type looked at the corruption of those who embraced it. The best example is Sergei Snezhkin's *An Extraordinary Incident on a Regional Scale* (1989). Snezhkin looks at the immorality inherent in the Komsomol, the communist youth league, in the Brezhnev era. The hero, Nikolai Shumilin, is the First Secretary of the local unit. He has just been promoted and he celebrates with a party in the Komsomol sauna, which turns into a drunken orgy. Meanwhile, someone breaks into the main office and steals the Komsomol banner. When a unit loses its banner, it has to be disbanded, so if it cannot be recovered Shumilin's career will come to an abrupt end. This flimsy plot provides the background for an analysis of the bleak reality behind the official proclamations of the Brezhnev era about youth being the shining hope of the socialist future. Its supposed vanguard turns out to be devoid of any communist idealism, although it spouts the right pledges and sings the right songs at the bacchanalian event with which the film begins.

Shumilin has both a wife and a lover, and a distinctly misogynistic attitude towards both. In the midst of making love to his wife, he finds himself wishing she were dead. So he heads off to find solace in his lover, and brutally rapes her on the kitchen table. She has just been mincing meat, and blood oozes from her fingers as Shumilin thrusts into her. Her cries mingle with Brezhnev's voice, which is booming from the television.

Vida Johnson has described this rape as one of the most well-motivated sex scenes of contemporary Soviet cinema. Sexual violence symbolizes, she suggests, 'the political and social impotence of men in a system which has systematically stripped them of power: they do to the women what the state has been doing to them'.[36] This is certainly what the director wanted us to think. The voice of Brezhnev, intertwined with the victim's screams, indicates that what Shumilin was really 'fucking' was the Soviet system. We have had repeated examples of female characters being used throughout Soviet history to represent Mother Russia and the heights of morality. Now, it seems they are being offered as symbols of the Soviet state and its distorted values.

To portray violence against the state in this manner is rather disturbing, however, at least to this viewer. Sociologists in the West have long explored the relationship between violence on the screen and violence on the streets. They do not claim a causal connection between them, but they do argue that the cumulative effect of such images helps to create a climate in which violence becomes acceptable. The repeated portrayal of women as the sources and recipients of male anger and frustration, and the linking of violence and sex in people's minds, is hardly likely to improve women's status.

It is also questionable as to whether such scenes are well-motivated. Khlopyankina refers to a particularly brutal example in Gennadii Gladkov's film *The Burn* (1988). In this case the woman is a literal representative of the system, a prison inspector captured by a group of escaped prisoners: 'At first they cruelly beat her around the head. One of them prepares to rape her. Another places a cigarette lighter between her legs. Finally, they wrap the body in plastic and take her to the town dump ... But it turns out that the woman is not yet dead. She comes to her senses, and for a long time tosses futilely around in the rubbish, trying to free herself . . . '[37] Khlopyankina tries to understand the purpose of this scene, and concludes that it is has no purpose; it exists simply because it *can* do, because the old bans have been lifted. Those people who protested against the sex in *Little Vera* would have been even more horrified, she muses, if they had known what was in store for them next.

In the prominence of the youth genre in the first years of the Gorbachev era, we hear a clear echo of an earlier era of Soviet history. As we have seen, the directors who emerged during Khrushchev's Thaw also chose to look at the profound changes taking place in the society around them through the eyes of the young, those on the threshold of adulthood. In fact, *Little Vera* could be described as a latter-day version of Marlen Khutsiev's *I am 20*, the cinematic banner of the *shestidesyatniki* ('those of the sixties'). There are, however, some crucial differences between them. Khutsiev's heroes may be almost as unclear

as Pichul's about their own personal aims, but they still believe that the aim
of their country is to develop socialism. They have an idealism and an optimism
which is clearly lacking in Vera and her friends. They also have a strong sense
of respect for their parents' generation. Their parents may have followed a false
god in the form of Stalin, but the integrity of their faith is not questioned.
Yet with young people of the *perestroika* era, it is precisely their parents' lack
of integrity which so alienates them. Their hypocrisy, their adherence to
'double-think', not only resulted in their own moral deformity, but also that
of their children. The young hero of Savva Kulish's film *Tragedy in the Style
of Rock* (1988), whose father – a supposed pillar of the establishment – turns out
to be an embezzler, sums up the feeling: 'Children brought up on lies cannot
have high moral standards.'

Ironically, most of the new films about youth did not prove successful with
young people. Although the heroes wore the right clothes and used the right
slang, the films were ultimately seen as a view from the outside, from the very
generation which had been rejected. Semen Kheist, a self-proclaimed hippy
writing in the satirical newspaper *Krokodil*, described such films as 'simply one
generation's fantasies about another. Our respected film-makers listen to a few
rock groups, read a few articles in the press, talk with a few "informals", and
then see themselves as virtual experts on the lives of youth. They demonstrate
all possible variations on what is essentially a single theme, and then think
they have revealed the problems of an entire generation, or even of society
as a whole.' The lives of young people do not consist only of rock concerts,
youth subcultures and battles with the mafia, he pointed out. Until film-makers
addressed the whole range of issues which concerned the young, what was
called 'youth cinema' would amount to nothing more than titillation for the
older generation. [38]

Prostitution was another popular theme in films of the early Gorbachev era.
Before the advent of *glasnost*', the official word was that prostitution had ceased
to exist. From 1986, however, there were articles galore in the press about the
women who hung around railway stations offering themselves for five roubles,
or who worked the top tourist hotels for rather larger sums. [39] The cinema
followed close behind.

This interest in prostitution can be explained in much the same way as the
obsession with juvenile delinquency. At the top of the list was simple curiosity
in a subject which was formerly out of bounds. Many of the journalistic articles
had a distinctly voyeuristic tone: as Elizabeth Waters put it, 'Headlines such
as "Confessions of a Night Butterfly" show how quickly Soviet journalists have
been learning from the Western tabloids.' [40] Much the same has been said about
film-makers. [41] Films about prostitution also had obvious opportunities for sex
scenes. At the same time, just as deviant youth culture could be analysed under

the guise of social concern, the uncovering of prostitution could be linked to the campaign against corruption.[42]

There is another factor in the fascination with this subject which does not find its parallel in the curiosity about youth, however. Soviet society provided the majority of people with few opportunities for social advancement and little in the way of glamour. The lifestyles of the foreign-currency prostitutes offered both. They serviced only foreign tourists and businessmen, and accepted only convertible currency and Western goods. They hung around the high-class hotels, dressed in elegant foreign clothes, drove foreign cars and were able to buy (or get access to through bribery) country cottages. Compared with the heavy burden of the average Soviet women, their workload was light, and their earnings were such that this did not need to be a long-term career. A reporter from the Moscow youth newspaper *Moskovskii Komsomolets* found a mother showing her 15-year-old daughter the ropes in the Black Sea resort of Sochi: 'she can retire by the time she's 25', the woman explained.[43] While prostitution was seldom openly applauded in such articles, there was more than a hint of respect for these self-proclaimed 'independent businesswomen'.[44]

The early films on prostitution again adopted a documentary format. Sergei Baranov's *How Do You Do?*, released in 1988, was the first. It consisted mainly of interviews, not only with prostitutes but also with hotel managers and doormen; it observed women negotiating with their clients; it even allowed the audience some vicarious participation by means of an illicit tape-recorder hidden in one hotel room. The rock-star Petr Mamonov again appears on screen throughout the film, growling out songs about alienation. This was not an attempt just to entertain or titillate the audience, however. The film was concerned with understanding why, and how, prostitution still existed in a society which had claimed to have eradicated it. Its main objective, according to Baranov, was merely to show the truth. As he says himself in the film, echoing the hero of *Tragedy in the Style of Rock*, 'I think that the bitter truth is better than a sweet lie . . . when a person is told lies from childhood, it is easy to come to lead a double life'.

The film pointed to a moral indifference amongst virtually all segments of the Soviet population. 'Everybody does this,' says one prostitute, 'from schoolgirls to doctors of philosophy . . . if you give her money, no woman will feel this is not the place for her'. It also illustrated the hypocrisy which characterized Soviet society before *glasnost'*: one prostitute interviewed in prison explained that since prostitution was not supposed to exist, she had been arrested on the charge of 'currency speculation and stealing from foreigners'.

How Do You Do? also indicated the falsity of the old image of a society in a state of well-being. A prostitute talks of the impossibility for ordinary people of obtaining a reasonable life by any other means. 'I want to have a nice place to live, a car, to go to a seaside resort . . .', she explains to Baranov, then asks him, 'Do you go to a seaside resort? Of course you do!' The bleak picture she paints of life led by the average Soviet citizen contrasts with the positive images put forward by a hotel doorman and a hotel manager, relics of an earlier epoch. The doorman is confused about why women choose such a life since they 'went to the same good schools, read the same books, watched the same films, were brought up on the same good examples' as everyone else: 'What happened to the woman's honour, to the dignity of the Soviet woman?' The hotel manager echoes his words, arguing that prostitution 'is a disgrace to our Soviet system, our way of life'. According to Baranov, however, prostitution virtually *is* the Soviet way of life. Again, then, women – in this case, 'working women' – represent the country's state of morality.

The same idea is expressed in the first feature film on the subject, *International Girl*. A joint Soviet-Swedish venture directed by Petr Todorovskii, it became the biggest Soviet box-office success of 1989. Drozdova discusses this film at some length in her chapter in this book and I will just give the bones of the plot here. The story begins in Leningrad, where the heroine, Tanya, works as a nurse by day but once night falls she turns into a foreign-currency prostitute. She eventually marries one of her clients, a Swedish computer buff, and goes to live with him in Stockholm. At first this seems like a dream come true, but Tanya is acutely lonely in her adopted country; she discovers that attachment to the motherland cannot be destroyed merely by the material frustrations imposed by the Soviet system. She finally decides to go home, but dies in a car crash on her way to the airport.

Tanya defies traditional stereotypes of the prostitute. She is beautiful, intelligent and she loves her mother! She turned to the job not out of poverty or greed but because it gives her the chance to lead a better life. In any case, the implication is that there is little moral choice between the jobs on offer in the Soviet Union; the film is full of images of people using each other in order to survive. When Tanya's mother, who is unaware of her night-time occupation, asks her if she loves her husband-to-be, she replies in a distinctly off-hand manner that she will come to love him. 'But that's selling yourself!' her mother explodes. 'Correct,' says Tanya. 'But how many of us do not sell ourselves?' In other words, prostitution – on a metaphorical if not a literal level – is a way of life in the Soviet Union.

Critic Viktor Gul'chenko offers a rather different interpretation of the film. He sees it as a Cinderella tale for the 1990s which reflected the current concerns of society. Film-makers no longer sought their Cinderellas amongst 'cooks who are learning to govern', as they did in the past, because this would be inappropriate in the moral climate of the present day. The chronic shortage of consumer goods produced a change in values, the emergence of a petty-bourgeois mentality in which the acquisition of 'things' became all important. The 'Cinderella of the factory', whose dream was to enter management, had turned into the 'Cinderella of the Street', whose dream was to enter the good life.[45]

With the growing commercialization of the film industry, Soviet film production turned increasingly to what could be described as the 'adventure genre'. Many films of this type are frank imitations of American 'cops and robbers', transposed to the Soviet situation. Again, the 'mafia' plays a prominent role. One typical example of this genre is Rudolf Fruntov's *Fools Die on Fridays* (1990). Andrei is a former policeman who discovered a mafia group operating within the police force. When he came close to identifying its members, he was arrested on a fake charge of police brutality. After three years in prison he is free again, but finds the mafia back on his tail. He seeks refuge with a beautiful young woman called Yanna, but she turns out to be enmeshed in the mafia herself, exchanging her body for an apartment full of imported Western goods. This does not make her an unsympathetic character, however, since prostitution is presented as a legitimate choice of career for a Soviet woman, so Andrei sets out to save them both. Although the film works well enough as an adventure tale, at times the plot seems little more than a background for the film's main object - sex. It is replete with scenes of orgiastic parties at the mafia's country dacha, with the multifarious couplings of Andrei and Yanna. The film's promotion literature proudly proclaims that its star actress was the winner of the second prize in the Soviet Union's first beauty contest, and the audience is offered the chance to judge for itself; in one scene the camera moves slowly, languorously, over Yanna's body as she lies in a sauna, exploring it inch by inch. What feminist film theorists have said of dominant Hollywood cinema can be applied equally to this film, and many others of the late *perestroika* era. The camera represents the eyes of the male spectator, for whom the woman is the object of 'the gaze', of sexual pleasure in looking. Women in the audience have little choice but to identify with this male objectification of woman.[46]

The Assassin (1990), by Viktor Sergeev, is unusual amongst films of the 'adventure' genre in that its protagonist is a woman. Ol'ga is a news photographer, who lives by herself in a large flat in Leningrad (as it was then). The film begins with her return to the city from a party at a country house, where she was subjected to some kind of sexual abuse (we are given no details) by four men. She is determined to get her revenge. Rather than turn to the police - films of the late Soviet era reflect a general disillusionment with the official security services - she takes the law into her own hands and hires a member of the local mafia to punish her abusers. The mafia can decide themselves what form the punishments take. Ol'ga specifies only that they should be sufficient to make the victims remember forever what they did to her. This turns out to be a fatal mistake.

The first punishment is the gang-rape of the teenaged daughter of one of the men. Ol'ga is brought to witness the good work of her employees; she is horrified, but all the same phones the girl's father and tells him to warn the others to expect equally grisly punishments. They meet, panic-stricken, to discuss what action to take. They decide to dispatch their youngest member, a post-graduate student called Andrei, to persuade Ol'ga to abandon her revenge. In anger she stabs him, but then repents and gets a doctor friend to treat him. The doctor tells her Andrei cannot be moved for some time, so Ol'ga is forced into acting as reluctant hostess to her one-time abuser. She begins to fall in love with him.

In the meantime, the second victim is kidnapped and given a series of morphine injections until he is reduced to a state of hopeless addiction. Ol'ga, fearful now for Andrei's safety, tries to call the mafia off, but inexplicably they insist on finishing the job she commissioned them to do. The third victim's car is sabotaged and he has a fatal crash. Ol'ga desperately moves Andrei from one hiding place to another in an attempt to save him. She fails, and he is stabbed to death. The film ends with Ol'ga shooting first the mafia boss, then herself.

As a thriller, *The Assassin* works very well. Nonetheless, there are some highly disturbing aspects to the film. To begin with, there is the alteration in Ol'ga's status. She begins by controlling the situation but ends up its victim. In this respect, she can be likened to the independent women of Hollywood's Film Noir in the 1940s; they too challenged male authority, and they also paid for this, either by being killed or by being 'neutralized' through their union with the male hero.[47] Both fates are heaped on Ol'ga.

Andrei's character is also rather worrying. Recuperating in Ol'ga's apartment, he proves himself to be a real charmer – as Ol'ga fondly murmurs, 'he's just a child'. His part in the supposed sexual abuse at the start of the film becomes impossible to understand – unless such abuse is seen as nothing more than a male prank, a mere sexual misdemeanour.

Finally, the film contains a number of juxtaposed images which seem to contrast Ol'ga's dangerous involvement with the underworld with more appropriate female pursuits. Her first meeting with the mafia boss takes place in the restaurant which he manages; while she is outlining her proposals for revenge, the camera moves to a troupe of female dancers rehearsing on stage. Their femininity seems to jar with Ol'ga's far-from-feminine plans. Flashbacks to Ol'ga's innocent pig-tailed childhood also provide a sharp contrast with the cruel world she now inhabits. This is a familiar trick which we first saw used by Eisenstein in *October* (1928), when he showed his disdain for women soldiers by juxtaposing a scene of women at bayonet practice with a statue of a mother teaching her child to walk. It could be argued that Sergeev's implication, like Eisenstein's, is that women should get back to doing that which nature intended for them.

Another thriller which places a woman in the forefront of the action, and gives her a similarly unfeminine role, is R. Odzhagov's *Seven Days After Murder* (1990). A young woman, Darya, is murdered at the country home of her father, who is a wealthy government official. The family's trusted, long-time chauffeur, an Azeri called Ralf, is charged with the murder; it transpires that he had been in love with the victim and was supposedly consumed with jealousy when she married someone else. However, this turns out to be too facile a verdict. As the plot unfolds, we discover that Darya was a drug addict, getting her supplies both from Ralf and from her elder sister, Lena, a medical doctor. Both sisters had had illicit affairs with the driver, who turns out to be the real father of Lena's small child. Lena is in fact the killer, having murdered Darya in a fit of jealousy when she found her in bed with Ralf. To her credit, she is not happy at the thought of Ralf taking the blame for her. All the same, the final scene has her casting a lascivious eye over the family's new driver, a young Uzbek man: Eastern men, it seems, are her weakness.

Once again, then, the film exposes the hypocrisy of Soviet society – and especially of its 'basic cell', the family. The warmth and support it exudes at the start of the investigation is a mere façade; underneath it is a mass of vices, hatreds, jealousies and hugely inflated egos. It is no coincidence that Lena is the epitome of moral collapse. Once again, woman represents a standard of morality; in this case, she indicates the complete lack of morality in contemporary Soviet society.

Most of the films which made waves in the Gorbachev era were directed by men. However, there were a number of interesting films by female directors. Lana Gogoberidze's first film of the era was *Turnabout* (1986), which consisted of a number of interwoven female narratives. At the centre is Manana, a once-popular actress who is unable to accept the fact that she is growing old. Then there is her adult daughter, an artist. There is also an old aunt, feeling vulnerable and confused after the demolition of her home. There is a dying woman in hospital, who worries about the fate of her illegitimate daughter. Finally, there is Manana's old friend Rusudan, a successful but lonely career woman who suffers from unrequited love.

As the film develops, it turns out that these seemingly disparate lives are connected with one another by unexpected threads. The man who demolished the aunt's home, Andro, is an old fan of Manana; Rusudan finds out about the orphaned child, and decides to resolve her loneliness by adopting her;

Andro turns out to be the child's secret father (he is married to someone else), and he decides to claim her. Throughout the film, Gogoberidze intercuts her gentle psychological analyses with scenes of a psychology class discussing the image of a woman in an old film. *Turnabout* bears some similarity to *Some Interviews on Personal Questions*, though it lacks the bite of this earlier film. The interconnection of women's destinies in *Turnabout* serves a similar function to the interweaving of Sofiko's life with the interviews she is conducting; and both films point to the social basis of seemingly individual problems. However, *Turnabout* is a softer, more lyrical tale.

Inessa Tumandzhan's *Commentary on a Search For Mercy* (1988) is an interesting combination of a virtual documentary inserted inside a fiction film. The plot is about a high-up government official who has received a ten-year prison sentence for accepting bribes. For technical reasons he cannot begin serving his sentence until he has been officially removed from his post, which will happen the next day. So he has one last day of freedom, and roams round Moscow drinking in the world. This is Moscow of the *perestroika* era, and what he sees, as if for the first time, is the underbelly of Soviet life. The city teems with bored, disaffected youth with nowhere to go and nothing to do. In one bar, a young woman explodes with anger when she suddenly realizes the other women there are all prostitutes looking for clients. 'All the bars are like this,' she yells, 'there is nowhere for young people to get together!' Corruption, youth alienation, rock music and prostitution - the familiar features of *glasnost'* cinema - all feature strongly in this film. It attempts to deal with them with a sensitivity not always present in Soviet cinema of those times, however.

The female director who caused the most controversy in Gorbachev's day, as she also had in that of Brezhnev, was Kira Muratova. She returned to directing after a gap of almost two decades with *The Asthenic Syndrome* (1990). However, even in the more liberal climate of the Gorbachev era, her work still provoked sufficient controversy to deny it general release, and it has appeared on the screens only of a few private cinema clubs. As Marina Drozdova explains in her chapter in this book, one of the film's main features is to show an inversion of gender roles, contrasting the passivity of the male hero with the aggression of the female protagonist who appears in a sub-plot. This is a woman who swears ferociously, who seduces a stranger and then, thinking better of it, kicks him out of bed. It is worth pondering the fact that this film has not been given general release, in contrast to those depicting violence against women by men.

Our discussion of Soviet cinema comes to a logical conclusion at this point. Gorbachev resigned as president in December 1991, and the Soviet Union was declared officially dead. Eleven of the fifteen former Soviet republics have turned themselves into a Commonwealth of Independent States, the exceptions being the three Baltic republics (which have gone their own way) and Georgia (which has been plunged into the throes of civil war). Tensions are already developing between the leaders of some of the Commonwealth's states; but predictions about the future are, thankfully, beyond the scope of this book. Indeed, they are virtually beyond the scope of anybody. In the words of Igor Zakharov, a prominent Russian journalist, 'There are so many varied, unconnected, contradictory and spontaneous events taking place simultaneously all over Moscow - and even more so all over this huge country - that, even in my privileged position on *Nezavisimaya Gazeta* [*The Independent Newspaper*], I understand very little of what is going on.'[48]

What general observations can we make about the representation of women in the motley assortment of films we have offered from the final era of the Soviet Union? How do these fit into the pattern of images of women throughout the history of Soviet cinema as a whole? In the conclusion to Part I of this book, we will glance back over the seventy years of the Soviet Union's existence, and try to draw some broad conclusions about the representation of women in its 'most important art'.

CONCLUSION

Before we discuss the representation of women throughout the seventy-four years of Soviet history, we should begin by recalling some of the most important features of the cinema as a whole. As we have noted throughout these chapters, until the onset of *glasnost'* and *perestroika* film-makers had little choice but to adapt to the prevailing ideology in whatever period of history they found themselves. Accordingly, their films constitute a fascinating mirror of political reality, but a far from faithful reflection of social reality. Reality is a slippery concept at the best of times, however, and our understanding of it is a largely subjective matter. Yet given the Soviet Union's professed commitment to realism in the cinema, it is interesting to see how broadly the term has been interpreted.

The leftist film-makers of the 1920s were theoretically pledged to realism, yet the reality they served up to their audience came in a far from raw form. This was partly because it was filtered through their own political perspectives, and partly because of their interest in developing the cinema as an art as well as a tool of education, which led to experimentation with the creative editing techniques known as montage. Accordingly, what they actually filmed underwent considerable transformation before it was offered up for audience consumption.

Such creative interpretations of reality were nothing to what followed in the Stalin era, however. Yet Stalinist cinema presents a curious contradiction. On the one hand, it can be seen as a complete divergence from real life, the presentation of an idealized vision of life as if it were reality. On the other, it can be seen as a true reflection of the bizarre reality which actually characterized Stalin's Soviet Union. Against a background of show-trials, executions and overflowing labour camps, people were convinced that they were creating Utopia; while famine took hold in the countryside, an atmosphere of perpetual merriment was cultivated in the cities by great sports events, May Day processions, vast military parades. The fairy-tale dichotomy of heroes and villains which entertained Soviet citizens in cinema halls prepared them for the brutal suppression in real life of anyone suspected of doubting the system. Hence, the films of this era both reflected and helped to create the myths about society on which Stalin's vision of socialism was based.

In the Khrushchev era came a reversion to a more genuine understanding of realism. The changes society was undergoing were explored mainly through the eyes of the young (as they would also be in the Gorbachev era, more than two decades later): a new generation confronting a new world. The heroic themes of the Stalin era were replaced by the small-scale problems of their everyday lives, and the grand Stalinist landscapes were reduced to the cramped and shabby realities of urban life. This process underwent a limited reversal after Khrushchev's demise, with a return to a more positive image of Soviet life. All the same, the fantastic illusions of Stalinist cinema were not revived in the Brezhnev decades. Against the backdrop of relative prosperity and well-being, it was now acknowledged that certain social problems did exist. In contrast to the heroic actions of Stalinist stakhanovites, a concern with the psychology of the heroes was now paramount. The creation of the new Soviet person could not be achieved, it seemed, without some personal trauma.

The range of permissible discussion was rapidly expanded in the interim years between Brezhnev's death and Gorbachev's rise to power. The 'second economy' made its first appearance on Soviet screens; so too did the corruption and inefficiency of the Soviet bureaucratic apparatus. This interest in the underbelly of the socialist dream became the main feature of cinema of the *glasnost'* era. The negative aspects of society tumbled across the screen: youth alienation, prostitution, moral anarchy, criminality, drug abuse and - with increasing frequency - violence against women.

Much of the moral chaos depicted on screen in the final years of Soviet power has been blamed by Soviet writers (including, as we shall see, the contributors to this book) on the once-celebrated 'collective' or 'mass'. Beneath the façade of collective responsibility its exact opposite is said to have developed: collective irresponsibility. Script-writer Natal'ya Ryazantseva goes still further and suggests that the basic essentials of human behaviour, such as honour and dignity, were destroyed when they were detached from the individual: 'In our country, the word "honour" has been mutilated for bureaucratic purposes. It has been turned into "the honour of the enterprise", "the honour of the collective farm" - that is, it has been turned into nothing.'[1] She points to a phenomenon which has recently received considerable attention in the Soviet press, that of mothers abandoning newborn babies who are handicapped in Soviet hospitals. This, she suggests, is an act of revenge against a system which consistently denied people any personal responsibility.[2] However, even if the desire to find a scape-goat for the pains of the past is understandable, it can surely be argued that too many of society's ills are being placed at this door. Abandonment of children is hardly unknown in the West, despite the fact that the stress has been on individualism rather than collective responsibility. Nor is it hard to find other reasons why an already overworked and under-financed woman cannot face the additional burden of a child with profound special needs.

At the outset, we discussed the fact that the cinema has, from the very beginning, been credited with a particularly powerful influence over its audience. Accordingly, Soviet leaders consciously employed the cinema as a weapon of propaganda and as a tool in moulding the 'new Soviet person'. What Victoria Bonnell has said of the early Soviet political poster applies equally to the cinema: 'Through mass propaganda, the Bolsheviks sought to establish the hegemony of their interpretation of the past, present and future – their own master narrative – and to inculcate among the population new categories for interpreting the world around them.'[3] Allegorical images of women were common in political art in the immediate aftermath of the revolution, inspired both by pre-revolutionary Tsarist art and the iconography of the French Revolution. These later gave way to more realistic representations of the woman-worker and peasant, but the allegorical woman was revived whenever it was deemed necessary. During the Second World War, for example, much use was made of the female figure to represent the motherland; this was an appeal to people's patriotism in order to encourage them into ever greater efforts and sacrifices. A recent visitor to Moscow would be in no doubt that allegorical representations of women are still in use. In the satirical posters displayed on Prospect Kalinina in 1991, the figure of a woman was used to represent Russia, the economy, culture, poverty, ecology and so on.[4]

Of course, films do not lend themselves to the same blatant allegorical representations to be found in posters. Nonetheless, we have suggested throughout this account that female characters have often functioned on a symbolic level as well as on a simple narrative level.

In the 1920s, there were a number of explorations of the 'new woman' on screen. While the depiction of the working woman was far from universal, many films did contrast the old pre-revolutionary female 'victim' with a more self-assured and independent image of womanhood. But there was often more to these images than first met the eye. In Pudovkin's *Mother*, for example, we find a clear example of the influence of France's Marianne, the French symbol of civic virtue. In case we fail to notice, the sound-track, added by Mosfilm in 1968, helpfully provides a snatch of 'La Marseillaise' as the mother holds the Red Flag aloft and gazes into the glorious future. Kozintsev and Trauberg's

New Babylon also contains some allegorical female images. These are unambiguous in the nightclub scenes, in which France and Paris are both personified by women. However, it could also be argued that Louise represents the conscience of revolutionary France - or, indeed, Marianne again. As we have seen, in a number of films of that era it could be said that women represent the Russian people and/or the new society.

In the 1930s, with Stalin's rapid industrialization drive, women were drawn into the workforce in vast numbers. This situation was reflected on screen. Although the majority of 'positive heroes' were male, we have seen examples of women depicted in such professions as teacher, pilot, even the head of a collective farm. (There was no discussion, however, of how they managed to combine these new roles with their old domestic functions, the burden of which Stalin had done little to reduce.) At the same time, we find a particularly clear example in 1937 (in Vertov's *Lullaby*) of women symbolizing Russia. In films about the Second World War (as in political posters of the same era), such symbolic images proliferated.

In the Brezhnev era, the emergence of a new genre of film about domestic life led to a preponderance of images of women. The so-called 'demographic crisis' - the drop in the birth-rate, especially in the European republics - had led to discussions in the press about the negative consequences of women's employment. (Soviet texts generally refer to women's 'emancipation', suggesting that employment and equality were entirely synonymous.) These discussions were reflected on screen. One of the major cinematic themes of the 1970s was the double-life of the Soviet woman, straddling the often conflicting worlds of public and private production. The practical and emotional difficulties which this brought about were no longer ignored, as in the Stalin era, but became the focus of film-makers' attention. The articles in the press pointed to a single solution - reducing women's work contribution and encouraging them to prioritize motherhood. Film-makers generally came up with more complex conclusions, but the predominant message was still that there had been a high price to pay for this 'emancipation'.

Some of these images, it could be argued, constitute a new development in the familiar symbolic representation of women on screen. In the early years of Soviet cinema, we saw many examples in which female characters represented the Russian land, its people and its eternal values. I noted one film from the Brezhnev era in which this was clearly still the case: the heroine of Gleb Panfilov's *The Theme* represents the land, the creative impulse and the very soul of Russia. However, there are a number of others in which women symbolize not Russia but the Soviet state and its distorted values.

The onset of the Gorbachev era led to more open discussions about Soviet history, and submerged hostilities towards the State began to emerge into the open. At the same time, many of the films which had been shelved in the Brezhnev era were put on general release for the first time, and these included some of those films in which female characters represented the Soviet state. Hence, women found themselves in the position of representing something on screen which now provoked open anger and bitterness on the part of much of the population.

Films made in the Gorbachev era answered this unspoken challenge. Many of the films released in the final years of the Soviet Union's existence continued to offer women as symbols of the old regime, but with some new adaptations. Directors of the Brezhnev era had not been unsympathetic to their heroines; their values may have been misguided, but they were sincere. Now these confused values gave way to total moral bankruptcy. Furthermore, anger towards the Soviet state was expressed on film by violence against the women who had come to represent it, a violence generally depicted in sexual terms. This, we could argue, was the logical but alarming conclusion of the long tradition of using women to depict the country and its morality.

This is not the only reason for depictions of violence against women, however. In many cases, woman herself is evidently the intended victim, and not just woman-as-symbol. Why should this be? At the risk of oversimplifying a complex subject, we can borrow some insights from feminist analyses of Hollywood's Film Noir. In the 1940s and 1950s, Film Noir brought the sexually independent women onto the screen. This female independence presented a serious challenge to patriarchy. The traditional order of gender relations was based on a dichotomy of active male/passive female; the independent, active woman threatened to subvert this. Although this was not the subject of the film's plot, the hero's quest to annihilate this threat formed a sub-text, a kind of subconscious layer of the film. How could the woman be dealt with without interrupting the surface narrative? Before the women's movement, this was a fairly easy matter since women who were sexually independent were automatically considered bad, and inevitably moved in bad circles. Hence their destruction was easily explained and justified within the film narrative. If they were not made safe by being married off, they were murdered; as Ann Kaplan puts it, '[t]he gun or knife stands in for the phallus which must dominate [the woman] by eliminating her'.[5] The women's movement gave women the confidence to lay claim to their own sexuality, and to reject this definition of themselves as necessarily bad simply because they were sexual. This meant that the reason for their punishment became necessarily more open. They were now more obviously paying the price not for being bad, but just for refusing to remain passive. The phallus started to be used as a weapon in a more literal way. As feminist film theorists have noted, there was a sudden glut of films appearing in the early 1970s which depicted women being raped.[6]

Some two decades later, sexually independent women began to appear on Soviet screens, and there was a simultaneous onslaught of male violence against them. However, we cannot point to exactly the same factors in the Soviet situation. There is nothing yet which constitutes a women's movement, for although independent women's groups have begun to emerge, they remain very fragmented. All the same, there is evident concern that patriarchy is under threat. We have discussed the 'demographic crisis' which began in the Brezhnev era, in which the 'masculinization' of women was said to be posing a threat both to Soviet manhood and to Soviet society. Could this lie, on a subconscious level, behind the scenes of rape and violence against women, which began to appear as soon as the cinema was released from censorship? As if to provide us with a clue, there are cases where a clear link is made between the phallus and the weapon. The heroine of Abai Kaprykov's *Blown Kiss* (1990), for example, is a nurse whose fiancé refuses to consummate their relationship until they are married. In her frustration, she seduces a patient in her hospital; she then attempts to kill herself by pointing a hunting rifle *between her legs*.

The few active women who have appeared in films of the later Soviet era have suffered the same fate as their counterparts of Western film tradition. Their independence rarely lasts. Either it turns out to have been an illusion from the start, based on a sexual relationship with a man (as in *Fools Die on Fridays* and *International Girl*); it is relinquished when they fall in love with the hero (*The Assassin*) or it ends with their death, or near-death (*Little Vera*, *International Girl*, *The Assassin*, *Blown Kiss*). The one woman who seems in no danger of dying is Lena in *Seven Days After Murder*. Here, the woman epitomizes the moral collapse which many people feel is consuming the country. Since the pessimistic message is that this state of affairs is not likely to end in the near future, Lena has to be allowed to survive.

There are other possible reasons for the proliferation of images of violence against women. It could simply be that the cinema, having turned its back on Socialist Realism, embraced a different kind of realism with a vengeance. In place of the former idealization of society, negative aspects tumbled across the screen as soon as they had a chance. Not only violence against women but, as we have seen, youth alienation, prostitution, criminality and other forms of 'social disease' became the basic themes of cinema in the Gorbachev era. Certainly, these problems do exist. However, it could be argued that the pendulum swung too far in this direction, and that the past idealization of Soviet society was replaced by its total condemnation.

Whatever the reasons behind it, the depiction of violence against women on screen, and the equation of sex and violence, is a disturbing development in late Soviet cinema, and not one which is likely to promote women's equality. If a more optimistic frame of mind emerges from the disintegration of the

Soviet Union and the creation of a new society (or societies) in its place, perhaps these negative images will transmute into a more positive view of gender relations. However, for the near future I am not hopeful.

PART II

Women on the Screen

We will turn now to the Soviet film critics for their views on the images of women portrayed on their country's screens. We begin with two chapters by Maya Turkovskaya, one of the best known and best qualified writers on the theatre and cinema in the Soviet Union. Born in Moscow in 1924, Turovskaya was an undergraduate both at the philology faculty at Moscow State University, and the State Institute of Theatrical Art. She then went on to do post-graduate research at the Leningrad Institute of Theatre and Music. She has published extensively both in the Soviet Union and abroad, and given papers at a number of international conferences, including the *Fourth International Congress of Soviet Studies*, held in Harrogate in July 1990.

The first of Turovskaya's chapters in this book provides a springboard for those which follow, since she sets representations of women on screen within the broader intellectual and cultural context. She looks at debates around the 'Woman Question' both before and after the revolution, and the image of women which they spawned in literature as well as on screen. She discusses the views of the pre-revolutionary Russian intelligentsia on how women's emancipation was to be achieved, and looks at the first manifestations of independent women. She explores the promises of the fledgling revolution, then turns to the rather more dismal reality which followed those promises. The revolution, she argues, did little to alleviate the appalling burdens placed on Russian women. Unlike their Western counterparts, they had no time to develop a sense of self-awareness, to become aware of their sex 'as an issue'; they were too busy with the debilitating problems of daily life. In the harshness of their lives, the femininity rejected by Western feminists seemed to them a longed-for luxury. This difference goes some way towards explaining why the greater openness and relaxation of the 1980s encouraged not feminism but a series of images of women which seem to fly in its face – beauty contests, pornography and paraded prostitution. The different circumstances of women in the Soviet Union and the West have ensured that they have always been out of step - that they have been concerned with different aspects of the 'Woman Question' at any one time. The present time is no exception.

Turovskaya's second chapter is an edited version of a talk she gave at a women's film festival in San Francisco in 1988, and explores the much debated concept of a specific 'Women's Cinema'.

Oksana Bulgakova is the author of the following chapter (Chapter 13). Originally from the Soviet Union, she now lives in Berlin, where she has developed a reputation as a film critic, script-writer and an expert on film theory. She writes on the changing image of the film star in the various periods of Soviet history.

Elena Stishova lives and works in Moscow. She is the head film critic of the journal *Iskusstvo Kino* (*Cinema Art*). Her chapter is concerned with the mythologized image of Soviet womanhood on screen, particularly in the figure of Klavdia Vavilova in Aleksandr Askoldov's *The Commissar*.

Dilyara Tasbulatova, a film critic from Alma Ata, in Kazakhstan, looks at the image of women in Kazakh films.

Marina Drozdova graduated from the Faculty of Journalism at Moscow State University in 1986. She has since published articles in the journals *Iskusstvo Kino* (*Cinema Art*), *Sovetskii Fil'm* (*Soviet Film*) and *Sovetskii Ekran* (*Soviet Screen*). She looks at the image of young women in films of the *perestroika* era, and in particular at the sex scenes which form such a prominent part of these films.

9 WOMAN AND THE 'WOMAN QUESTION' IN THE USSR

Maya Turovskaya

The 'Woman Question' is concerned with the same circle of problems in both Russia and the West. Yet we have almost always been located at different points on that circle. I believe that this is mainly due to historical differences.

Boris Pasternak once wrote: 'Being a woman is a great labour, a mad heroism'. This seems to me a uniquely Russian saying. The fate of Russian women has always been particularly hard, especially for women of the peasantry. The Russian poet Nekrasov wrote that:

> Fate had three harsh burdens.
> The first was to marry a slave.
> The second – to be the mother of a slave's son.
> The third – to submit to a slave, up until one's grave.
> Each of these dreadful burdens
> Was cast upon the woman of Russian soil.*

The Russian peasant woman was liberated from these three forms of slavery not long ago – a mere 130 years.† Of course, women of the nobility and of the intelligentsia had rather different destinies. Yet these also differed from those of their Western counterparts. Women held a significant position in

---

*From N. A. Nekrasov, 'Moroz: krasnyi nos' in *Izbrannye proizvedeniya* (Leningrad, Lenizdat, 1972 p.164). The original Russian reads as follows:

Три тяжкие доли имела судьба,
И первая доля: с рабом повенчаться,
Вторая – быть матерью сына раба,
А третья – до гроба рабу покоряться,
И все эти грозные доли легли
На женщину русской земли.

†Editor's note: This is a reference to the emancipation of the serfs, carried out in 1861.

aristocratic society. This is clear from the poems of Pushkin, which every Russian knows and which have the same significance within our culture that the plays of Shakespeare have in the English language. Note, for example, the images of Tat'yana and Ol'ga in *Eugene Onegin*. Like those of peasant women, the lives of women of the intelligentsia were influenced by serfdom, though in a different way; the intelligentsia characteristically carried a sense of guilt about the Russian people, and women as well as men took this 'dreadful burden' on themselves.

The 'Woman Question' came to the fore in Russia at the beginning of this century, as it did elsewhere. But in Russia it did not take the form of a separate suffragist movement. It developed, instead, as part of a broader intellectual movement. A. Amfiteatrov, an essayist and publicist, was a typical champion of the Russian women's movement in the early twentieth century. He summarized the liberal ideas on this theme in an interesting collection of articles entitled 'The female "exclusion from the system"'. The word he used – 'Nestroenie' – does not exist in the Russian language; the author invented it as a way of conveying the idea that women's issues had reached a turning point in the unsettled social situation which had emerged at the start of the century. He deals with various aspects of the 'Woman Question'.

The arrival of this 'questioning state' was facilitated by the appearance of the 'young lady' in Russia, the *baryshnya*. She found herself in that state of relative freedom which now existed between childhood and marriage, though one still tempered by a strict sexual morality. Girls were not married off at such a young age now, and so did not go straight from their childhood to the altar. A breathing-space had appeared, which made possible the development of self-awareness. In time, this personal development entered into the social sphere, and turned into the 'Woman Question'.

In a lecture delivered in Paris, Amfiteatrov compared the young lady in France with her Russian counterpart. He noted that instead of receiving the old-fashioned, sentimental kind of education which prepared them for nothing but the role of wife, girls in Russia were turning into revolutionary types: students, people seeking (in one form or another) a social role. It is easy to agree with this observation. The young lady of Russia dashed not to her ballet class but 'to the people'. She taught peasant children; she became a doctor; she even planted bombs.

One of the members of the People's Will, an organization set up to destroy the Tsarist government, was a woman, Sof'ya Perovskaya. The daughter of a general, she was hanged in 1881 (at the age of 28), along with four men, for the execution of Aleksander II. Another well-known woman, Sof'ya Kovalevskaya, who lived from 1850 to 1891, was an outstanding mathematician and scientist. She was certainly an exceptional character, yet one could also say that she was flowing with the tide of those times. In the letters and diaries of the women of that era (many of which have been preserved in the archives), there is much that is both personal and social, so that it is difficult to distinguish between the two.

Of course, social emancipation goes hand in hand with greater sexual freedom. This is reflected in the literature of writers such as Amfiteatrov, and of Verbitskaya, the author of a number of rather trivial novels about the 'new woman' which were very popular at the turn of the century, in particular *The Key to Happiness*. It is also evident in the plays of V.I. Nemirovich-Danchenko, the founder of the Moscow Arts Theatre. In short, sexual freedom was a feature of the whole field of the 'issue-conscious', 'popular' and sometimes almost gutter culture which blossomed at the turn of the century. The 'woman of destiny' was generally at the same time 'forward'. She was opposed to hypocrisy and inequality both in social matters, and in the sphere of sexual morality.

But it did not matter how many 'lionesses', how many 'emancipesses' appeared in the pages of novels and on the stages of theatres. In the eyes of society, the concept of sacrifice was still more important, more worthy, than the concept of womanhood. A woman's erotic appeal was never her most important quality in Russian culture. She performed the function, primarily, of a moral standard. The 'Russian at the *rendez-vous*' – that is, the man – was generally portrayed as her inferior in this sense. If one does not bear in mind this female halo, this idealization of the woman, it is impossible to understand the image of the Russian woman which is part of our national heritage.

The 'Woman Question' was not solved, of course, by the *baryshnya,* the young lady who went 'to the people' or who went into medicine. Inequality with men existed here, too. In order to study, a Russian woman had to go abroad; most often she ended up in Germany or Switzerland, which offered inexpensive opportunities for study. Even when special schools and courses began to open for women in Russia, it was not easy to squeeze through their narrow doors.

There was another aspect of the 'Woman Question' which appeared, during the climate of rapid urbanization, alongside the right to education and the right to an independent life: this was female prostitution. That same Amfiteatrov devoted a significant portion of his book on women to this theme. Within the parameters of Russian culture, prostitution has never been portrayed as the 'oldest profession'. It has always been seen as a fall from grace, a loss of honour. The first heroine of Russian sentimentalism, Nikolai Karamzin's 'poor Liza', drowns herself after being seduced by the shallow Erast. (Karamzin was a friend of Pushkin, though many years his senior. He was noted in particular for his book *The History of the Russian State*.) The 'infernal' women of Dostoevskii's novels – Nastas'ya Filippovna in *The Idiot*, for example, or Grushen'ka in *The Brothers Karamazov* – took revenge on society for their fall. The early Russian cinema, like literature, created images of the female seducer, the female sacrifice. The pre-revolutionary actress Vera Kholodnaya was the embodiment of these images.*

There were, of course, attempts to achieve the moral salvation of the 'fallen'. Sometimes this took place on an individual level, prompted by that 'guilt about the fate of the people' which formed part of the moral code of the intelligentsia. Alternately, it took place on a social level, in the form of a social Utopia. An example of this can be found in the workshop for women set up by Vera Pavlovna, in Chernyshevskii's famous novel *What is to be Done?*, which became the revolutionary manifesto for a whole generation of young people. (Incidentally, Vera Pavlovna also became the symbol of female sexual freedom, albeit one with an ideological lining.) There were also philanthropic attempts, for the most part initiated by women, to improve social conditions and treat these social victims.

Amfiteatrov did not share these illusions about saving the 'fallen', nor about philanthropy in general. Perhaps he represents more accurately the liberal understanding of how the 'Woman Question', including prostitution, could conclusively be solved. He viewed prostitution as a social evil, a consequence of women's lack of equality in society. The fallen woman was frequently a poor girl, from a peasant background, who entered domestic service. She was then seduced by the master of the house, or by his son, or by someone else from high society. Afterwards she was tossed out onto the streets. Such scenarios were the result of the social structure which did not allow her adequate or sufficiently well-paid work. According to Amfiteatrov, when legal marriage takes place in conditions of inequality, this just amounts to a more polite form of women selling themselves - i.e. it is legalized prostitution. Amfiteatrov called the woman without legal rights 'sexual merchandise', something to be bought and sold. He suggested - not without justification, as it turns out - that the 'Woman Question' would become the next great movement of the twentieth century. In his view, the final resolution of the issue rested on women gaining absolutely equal rights. In other words, by means of social reform, female 'nestroenie' - their virtual exclusion from the system - would be transformed into a general 'ustroenie', or all-embracing social system.

One of the films made by Chardynin in the years leading up to the revolution was called *The Woman of Tomorrow*. Chardynin attempted to challenge the image of the eternal female victim; he put in its place a woman doctor who, possessing both social and spiritual independence, not only did not become 'sexual merchandise' in marriage, but proved herself stronger than both of the ill-starred men in her life (one shot himself, the other declined into

*For a fuller discussion of Kholodnaya and the characters she portrayed, see Chapters i and ii.

degeneracy). She went on to find an equal partner in the shape of a doctor colleague.

Like many of the other Utopian aspirations of the Russian intelligentsia, hopes of achieving women's liberation through the granting of equal rights were destroyed by the practical realities of the Russian revolution. I have always thought that there should have been some sort of decree on women's rights after 1917, in just the same way that there was a decree on land. But no such women's freedom charter has been discovered among the documents of the revolution. The Utopia envisioned by Amfitreatov was ushered into existence with no fireworks, in a mundane way, in the form of a clause that was added to legal documents quietly asserting women's equality – 'regardless of sex, nationality etc.', was the wording. At the same time, however, class inequality received much more attention; benefits were granted to the working class, and various privations imposed on the former 'exploitative' classes. Hence, if we recall the words of the poet Nekrasov, the weight of 'dreadful burdens' were once again, albeit in a new way, placed on the shoulders of 'the woman of Russian soil'.

All the same, in theory – and to some extent in practice – the first decade of the revolution did witness the so-called emancipation of women. This was particularly true for women in the Eastern republics of the Soviet Union, who had previously been forced to wear the veil. Disputes took place about the nature of 'free love' between equal partners. Chernyshevskii's Vera Pavlovna, with her workshop, her two men and her portentous 'socialist dream' (which was ridiculed at the time by Dostoevskii) became an example for many women. Among these was Lily Brik, the lover of Mayakovskii.

This new state of affairs was broached indirectly in A. Room's celebrated film *Bed and Sofa*. The heroine is no intellectual (the action takes place in a petty-bourgeois milieu, as hinted by the film's Russian title, *No. 3 Meschchanskaya Street* – Meshchanskaya means bourgeois). Yet she leaves both of her men in order to give birth to her child alone, to take responsibility for it herself.

The heroine of Pil'nyak story *The Birth of Man* is independent and free-thinking, but despite her supposed equal rights she too falls into the same trap of nature. The problem of unwanted pregnancy was not one which had formerly received the serious consideration of the standard-bearers of women's equality. The existence of wet-nurses and servants had made it possible for the pre-revolutionary 'woman of tomorrow' to bring up her child 'off screen'. Revolutionary reality, having made accessible to the masses the image of the working woman (my own mother, for example, was a doctor), brought a new range of issues to the 'Woman Question'.

The Soviet man was not in a position to support a family, even if he wanted to. (Nor, indeed, is he to this day.) Female labour, not only in the countryside but also in the city, was an economic necessity. The working woman had become the norm in all social classes. The complete chaos which the revolution and civil war had wrought on the economy did not make things any easier. The working woman was physically incapable of maintaining a household without outside help. Hence, in place of the servants of the past, the wet nurses, maids and cooks, there appeared a new social institution – the domestic worker placed in the meagre and overcrowded conditions of a communal apartment.

If the working woman as a mass phenomenon was a child of economic necessity, then the domestic worker was a victim of the forced destruction of the villages. In my family we had a succession of such women, with two of them living almost their entire lives with us. One, Polina, who had come from a dispossessed kulak family, lived with my parents' family for almost forty years. The other, also called Polina, and also from the countryside, has been with me for twenty-five years. More often than not, however, such employment was a temporary state. Girls went on to work in factories or to become students – if they could get a place in a hostel. This was not so easy. Indeed, it was often the lack of available accommodation which had driven them into domestic service in the first place. The film *House on Trubnaya Street*, made in 1927 under the direction of Boris Barnet, and Arbuzova's play of 1939, *Tanya*, both dealt with the fate of such girls. G. Aleksandrov's film *The Bright Path* (1940) is one of most obvious films that was inspired by Lenin's dictum about every cook learning to govern; the heroine begins as a domestic, becomes a textile worker, and goes on to be a member of the Supreme Soviet, defeating the 'wreckers' who threaten the revolution. Yet in reality, society needed domestic workers to stay where they were. In the large cities, the working woman who also had a family could not have survived without her; nor vice versa.

Alas, prostitution did not disappear with the establishment of equal rights. In 1927, O. Freilikh made a film called *Prostitute*, which was part feature film, part popularized documentary, about the fate of three women who had ended up on the streets. The attitude towards the problem had changed profoundly, however. The 'fall' was no longer seen as something final, irreversible. A woman could change her fate, could shape her own destiny, by taking a job.

Yet the type of employment offered to women was often hard, physical labour. The so-called 'Dictatorship of the Proletariat' – however nominal its achievement – had given birth to a new prejudice. The work which was most respected, and most often portrayed in films, was physical labour. Women strove to master male professions. Women pilots, parachutists and tractor drivers became the heroines of the day. This is especially notable during the cinema of the 1930s. The machine-gun operator Anna, from the 1934 film *Chapaev*, directed by the so-called Vasiliev brothers (who were not really brothers, though they shared the same surname), is one popular example.

Sexual freedom not only ceased to be encouraged in the 1930s, it was no longer even a topic of discussion. Women's role in the family returned to much the same old mould. Femininity, as such, became almost a 'negative' quality. In the play by Arbuzov, *Tanya*, the heroine gives up her studies at an institute for the sake of her husband, though he then abandons her because of the 'petty-bourgeois' attitudes he claims she has. (In the end, incidentally, she becomes a doctor and saves the life of his child.) The woman's erotic appeal was completely forgotten. The only real 'star' of Soviet cinema in the 1930s, Lyubov' Orlova, continually had to conceal her healthy sexuality under the guise of a simpleton.

As early as the 1920s, in place of the 'worldly' heroines of the past, a new type was created on screen – the strong peasant woman. Even beautiful actresses such as Emma Tsesarskaya and Alla Tarasova, of the Moscow Arts Theatre, had to hide their beauty beneath the rough boots, scarves and quilted jackets of the peasantry and enter into equal combat with men on male territory – either in the form of physical labour (as in the 1940 film *Peasant Women,* directed by V. Batalov) or fighting in the war. The development of such a tradition came in very handy during the Second World War. Even the gentle Marina Ladynina in Pyr'ev's popular village comedies donned working boots and performed great feats of labour, while the 'Komsomol goddess' Makarova displayed equally phenomenal work enthusiasm. The apogee of the new female image was Vera Maretskaya in *Member of the Government,* made in 1939 by A. Zarkhi and I. Kheifits – an oppressed peasant woman who learns to direct a collective farm, goes on to denounce an enemy of the people (something almost obligatory in films of this era), and finally, though almost losing her husband in the process, enters the Supreme Soviet.

In reality, even in the urban environment (which was somewhat easier than the countryside), the 'emancipated' woman eventually came to see her emancipation as a burden. She was worn down by a combination of strains – the excessive workload, the difficulties of everyday life, traditional morals and congested living quarters. (I remember meeting my dates at the chemist, under the clock, at the skating rink – there was no other place.) Eventually, women came to look back on the era when they were 'sexual merchandise' as almost one of privilege.

Nekrasov once wrote that the Russian woman was prepared to:

> Stop her horse in mid-gallop
> And enter a burning hut!*

*From Nekrasov, 'Moroz: krasnyi nos', op. cit. The original Russian reads as follows:
    Коня на скаку остановит,
    В горящую избу войдет!

In our time, however, Korzhavin makes a different observation about his female contemporaries. He sighs:

> She would prefer it to be otherwise -
> To have leisure to put on an expensive gown.
> But the horse goes right on galloping,
> And the hut is still burning, still burning . . .*

During the war, the following rhyme was heard everywhere:

> I am a horse, I am an ox -
> I am a woman, I am a man . . .†

This is not far from the truth.

Of course we did everything we could, everything we were allowed, almost by instinct. We tried to dress smartly, we had romances, we brought up our children. But we simply did not have time to become aware of our sex, to see it as an issue. Both the rapid freezing-over of the 1960s Thaw and the difficulties of everyday life prevented us from acquiring this self-awareness. Only in the 1980s did dreams about female erotic appeal begin to tumble out of our subconscious, out of the underground, like the frozen sounds from the horn of Munchausen. Yet in contemporary films, in the arrival of Soviet beauty contests, in the ostentatious apparel of our new breed of prostitutes - the 'International Girls' - these dreams have turned into something grotesque and backward. While feminism was developing in the West, we were busy battling for a more comfortable life. So once again, we now find ourselves at different points on the circle.

Она бы хотела иначе –
Носить драгоценный наряд,
Но кони все скачут и скачут,
А избы горят и горят.

Я и лошадь, я и бык
Я и баба и мужик

10 'WOMEN'S CINEMA' IN THE USSR

Maya Turovskaya

What do we actually mean by 'women's cinema'? Are we referring to films which are directed by women, or films which address issues or themes which are of particular concern to women? In the Soviet Union, these are not necessarily synonymous.

If we mean by 'women's cinema' films which are directed by women, then the phenomenon began in Russia very early on. In 1916, Ol'ga Preobrazhenskaya – a stage and screen actress who had already starred in a number of pictures – made her debut as a director with a film called *Baryshnya-Krestyanka*. Translated literally, this means something like 'noble-peasant girl'. It was based on a novel by the great nineteenth-century Russian poet, Aleksandr Pushkin.

A year later, the October revolution took place. This led to radical changes not only in the practical possibilities which were open to women but also in their self-confidence and self-awareness. They achieved equality with men, at least in a formal, legal sense. Of course, it was not possible for all women, at once, to fully realize and use this equality, but step by step, as their social consciousness was transformed, a consciousness which embraced the cinema and the arts in general, the concept of the 'new woman' came into being. This concept had not sprung from nowhere. It had its antecedents in such famous women of the revolution as Larisa Reisner, who lived from 1895 to 1926 – a great beauty who was a journalist, political activist and writer – or Aleksandra Kollontai (1872–1952) – one of a handful of women diplomats, who was the Soviet Ambassador to Sweden and then Mexico. The concept was, all the same, a prototype, and became the object of heated discussion.

Yet in the early years, 'women's cinema' and the image of the 'new woman' did not go together. It was male directors who generally made films about women's liberation. The most famous and controversial was *Bed and Sofa*, by Abram Room, based on a story by Viktor Shklovskii. This film addressed the concept of 'free love', as it was called then, and examined the relationship between one woman and two men. In the end, having discovered that she is pregnant, the woman leaves them both; she means to assume full responsibility for her own life as well as that of her child.

At this time, Ol'ga Preobrazhenskaya was making films for and about children. *Fedka's Truth* came in 1925, *Kashtanka*, based on a story by Chekhov, in 1926, and *Anya* in 1927. Women in our country have often made films for children. This is significant, since it means that as well as conducting professional work in the cinema, they were also participating in the traditional female role of upbringing. However, in the same year that *Anya* appeared, Preobrazhenskaya also made a film for adults, *Peasant Women of Ryazan*. As well as being her first really big success, this can be considered the first 'women's film' in both senses of the term – it was directed by a woman, and it addressed woman's *dolya*. This word has no direct translation in English, it means something like 'fate', but with a shade of sadness, a tinge of sorrow. The fate of Russian women was at all times harder than that of men, especially in village life. This film uses the traditional structure of a melodrama, something which has always been very popular with Russian audiences, and this preference was not changed by the revolution. The style is that of a *lubok*, which is a kind of folk comic-strip of old Russia, consisting of primitive pictures with inscriptions. Early Russian cinema inherited much from the aesthetics of the *lubok*.

The story is based on *snokharchestvo*. Again, this word has no English equivalent. It refers to the practice of the master of a patriarchal household sleeping with his daughter-in-law. In this film, it is used both as a narrative trick and as an attempt to reflect the reality of everyday village life.

There are two distinct female types portrayed in the film. One is the poor bride Anna, whom old Shironin weds to his weak-willed son, Ivan. Then, when Ivan goes off to fight in the First World War, Shironin rapes her. The other type is Shironin's own daughter, Vasilisa – a strong, freedom-loving woman, a complete contrast to Anna. Vasilisa indulges in love outside marriage and has set up an orphanage for homeless children in a country mansion. She is the 'new woman'. (She was played by Emma Tsesarskaya, who went on to become a star of the peasant films of the 1930s.) Incidentally, the film was made in the same year as *Battleship Potemkin*, yet in contrast, it refers to the war and the revolution only indirectly.

Despite her depiction of the new woman, Preobrazhenskaya still belonged to the old cinema, with its traditional narratives and styles. At the same time, however, a genuine 'new woman' appeared in the Soviet cinema – indeed, was one of its founders. This was Esfir' Shub. Preobrazhenskaya had come to the cinema by way of the theatre; she had been a pupil of Stanislavskii, at the Arts

Theatre. Shub, however, took a completely different route. She was a graduate of the Higher Women's Institute in Moscow where her teachers were the renowned philologists N. Veselovskii, P. Sakulin and F. de la Bart. Under their guidance, she studied Dante, Dostoevskii and Heine, and in 1918 got a job in the Theatre Department of the Peoples' Commissariat for Education. She became personal secretary to the great director and leader of the 'October Theatre', Vsevolod Meierhold. While working at the Theatre Department, she met a young man who had just returned from the front (this was the time of the civil war), and with whom she developed a passion for this new art form, the cinema. His name was Sergei Eisenstein.

Shub did not go to the cinema school (where Preobrazhenskaya was one of the teachers). Instead, she went straight to work. Her approach may seem strange; she re-edited, or literally re-cut, foreign films for Soviet audiences, and wrote new texts for them. There were two reasons for this practice. One was simply that there was a chronic shortage of film stock in the Soviet Union, and this method got around the problem of finding film to shoot with. The other was that foreign films were considered 'bourgeois' in their original form; they had to be remade in such a way that they would serve the proletarian revolution. This was exactly what Shub did, both by herself and in collaboration with Eisenstein. The famous film by Fritz Lang, for example, *Doctor Mabuse*, was re-edited by Shub and Eisenstein as *Gilded Gold*. Unfortunately we have been unable as yet to find a print of this interesting product.

So Shub became a professional film-editor, and a revolutionary artist. While Preobrazhenskaya's roots were in the old Russian theatre, in the studio-based cinema and in melodrama, Shub's influences were Meierhold and the film-chronicle or documentary footage. She formed part of the new revolutionary intelligentsia.

For Shub, the cinematographic ideal was the documentary. This was the case also for Dziga Vertov. There was a big difference between them, however. Vertov created his documentaries according to the laws of poetry. Shub, on the other hand, was the inventor of the art of film-making which later became known as 'montage', or compilatory film. She was also the first to think of using old film-chronicle to create new films. When the film archive of the Russian Royal Family came into her hands, she cut from it her first and most famous film, *The Fall of the Romanov Dynasty*. (She also got some of the footage for this film by actually purchasing it from American firms.) This film was made in the same year as Eisenstein's *Battleship Potemkin* and Preobrazhenskaya's *Peasant Women of Ryazan* – 1927, a key year for the Soviet film industry. (I should perhaps note here that the script for *Battleship Potemkin* was written by a woman – Nina Agadzhanova.)

While *Peasant Women of Ryazan* answered all of the requirements of pre-revolutionary Russian cinema - melodrama, *lubok* and emotional appeal - *The Fall of the Romanov Dynasty* became a manifesto for the new, revolutionary cinema. It was based on the theoretical declarations of Kuleshov, Eisenstein and Vertov (though there were arguments between these artists) that it was necessary to show real life on screen, to appeal to the intellect, and to do so by use of montage.

We have seen, then, that 'women's cinema' had already, by 1927, rightly claimed a significant position for itself in the Soviet film world. Women's legal equality with men was being followed, in great strides, by equality in practice. It is interesting to note, though, that the first image of the 'new woman' was produced by Preobrazhenskaya, though she herself was from the old school of film-making.

In fact, 'women's themes' were at that time very popular in the cinema. There is nothing strange in this. Women were, after all, the most down-trodden people in Russia. All the same, this theme did not become a distinguishing feature of films made by women. Preobrazhenskaya continued to make films until 1941 (often in consort with other directors), but *Peasant Women of Ryazan* remained an exception as it was the only film she made which tackled women's fate.

How can we explain this? The idea of 'equality' presupposed, among other things, that women should be exactly the same as men. Accordingly, they strove to master all of the most difficult professions. On one side of the coin, we have women who became pilots and parachutists; on the other side, women working in the *Metrostroi* (constructing the underground transport system) or at the great furnaces melting metal. (We are still dealing with the effects of such 'emancipation'; women are working where they should not be, where extremely demanding physical labour is required.) In such a climate, it did not seem appropriate for women to make films about distinctly women's themes.

Even today, women in intellectual professions are proud when they are complimented on having a 'man's brain' - or, in the case of a film director, a 'man's hand'. The idea of women expressing their own concerns is still resisted, if not openly laughed at. This is all the effect of the 'equality' of the 1920s. When women in the Soviet Union called themselves 'equal partners', they actually ended up losing rather a lot. Now, it seems that to be recognized as an 'equal partner' is the dream of many women in the West. Their daughters will not thank them for it.

I would like to mention one more film of the 1920s which was directed by a woman, *The Glass Eye*. This film is not very interesting in itself, but it is still significant for a number of reasons. Firstly, it was directed by Lilya (or Lily) Brik, who was Mayakovskii's famous love. She was seen as the very image of the emancipated woman, even though she did not actually 'achieve' much: she did not become much of a director, nor much of an actress (though Mayakovskii made a film in which she starred, called *Chained by a Film*). Yet the story of the film *Bed and Sofa* was inspired by Brik's life. Secondly, Brik cut the compilative material in her film with drama scenes in which Veronika Polonskaya, Mayakovskii's last love, appeared. The film is, then, one of the curiosities of women's cinema.

Glancing through Esfir' Shub's filmography, it would seem that there are no films about women. However, this is not so. Among her projects for films which were not completed, we find the script for a film which was simply to be entitled *Women*. The film was conceived as a documentary, but with a story-line. It included the full set of ideals concerning women's equality. It made a mockery of the sentimental stories of the old cinema, and inserted in their place images of the 'new woman'. The heroines were not actresses but real people whom Shub had sought out for use in the film. There is the female head of a village Soviet, or council. There is the working-class woman who is studying English, and engages in sport. There are women working on the construction of the metro. There are foreign tourists, rich but unsophisticated, even rather foolish. There is a Black woman, Mildred, who has come to the Soviet Union to take part in the real life of Soviet women. The film also looks at the grave social problems of that time: prostitution, homelessness amongst orphaned children. It even includes a suicide committed for love! Those who want to understand how Soviet women felt about themselves in the early years of the revolution would do well to read this script.

It may seem paradoxical that this film did not appear on the screens. However, Shub had begun the project in the beginning of the 1930s. By then, compilative revolutionary cinema was considered dubious and was strongly criticized. Films of quite another type were being promoted - commercial, mass-culture films, with simple plots and simple styles. In this climate, Shub's more intellectual work remained on paper.

Women directors who worked in the 1930s, such as Vera Stroeva, Yuliya Solntseva and Margarita Barskaya, did not, in principle, distinguish themselves from men. Vera Stroeva was married to a director, Grigorii Roshal', and together they were as complex a pair of directors as Larisa Shepit'ko and Elem Klimov were later to become. Unlike the Klimovs, however, they sometimes worked together. One of their best films, *Petersburg Night* (from the story by Dostoevskii), was made in collaboration in 1934. Yuliya Solntseva was also married to a great director, Aleksandr Dovzhenko; she became a director in her own right only after his death, when she began to make films from his unrealized scripts. (*Poem about the Sea*, made in 1958, is one of her films.) Before this, in the 1920s, she was an exotic film star - it was she who played the Martian princess in the science fiction film of 1924, *Aelita*.

Margarita Barskaya made only one film, *Torn Boots* (1933). Nonetheless, her contribution was important. This film was greatly loved by people of my generation in our childhood. (It has to be said, however, that the film now looks rather weak.) Barskaya was also the wife of a director, Chardynin, who was well known in the years before the revolution. At that time, she was a none too talented actress. However, she has gone down in the history of Soviet cinema as one of the pioneers and initiators of children's cinema. Preobrazhenskaya also made some films for children, of a rather didactic nature, but *Torn Boots* is the really novel achievement amongst children's films. Barskaya was one of the first to film real children, and not just single child-stars, but big groups of children, ranging in age from one year 3 months to 13 years (the film's main character, Bubi, was 3 years old).

Barskaya's fame is not based only on the making of this one popular film, however. In 1930, she opened the Laboratory for Children's Cinema, and later, in 1936, she founded a special studio, Soyuzdetfilm, dedicated to the making of children's films. Hence children's cinema – which could be described as a special branch of 'women's cinema' in the Soviet Union – was the particular achievement of Margarita Barskaya.

Moving to the present day, we now have many women directors. As a rule they are graduates of VGIK, the All-union State Institute of Cinematography. There are several names amongst them who count not only among the best in women's cinema but in Soviet cinema as a whole. There is Larisa Shepit'ko, who was tragically killed in a car crash at the height of her career; Lana Gogoberidze; Kira Muratova, who to our joy has recently returned to active work in the cinema; and Dina Asanova.

Dina Asanova – who, like Shepit'ko, died tragically early – was a very original director. Her work is interesting for a number of different reasons. One of these is that, although she worked in Russian cinema, she was herself Kirgizian, and began her career in her national studio, Kirgizfilm. Now, few of the republics do not have women directors working in their film studios. (The most celebrated of the non-Russian female directors is Lana Gogoberidze – Georgia has produced a number of women directors, the first of whom was Lana's own mother.)

Dina Asanova's particular interest was films about teenagers. She was very fond of young people and worked very well with them, even those who are generally considered 'difficult' (both in our country and in the West). Her films *Woodpeckers Don't Get Headaches, The Restricted Key* and, in particular, *Tough Kids*, were important not only from a cinematographic point of view, but also in terms of their social comment. Young people watched them eagerly and discussed them heatedly. Asanova touched on a range of complex issues before any form of *perestroika* had begun, and she did so completely on her own initiative. Curiously, one of her weakest films was the only one which had a 'women's theme'. This is not coincidental. Dealing with specifically female problems is not an easy thing in our cinema.

Larisa Shepit'ko (a strikingly beautiful woman, incidentally, who could have become a great film-star, the Greta Garbo of Soviet cinema, if she had so chosen) made two films about women. The first was *You and Me*, made in 1971, which was not particularly good; and the second was the first-class *Wings*, made in 1976. The latter is a very objective portrait of a generation of women who have achieved equality, record achievements and equal partnership with men. I will not say she was actually hostile to this generation, but certainly she was less than enthusiastic. Sometimes she shows sympathy for her main character, sometimes not – but at any rate, she certainly does not identify herself with this character. Paradoxically, Shepit'ko was herself seen as the embodiment of equality and even of female competitiveness with men. She refused to recognize the concept of 'women's cinema', in fact, she even considered the notion humiliating.

Lana Gogoberidze is the complete opposite. She not only sympathizes with the idea of women expressing themselves on screen, but herself provides the best examples of this. Her film *Some Interviews on Personal Questions*, made in 1979, has been shown around the globe. The film can justly be regarded as a model of female self-expression, although it contains only a few actual autobiographical motifs. (The heroine's mother had been arrested during the years of Stalin's terror, as had Gogoberidze's own mother; her aunts rescued her from an orphanage and brought her up, as was also the case with Gogoberidze.) In my view, this film is the first in Soviet cinema which can properly be called a real 'woman's film'.

Now that we have been re-acquainted with the work of Kira Muratova, however, we can place her in the same category. Kira Muratova is a very original director whose films we have finally seen twenty years late. *Brief Encounters* (made in 1968) and *Long Farewells* (1971) are female through and through, and not only in their themes, but also in their outlook on life.

Today, then, we have a real and serious women's cinema in both senses of the term – films which are made by women and address women's themes. All the same, one still needs considerable courage to speak aloud about this, even in our film-makers' union. Lana Gogoberidze has this courage. Not only does she make women's films (her most recent film, incidentally, *Turnabout*, is a sympathetic portrait of an old actress, a former star); she also talks about, and organizes for, women's cinema. At the 15th Moscow Film Festival it was decided to create an international organization of women working in film, and Gogoberidze became its first president.

It would, perhaps, be logical to stop on this optimistic note. However, there are a few more points I would like briefly to address. Although I realize that the term 'women's film' is usually applied to films which have been directed by women, our experience shows that the role of women script-writers is hardly less important. In general, the personal role of the script-writer in our cinema is more significant than it is in the West. In Russia, a script-writer is seen as a distinguished author. The script has a life independent of the film; it may be published whether or not it is filmed, and regardless of whether the film is successful. Furthermore, films 'about women' often owe their existence to the efforts of women script-writers. Some of the popular Soviet films on women's themes such as *Member of the Government* (1940) or *Village Teacher* (1947) were made by male directors, but from scripts written by women – in these cases, Katerina Vinogradskaya and Maria Smirnova respectively. Hence it is my feeling that Women's Film Festivals should show retrospectives not only of films by women directors but also by women script-writers.

We should also note the contribution made by women film critics. The role of women in this area of the film world has been especially significant; and all the more so because, as we say in Russia, they are 'multi-loom weavers' – they are working on many different things at the same time. I, for example, am primarily a critic, but was also a script-writer for Mikhail Romm's famous film *Ordinary Fascism*** and for a number of documentaries. I also did the film-editing, in a Bulgarian television studio, for two programmes in the documentary series *Cinema and the Stars*. This was, incidentally, about the image of women in the American cinema; the programmes I worked on were called *Tales of Old Manhattan* and *Beloved of All America*.

I am by no means an exception. I should mention above all Neya Zorkaya, who is an historian both of pre-revolutionary and post-revolutionary cinema. Inna Solov'eva and Vera Shitova are also accomplished critics and scholars. At the same time, however, we must be aware that women critics in our country do not see themselves as being in the business of 'women's criticism'. They regard it as a great compliment when it is said of them that they have 'a masculine hand'.

Women not only make films: they also write – among other things, about women and films. It would, accordingly, be interesting to organize presentations and retrospectives not only of films, but also of books. I am, however, a representative of 'the most reading-oriented country in the world'; perhaps I will not be understood in the more 'audiovisual' countries!

---

*Editor's note: This was scripted by Maya Turovskya and Yurii Khanyutin, who were both known primarily as film critics, and released in 1965. It sought the psychological roots of Nazism in the social instability of Germany in the 1930s, and the feeling of inferiority which this spawned.

11 THE HYDRA OF THE SOVIET CINEMA

The Metamorphoses of the Soviet Film Heroine

Oksana Bulgakova

One of the conscious pre-requisites for the creation of heroes or heroines of the screen is the notion of the social stereotype. The alteration of these stereotypes is caused by the arrival of a new epoch, which puts forward a new person as the ideal. This essay will explore the development of the most enduring images of the Soviet heroine through the seventy-year history of Soviet cinema.

FROM 1910 TO THE 1920s: TAKING LEAVE OF THE 'QUEENS OF THE SCREEN'

The change in the image of the film heroine which took place in the early years of the revolution - from the heroines of pre-revolutionary films, to the new woman of the Soviet era - was particularly striking. When the old social structure was overthrown, and the old social strata mixed up, the cinema was for a time virtually extinguished. But it gradually returned to life, peopled by new faces. (This happened not just because the old film stars of the 'Golden Series'* were simply removed from the posters: many of them had emigrated, such as Natal'ya Lisenko, Vera Karalli and Natal'ya Kovan'ko. Vera Kholodnaya had died.)

A beautiful, delicate woman with a classically perfect face, narrow eyebrows, a poetic curl in her hair - 'a suffering victim of passions and circumstances'[1] - is obliged to give up her place to a woman worker and peasant, a soldier, a woman from the lower classes. A woman of the revolution. This woman is literally moving from a basement to a palace - and at the same time, she is taking over the film-palace. This sharp change in the social status of the film

*Editor's note: This was the name given to a series of pre-revolutionary cinema hits.

heroine was a necessary step. It also resulted in a liberation from the strict conception of female beauty which prevailed in the past, and gave freer rein to the social role and behaviour allowed of her.

In the recent past, before the revolution, the cinema had concentrated on tales of seduction and temptation. It had explored the unhappy love affairs of governesses, circus stars and aristocrats in dramas of jealousy, tragic misunderstandings and self-sacrifice. Evil was personified by villains intent on destroying the heroine's happiness. The cinema openly seduced the audience with its splendid queens of the screen, who were under the sway of mystical forces and fatal passions. It is interesting to note that no virtuous Cinderellas, no optimistic Mary Pickford-types, gained a foothold in the Russian cinema. Neya Zorkaya, our renowned researcher on the silent film, noted that while there certainly were Russian versions of the Cinderella story, the heroines did not end up at the altar with their Prince Charmings. On the contrary, they had to pay for their brief moment of luxurious and illusory happiness with suffering, illness and death. [2]

The standard of female beauty in those years, the stereotype of the film heroine, was personified by Vera Kholodnaya. She appeared on screen as a melancholic mixture of woman and girl, though often with the features of a *femme fatale* (depending on the story), infused with suffering virtue. [3] The heroine which Kholodnaya played always surrendered passively to her fate, which took the form of a male tempter. The subject of the tale was always seduction, the drama of adultery. Socially, she came from the lower middle class. She was the wife of a low-level clerk, an orphan taken in by a millionaire or a circus performer. In the course of the film, her modest life was transformed and she moved up to a 'higher position' – she became the mistress of a rich aristocrat. Her clothes also underwent a transformation. Instead of the white English blouse and muslin dress of a young lady, or the modest, old fur coat of a student, our heroine was now decked out in low-necked evening gowns, necklaces and bonnets with ostrich feathers. Her setting became the salon, the boudoir and the country villa; she was surrounded by bottles of champagne, bowls of fruit and telephones. Ruin, inheritance, marriages contracted for money and the passing of false cheques provided the detail of these stories. The heroine was tempted, abandoned and finally died, bitterly regretting her unfaithfulness to her husband. Vice was beautiful, aesthetic and . . . fatal. The leap to luxury, to the 'light', ended for the heroine in the darkness of the grave.

The philosophy of such films was always the same. It was based on petty-bourgeois dreams and fears. They warned us: Be satisfied with the fate you were given, wealth is the source of evil and in poverty lies the security of virtue. It is interesting to note that it was this kind of heroine – the victim of someone else's sensuality – who became the most popular in Russia, rather than the image of victorious innocence exemplified by Pickford. Perhaps this is because Pickford made her debut in the Victorian era, while Kholodnaya's glory coincided with the years of the First World War, which so completely changed the climate of society.

But the boundaries within society itself were more strict. Hence the path from housemaid to countess, from dishwasher to millionairess, from baker to president, could not easily be trod, even in the cinema. This type of heroine, with her poorly developed sense of self-awareness, who was accustomed to her own subordination and allowed her fragile femininity to be trampled on, is an indication of the level of women's emancipation in Russian society of that era, which rested firmly on patriarchy, and admitted less than 4 per cent of the 'weaker sex' into higher education. But this 'victim of her own social standing' was mourned by cinema audiences. And their compassion was the first step on the path to changing her social standing.

Vera Kholodnaya's appearance, with her delicate, classical, stone-like profile, combined the physical traits of a child – a clear forehead, huge bright innocent eyes – with the sensuous mouth of a vamp. Kholodnaya, the wife of a small-time lawyer, rose suddenly to the heights of a stormy fame and died at the age of 26 in 1919. This was, coincidentally, the year of the birth of Soviet cinema, celebrated in August with the Decree on Nationalization of the Cinema Department.

After the revolution, the traditionally beautiful film actresses did not immediately disappear, but the films they appeared in underwent a distinct change. Melodramas became a way of 'exposing social evils'. The role of fatal forces was now allotted to the former regime, which also took on the blame for destroying the happiness of the heroes:

> The hero-lover . . . adopted heroic poses in the casemate, while tears tumbled from the queen of the screen, a victim of Tsarism.[4]

Hence the salon melodramas underwent their own socialist revolution: the tempters were exposed as 'relics of the past' or as members of the White Guard [counter-revolutionaries].

The Soviet film beauties of the 1920s, like Ol'ga Zhizneva, Vera Malinovskaya, Yuliya Solntseva and Nato Vachnadze, were depicted as relics of a past beauty, as something exotic which somehow remained in this new life. They played romantic heroines and beautiful adventuresses in films based on exotic stories of the past, or about life in the 'golden but decadent' West. They also took on the parts of bourgeois ladies of these new times – the wives of Nepmen, seducing 'Party men' and 'Commissars' with their boudoir beauty, wheedling credit out of them to finance their husbands' shady transactions. Only in such

a context was it possible to offer the old melodramas about temptation, passion
and the large sums of money which go with them. But the appraisal of such
heroines changed. They were no longer melancholy victims who could arouse
the sympathy of the audience. Instead of being seduced, they now did the
seducing, the deceiving and the betraying (or else were used by their husbands
as the instruments by which to do this); their prey were honest and
inexperienced Party members – men freshly returned from the trenches of the
Civil War, who found themselves caught up in *The Poison of the New Economic
Policy* (such was the name of Boris Svetozarov's film, made in 1924). Their beauty
was forbidden fruit, their sensuality destructive. In the films of this new era,
the 'dangerous beauty' appeared as the negative counterpart of the 'positive'
female revolutionary and lawful wife. The lady of the past became de-classed
and found herself in the role of prostitute (*Prostitute*, 1927) or thief (*Devil's Wheel*,
1926). The beauties no longer changed their 'social standing', nor their clothes,
like Kholodnaya's heroines; from their first appearance on the screen they were
dressed in low-necked gowns against the background of a 'den of iniquity'.

But, in 1924, Aleksei Tolstoi and Yakov Protazanov returned from emigration
to make the first Soviet hit, *Aelita*. Alongside the more traditional portrayal of
lovers by Yuliya Solntseva and Nikolai Tsereteli (an exotic dandy in a tail coat),
there was a second couple, a comic soap-opera version played by Vera Orlova
and Nikolai Batalov. In this way, Protazanov contrasted the image of pre-
revolutionary Russian 'queens' with the model of the new Soviet heroes. The
main task of these new heroes was not to suffer from jealousy and evil forces,
but to 'make revolution' – even, if need be, on Mars.*

THE 1920s: THE TIME OF THE ANTI-STAR

The Soviet avant-garde insisted that the cinema get closer to life. It had to step
out through 'the roofs of film studios', beyond 'the heads of actors' and land
in the street. War was declared on any form of mystification. The avant-
garde cinema of the 1920s promoted a programme of documentalism in the
broadest sense, renouncing both individual intrigue and the individual hero.
Its call was 'Forward!' – towards a model of immediacy, a 'montage image of
the modern person'.[5] The frames were filled with the masses; and if a single
person stepped out from the masses, he was not an actor but a 'type', a 'socio-
biological hieroglyphic'. As Sergei Eisenstein put it, the hero's social biography

---

Aelita was the screen version of Aleksei Tolstoi's novel, which tells the tale of a Soviet engineer in post-
revolutionary Moscow who dreams that he builds a space ship and flies to Mars where he helps bring about
a second proletarian revolution!

and individual temperament were the messages clearly given by his appearance; the audience was meant to be able to interpret these 'instantaneously'.[6] Vsesolod Pudovkin defined the new principle of photogenicity:

A face which can grab the audience in only 2 metres of film - this is the model![7]

The face of this new hero, which was ardently promoted by directors, went round the screens of the world, filling cinema halls with strength, wildness and freedom. Dziga Vertov revealed the full significance of this face, and the sweaty, muscular body which went with it, by bringing it closer to the audience, magnifying it up to a coarse grain. An asymmetrical, irregular, roughly-hewn face, devoid of stage make-up. This was an aggressive challenge to the classical, smooth beauty of the past, with its delicate features, thickly layered make-up and 'demonic' eyes outlined in black.

Lev Kuleshov formed a new actors' workshop which consisted mainly of people who had not been accepted into film school on the grounds that they were 'professionally unfit'. Another new collective, the Leningrad Factory of the Eccentric Actor (FEKS), re-worked the 'old' characters into something new with the help of eccentricity and stylization. The social position of the 'queen of the screen' was eroded, but it was underscored in the new heroine. The former heroine could have appeared on postcards or advertisements or in fashion magazines. The new one was unthinkable in this context; for her, only political posters were appropriate. The 1920s struck a complete blow to the 'queens', replacing them with people who represented the masses. The women were not beautiful; nor were the men traditional lovers.

The hero and lover of *Aelita* had the usual themes to deal with - love, pursuit and gunshots. But the new hero, Nikolai Batalov, wore a great-coat, heavy boots and a *budenovka* cap on his head.* He worked for the revolution, and in an almost off-hand way, courted a proletarian woman who was a bonded servant. This man of the street was sure that the world belonged to him, and the audience could not fail to be caught up in the new confidence of the working-class strength. The hero, one of the masses, was treading the path of enlightenment, from a dark, repressed worker to a politically-conscious revolutionary and fighter; from a proletarian victim of society into a leader. If necessary, he would die for this.

This kind of story became the norm for screen heroines as well. Two examples can be found in the role played by Vera Baranovskaya in the screen version of Gorkii's *Mother*, made in 1927 by Pudovkin; and that of Marfa Lapkina in *The Old and New*, made in 1929 by Eisenstein. The first of these was set in

*A *budenovka* was a military cap used by the Red Army in the Civil War.

a city in 1905; the second in a village at the time of collectivization, when the first collective farms were being set up. In the first film, the heroine dies with a red banner in her hands, under the bullets of the Tsarist police. In the second, she is transformed from an ugly duckling, a repressed farm labourer who does not even own a horse, into the first female tractor driver. *New Babylon* (1929) is set in an earlier era, a half century before, but the heroine played by Elena Kuz'mina also undergoes a transformation. From a naïve shop assistant, she turns into a blazing Communard.*

The heroines of the 1920s turned from being victims of the regime and of circumstances, deprived of basic civil rights, to an awareness of their position and protest against it. The camera moved with them; from its position looking down on them from above, underlining their oppression, it began looking upwards from below, as if they were monuments.

Female 'anti-stars' of the 1920s were distinguished above all by their unattractiveness. Aleksandra Khokhlova (from Lev Kuleshov's workshop), Vera Baranovskaya and Elena Kuz'mina (from the Factory of the Eccentric Actor) were brought up in this cinema; they were reared on hostility to 'the star', 'the beauty', 'the queen of the screen'. So the naturalness of Marfa Lapkina, who was not a professional actress, was not so different from that of the heroines played by professionals. While everyone was delirious with delight over 'Greta Garbo's divine beauty', a reviewer described Kuz'mina as a 'hiccoughing monster'. But the anti-stars of the 1920s, with their troubled, hungry faces, were not worried about their lack of beauty, their hiccoughs, their torn dresses, their wrinkles or whether their wet hair was stuck to their faces. They were often to be found lying beaten in the mud, on the floor or in puddles. For these anti-stars were able to display such open passion, such anger and rage, that this raised them from their humble positions. Although many of these films were set in the past, they were still modern; they were concerned with the process of the re-education of the masses, and this did not end when the Bolsheviks came to power, it was only just beginning. That is why the 'growth and liberation of consciousness' was so vital, and formed the link between the cinema and real life. The purpose of the heroine and that of the plot were identical.

A controversy arose over what kind of heroine this new cinema should be promoting. The Leftists decisively attacked the beautiful Malinovskaya-type film stars, and yet the films in which they appeared were financed by the state film company, *Sovkino*, which did not make funding available for the

---

* *Mother*, based on Maxim Gorkii's novel, was about the development of the heroine's own political awareness as she supports her son in his revolutionary activities of that year. *The Old and New* is an idealized version of life on a collective farm. The star, Marfa Lapkina, was a real peasant woman. *New Babylon* was about the Paris Commune of 1871.

'proletarian pictures'. The audience also preferred to see what they considered beautiful rather than, as one worker remarked in a letter to a newspaper, the 'coarse words and actions you find in real life – just as if you were still in the factory'. Sergei Tret'yakov, a Leftist art critic, replied to this worker:

> The desire for elegance is very strong. Is it not precisely because of this that young Soviet girls, brandishing studio bags . . . rush on their spindly legs, at the end of a dull working day, to drama clubs and studios, to escape their own lives through the familiar images of empresses, duchesses, heroines, mermaids, temptresses, 'seagulls' and vampires? Is this not why the old-style beauties do not leave our screens, and men in the audience demand to see women with satin skins, dainty feet, the hands of aristocrats, delicate bones, noble profiles and perfect mouths? But do you not think it possible that this combination of attributes continues to reproduce the old feudal notion of the woman, as nothing more than a bed accessory? What sort of worker or friend is she, with her small feet, delicate bones, tender hands? She is exactly that kind of 'tender creature' for whom men abandon their coarse, tired wives, with their snub-noses, small eyes and heavy bones. But instead of dethroning these beauties for the sake of these coarse, heavy-boned women, the stereotype of womanhood shared by cinema-goers and film-makers ensures that thousands of comely maidens are moving as if hypnotised towards the beckoning lights [of the cinema theatres] . . .[8]

The Soviet avant-garde fought against this image of female beauty in the cinema, but the casting directors and producers fought against the avant-garde. However, the personal tragedies which resulted for individual actresses has been considered to lie beyond the limits of what is appropriate subject-matter for film history.

Aleksandra Khokhlova was one of the brightest new talents of the Soviet cinema. Innovative film-makers – especially Eisenstein and Shklovskii – hoped to turn her into the first original Soviet film-heroine. But this hope was defeated by the unshakeable notions held by producers, film promoters and audiences, of what kind of woman should appear on screen. Khokhlova was neither a beauty nor a vamp. She was thin to the point of looking eccentric. She had a huge mouth, her movements were almost grotesque and her hair stood out on all sides, forming a halo around her oblong head. She was a parody of the old-style seductive star. Indeed, Khokhlova parodied the very subject of seduction in her first memorable role as a 'countess' in *The Extraordinary Adventures of Mr West in the Land of the Bolsheviks* (1924). In 1926, Eisenstein wrote:

> Khokhlova scales the absolute heights of skill. And what's more, she has her own unique style . . . She is no 'Soviet Pickford' . . . America is well acquainted with the image of the petty-bourgeoisie and the 'bathing girl'. The very existence of Khokhlova destroys this image. Her bared teeth rip up the stencil of the formula

'woman of the screen', the 'woman of the alcove'. Having decisively rejected the demonic woman, the adventuress . . . I would like to plait her hair, dress her in a sarafan, and cast her in a series of grotesque but comical tales of town versus country. Khokhlova is the first eccentric woman on the screen.[9]

Yet it was exactly at this time that a request was made to 'remove' this unique film actress from the screen, on the grounds that she was too ugly, too scrawny.

In response, Osip Brik wrote the script *Cleopatra* especially for Khokhlova. It was a parody of the attitude that the bosses of the film industry had towards her. The script was about a variety show which made money out of the ugliness of an unfortunate prostitute called Cleopatra. It 'sells' her appearance, and its defiance of conventional notions of beauty, as a comic turn. But the actress falls in love and love turns her into a beautiful, inspired woman. The impresario is furious about this 'transformation' and tries to stop it - it might be the ruin of him!

But the film was never made. Mezhrabpom* - a film corporation which 'bought' Khokhlova's husband, Kuleshov - was adamantly opposed to the appearance of this skeleton on the screen. Thus the fate of the script, and of Khokhlova herself, was decided. In 1933, she exchanged her position in front of the camera for a new one behind it, and became a director.

The 1920s came to a close. The ideal of the 'anti-star' put forward in those years did not, in the end, catch on. It collided with traditional notions about the 'woman of the screen' which both cinema administrators and the general public still adhered to. During the transition to the 1930s, a new image of the Soviet film heroine began to take shape. It fell to Yakov Protazanov, once again, to come up with its concrete form. He paired Ada Voitsik, a young film-school student, with Ivan Koval'-Samborskii in the film version of *Forty-First*. The plebian type of the 1920s was blended with, and ennobled by, the smooth beauty of the old 'queen of the screen'. This image came to define the ideal of cinema beauty in the 1930s. This new pair of lovers offered by Protazanov prepared the way for a new type of hero. For the first time, actresses appeared in comedies of everyday life. The stark, exotic anti-stars of the 1920s were swept away, along with the whole era of silent film.

THE 1930s: 'THE BEAUTY OF SIMPLICITY' AND 'EXCEPTIONAL ORDINARINESS'

The heroines of the 1930s had to descend from the heights of ecstasy,

Mezhrabpom is the Russian acronym of Workers' International Relief, an international organization set up by Lenin in 1921. While its initial task was to provide financial support for striking workers and victims of natural disasters, it went on to develop a cultural wing which published periodicals and books, sponsored theatrical events and finally went into film production.

eccentricity and stylization, to the level of everyday life - they had to settle in the very neighbourhoods where the audience lived. Society had entered the period of the 'Second Revolution', and demanded from art a visual demonstration of an ideal life, a pledge to the audience that happiness lay not far in the future. The simple boy and girl next door - familiar and ordinary - had to be transformed into this ideal. They had to be romanticized, brightened up, elevated. The arrival of talking movies speeded up the process of transforming the images on screen.

This remodelling of the person was a reflection of real-life plans for the country as a whole. The atmosphere which the films of the 1930s created was meant to promote a new mood of social optimism. A leader had stepped forward from the masses. This was reflected in the cinema; a single actor became not only the hero of the action but the hero of life. Exceptional individuals were sought out and turned into stars. The country knew (indeed, it *had* to know, according to its leader) who was the best milkmaid, who was the first woman pilot.

The film heroes and heroines were no longer emaciated, consumptive revolutionaries. They were well-fed, clean-shaven, curly-haired citizens. Heroines wore make-up again and regained the right to be beautiful - as long as they preserved a plebian simplicity in their faces and their manner of dress. They were also granted a higher social position. This does not mean that they were raised from the lowest depths of the proletariat. On the contrary, they were the representatives of a new class. This class had gained the power, and the conviction of the rightness of its mission, to create a new society, a stable society - with a firm career in it for themselves.

The path of the heroine of the 1930s began where that of her 1920s predecessor had ended. From the victim who had just woken up to her position, she went on to become director of an enterprise, head of a government ministry or shock-worker (a person who overfulfilled his or her production target). This image appeared not just on screen, but in posters, paintings and sculptures. She was both a real woman and an abstract idea - the 'beauty of simplicity', the 'beauty of ordinary folk'.

So the 1930s advanced their own stereotype of womanhood. She was a member of the Party, or the Komsomol, and a stakhanovite. She was no primordial woman, but a fully-formed heroine with clear convictions, a developed character, with a mature appearance, a carefully moulded figure. Her sculpted contours were illuminated, and the director evidently admired them along with the audience. In contrast to the earlier periods of Soviet cinema, the camera no longer looked down on the heroine from above or up at her from below. It was on the same level, no higher, no lower. This was no bourgeois beauty of 'the alcove', but a worker. She was strong, with broad bones, prominent features and a sporty figure. Her hair was blonde, her teeth white; she had dimpled-cheeks and a contagious smile. She was a 'healthy' beauty. The young peasant woman of Russian folklore, the national ideal of beauty, played a considerable role in the creation of this image. (This Russian beauty, incidentally, was also despatched to the Central Asian republics, where there was a shortage of local actresses.)

The most important thing about these heroines was their immutable clarity, their whole-hearted natures, their absence of doubt, their optimism. This appearance was amplified by expansive gestures, resolute strides and loud, clear voices (essential for singing songs and addressing meetings). The heroine sang not only revolutionary songs but also lyrical and humorous ones. She received declarations of love, but in these films there was no hint of intimacy or sensuality. Even if the script-writer had given her children, she still remained somehow 'childless'. Her love could not be directed towards just one person but had to be shared out to everyone. If she did feel love for one person, it had to be of the platonic kind. Girlfriends of the 'boy next door' lose their erotic appeal. It is as if their very sportiness kills sensuality. The heroines were not interested in fashion, in new hair styles or in cosmetics. They could not seduce anyone.

Sensuality (in a very flimsy, veiled form) was now permissible only in women of the 'petty-bourgeoisie' – the 'boudoir' wives and daughters of the big bosses, who themselves did not work. These women were now portrayed in an entirely negative way. Although they emulated the former 'queens of the screen', they were actually a caricature of this type of woman. Soviet 'ladies of the alcove' were reduced to a comic stereotype. Instead of learning how to operate industrial machinery, they struggled against weight gain, fussed about their big noses, gazed at themselves too often in the mirror and were constantly changing their outfits.

Zoya Fedorova was one of the new young screen heroines of the 1930s. For fifteen continuous years this actress was cast in the role of a mischievous, snub-nosed, energetic, cheerful member of the Komsomol. She progressed from the roles of simple worker, fun-loving girl and stakhanovite (as in *Miners*, 1937) to factory director (*The Great Citizen*, 1938–9). Not once did she ever appear in a beautiful dress and she had to rely on natural prettiness instead of social charm.[10] She did not reach the 'unattainable brilliance' of a film star but she remained simple and accessible, and was accepted by the audience on the basis of her social optimism and her contagious conviviality. The audience's ability to identify with such a heroine was immense. Film-goers and admirers described her as their 'girlfriend' or their 'daughter'.

There was considerable discussion throughout the 1930s about the idea of the Hollywood star. In the Soviet Union this became inseparable from the image of Mary Pickford. This is probably because of her unerotic teenage image, which was similar to the type of prettiness being promoted in the Soviet cinema. The Soviet cinema offered a direct response to Pickford in the form of Lyubov' Orlova. She always played 'Cinderella' types, but in a distinctive Soviet version of the story. This sometimes took a light-hearted form, as in *Jazz Comedy*, made in 1934, where she played a housewife who became a stage star.

Or, it could be more serious, as in *The Bright Path* (1940), in which she became a stakhanovite engineer and a member of the Supreme Soviet. (She did not win a prince but she did get a medal!) In the 1938 film *To the Volga*, Moscow film-goers were introduced to a village postwoman, Strel'ka, whose simple, melodious songs resulted in her becoming a powerful, state-sponsored singer. In *Circus*, made in 1934, she played an American circus performer, who at the start of the film was found sobbing piteously in her dressing room because of fear for the future of her Black baby. By the end, she was marching alongside Russian athletes in a sports parade on Red Square, an equal amongst equals.

Marina Ladynina also appeared in such films. But unlike Orlova, Ladinina did not have to 'develop'. She started out as a shock-worker (*The Rich Bride*, 1937), as leader of a brigade of tractor drivers (*Tractor Drivers*, 1939), as a renowned pig-keeper (*Swineherd and Shepherd*, 1941), as a kindergarten teacher who becomes an anti-aircraft gunner during the war (*At Six p.m. After the War*, 1943), and as the chairwoman of a *kholkhoz* (*Cossacks of the Kuban*, 1951). Her one departure from this kind of job was in the film *Tales of the Siberian Land* (1948), in which she played a singer. Like her city sister Orlova, Ladinina was blonde, had dazzling white teeth, a broad smile, and a simple, artless life-style. She always played the same type of person: a stylized, folkloric image of the shock-worker. The films always followed the same pattern: they consisted of a socialist competition between who was good and who was better. This contest was complicated by little misunderstandings between lovers, but these were soon resolved, and the film invariably ended with a magnificent wedding and a noisy celebration of an excellent harvest.

The first film in the series, *The Rich Bride*, had precisely this theme. It was built around an 'artificial' triangle. This consisted of a young couple, both tractor-drivers and shock-workers, who were in love with each other and dreamt of getting married, and a wicked book-keeper who came between them. He also wanted to marry the female shock-worker and so tried to turn the young lovers against each other. He told the man that his girlfriend was backward; he told the woman that her boyfriend was lazy. Believing the book-keeper, they were furious with each other, and this spurred them into rivalry in their work. Yet at a critical moment, when the harvest was threatened by a storm, they came to each other's rescue, and the misunderstanding was resolved. The film ended with them being rewarded and married simultaneously. This pattern was repeated in each of the other films in the series.[11] The story was thickly interspersed with songs, sung with a rake slung over the shoulder, with a suckling pig in the arms, aloft a tractor . . .

Tamara Makarova worked in the same optimistic key. The strong, blonde-haired, sporty young women she played were in one case a doctor on an expedition to the North Pole, in another a member of the Komsomol, off to build a new city, and in a third, a peasant who had started reading Engels in order to improve her mind.

Vera Maretskaya, who started her film career in the 1920s playing comic parts (such as domestic servants and village idiots arriving in the big city), also took on this Lyubov' Orlova type of role in the 1930s. For some time she played frivolous ladies, but with the arrival of talking pictures the comedies gave way to a higher genre. By the end of the 1930s she was treading the by now familiar path of development: from backward domestic servant to professional revolutionary in *The Generation of Conquerors*, and from former farmhand to *Member of the Government*. Outwardly, she resembled Vera Baranovskaya, who had played the title role in the silent film version of Gorkii's *Mother*. But she demonstrated her heroines' development in a more down-to-earth, more life-like way. It was she who went on to play Gorkii's mother in the talking version of the film. Her 'type' was conducive to this role – it was more mature and less feminine than that of the light-weight beauties of the 1930s, more rough and womanish.

The songs from these films were used as radio signature tunes and epigraphs of their times. They reflected the 'sunny side' of the 1930s epoch: 'The USSR at work on the construction site'; the scale, the scope, the records, the sudden fortune of Aleksei Stakhanov. The fact that when these songs were on the air they were interspersed with reports of enemy plots, lists of opposition leaders who had been shot, reports about the Fascist takeover of Europe, the wars in Spain and Abyssinia, the annexation of Austria, seemed to disturb no one, neither the performers nor the listeners.

In the spreading, artificial atmosphere of joy and optimism, an ominous slogan appeared: 'the growth in the number of our successes is proportionate to the growth in the number of our enemies'. This was reflected in a new 'dark' side of films, with heroes dying, usually at the hands of class enemies, foreign spies or members of the right or left opposition. Hence, Lyubov' Orlova's role in the film *The Mistake of Kochin the Engineer*, of 1939, is concerned not only with the heroine's 'rising sun', but also with her death as the victim of dark forces.

So, having begun with those 'heavy-featured, wide-boned, small-eyed' boys and girls who lived next door to the audience, the cinema then moulded them into an ideal type of hero, imitating the methods of Hollywood. And it was no coincidence that just at that time the heroine and actress began to move closer to the idea of a film star, with a certain 'image'. The cinema screen had liberated the heroine from everyday life, it made her both romantic and legendary. From there, a stylized, conventional type of 'simple' girl, a Slavonic beauty, began to develop. But at the same time, social position and national identity were being 'washed away'.

The visual character of the epoch can be defined as one of 'representation'. Maya Turovskaya, a researcher on the Soviet cinema, has rightly observed that tall houses represented fabulous homes for the people who really lived in miserable barracks and communal flats; the Exhibition of Achievements, which included palaces for pigs and cows, represented the fantastic successes which were claimed for the nation. In just the same way, the scintillating, talented, energetic film beauties, clothed in a variety of social outfits, who sang and danced, posed coquettishly, cracked jokes and overcame any difficulties, represented the 'simple person'. The idealized heroines which they created, against idealized cardboard backdrops, had to convince the audience that in the Soviet Union, 'if ordered by the country to become a hero, *everyone of us* will become one'. In other words, even the simplest of people, someone who is just one of the crowd, turns out to be talented and heroic - exceptional - as if nature makes nothing ordinary.

This notion was reflected in art. For a long time, from the late 1950s, art asserted that a person had the right to be 'ordinary'. And yet at the same time it placed a huge complex in the mass consciousness about living an ordinary life; it promoted an idea that an 'anonymous, simple destiny' had to be rejected as something shameful. Strict, hierarchical value orientations, propagated by the cinema in an idealized form, were reinforced in real life in material ways. These consisted of enormous apartments, gigantic bonuses and glittering awards for exceptional individuals, who stood out against a background of equalized poverty.

In the 1920s, the film hero emerged from a de-classed mass, to be raised up to the level of class consciousness. In the 1930s, he started out with a degree of political consciousness, and went on to develop its full potential - from something already good, to something even better. As society was gradually 'purified' of its alien elements in the form of kulaks and the old intelligentsia, a new class stratification began: the commander on the one hand, the aide on the other; the enterprise director on the one hand, the worker on the other; the army general on the one hand, the soldier on the other. At the same time there was a division between overcrowded communal apartments or nice new ones provided by the state; between a place in an overcrowded tram or a private automobile; between a place in a food queue or private supplies.

However, the film heroines of the 1930s trod the path of development not as a 'way up' the social ladder. It was as if the social significance of this development did not exist in the cinema. It was absent from the consciousness of the heroines; it went unnoticed by the critics. The function of the cinema was to infect the audience with an optimism and confidence in society which bordered on mindlessness, an energy and a collective laughter which concealed backwardness and a lack of awareness. An open hatred of the enemy and of saboteurs was encouraged alongside a love of the Motherland and the Party, as personified by the leader of the country and reflected in the image of lesser Party leaders. The heroines called on the audience to model their own lives according to the stories shown on the screen, following the path that leads them upwards - though not in a social sense.

The 'triangle' of lovers of an earlier screen era was ejected from dramatic art, and replaced by a 'square'. There are two pairs of lovers. In the final scene, the suffering lover in the supporting role marries his girlfriend, at the same time as the main couple marries. The formation of the perfect couple, who are equals, took place at the same time as that compulsory registration of marriages was reintroduced into society, after the communes of the 1920s which called for free love and the banning of abortions.

The heroes had no time for love in these films, however. Duty and work pushed it out of the picture. Intimacy and sensuality were also absent. Love was celebrated on top of a tractor, a kiss took place only on the platform where awards were being given out. This is why the heroines – emancipated and enjoying equal rights with men on the screen, almost drunk with success – seemed somehow 'man-like', even though they were beautiful women.

The unique unattractiveness of actresses of the 1920s, who came from the streets and showed traces of degeneration (for example, Marfa Lapkina's failure of a nose gave a hint of syphilis, the main illness of rural Russia), had been transformed into healthy beauty. In comparison with the pre-revolutionary cinema, the film's ideal heroine had become that of a working woman, a sportswoman, a record-holder. The change in the stereotype, and the arrival of talking pictures, had led also to a change in the image of the actor, a rejection of the 1920s school of eccentricity and expressiveness. Actors played not just individuals but types, and these same types then appeared on posters and in sculptures, in which they were purified and elevated into new stereotypes. The heroines of the 1930s did not play complex, restless characters, but were open and direct. There was no contradiction between their pure outer appearance and their pure inner life. A friend was a friend and an enemy was an enemy. Enemies, on the other hand, were closed and impenetrable – mysterious types from the West. They were spies, White Guards, saboteurs, libertines. The 'vamp' could now only be played as a parody (and this was at the same time that the American film empire was turning Greta Garbo, Marlene Dietrich and Mae West into mythologized incarnations of Eros!). Yet immutable clarity and openness was forced off the screen by the end of the 1950s, and actors who had played the parts of heroes now had to become dogmatists. The old type had to be replaced by one who carried a different inner message, the clearness of a single meaning had to be replaced by a multiplicity of meanings.

During the first year of the war, Yulii Raizman's *Mashen'ka* appeared on the screen, with Valentina Koraveva in the title role. She was a strange heroine for that time, who did not 'catch on' – she was simple, unremarkable, attractive without being beautiful. She was a forerunner of the heroines of the 1950s – but she appeared before her time.

THE 1940s: PROFILES FROM MEDALS AND DAZZLING BLONDES

When the war broke out, the image of the hero was hardened into the profile on a medal. The cinema responded to the war in two different ways: either the hero was sent off on some monumental mission, or else he appeared in ever-more light-hearted musical comedies. He would be cast in the full-dress portrait of a great military leader or he would play a valiant serviceman in a love adventure while at home on leave. Both genres took the cinema further and further from reality.

Vera Maretskaya and Natal'ya Uzhvii, the old heroines of the 1930s, were used in the first type of film; both were martyred in tragic circumstances. In general, however, women did not take the lead roles in such films as often as men. The screen does not offer heroic histories of women in such quantity as it does of men, tsars and generals. The second type of film, that of the musical comedies, introduced cinema audiences to the dazzling blondes, Valentina Serova, Lyudmila Tselikhovkaya and Lidiya Smirovna. With the relaxation of wartime morality, they were allowed a hint of sensuality and eroticism. They moved the audience, they needed protection and thus the old femininity returned. Without doubt, Serova possessed an erotic charm. Tselikovskaya, who was 15 when she began to appear in films, played the 'weak' type who needed to be looked after, a 'charming child'. These heroines were no longer simple peasants, administrators, workers; instead they were students, singers and the young brides of husbands in shining uniforms. The main function of the new heroines was not to fulfil and overfulfil the plan, but to faithfully love and wait!

THE 1950s: THE SECOND FAREWELL TO BEAUTY; ON TO THE POETRY OF THE PROSAIC

In the early 1950s, the harsh postwar period, the granite leader and dazzling beauty of the war years were shunned. The heroine had to get closer to the audience, which was exhausted from the losses and the tragedies of war, and stunned by the death of Stalin and the revelations of the 20th Party Congress. A gradual re-evaluation of values, a re-thinking of the image of 'life's hero', of communism and of the cinema, produced a new face for the screen. It contrasted sharply with that of the 1930s, and met with unexpected success. At last, here were films which did not examine life which was festively unreal, historically pompous or heroically solemn, but ordinary prosaic existence. In place of monumentalism, brilliance and the abstraction of ideals, the camera looked at everyday life as if through the eyes of someone who had just returned from the war (or from a labour camp). It rediscovered the value of unobtrusive detail – the pleasures of family, of the birth of a child, of simple friendship. For the first time, heroes had to tackle difficulties not from outside (in the form of foreign enemies and saboteurs) but within their own lives.

It was, then, no coincidence that Lyudmila Gurchenko, who had made a brilliant debut in the musical comedy *Carnival Night,* and had been ready to displace Orlova, disappeared from the cinema for almost twenty years. Her type was no longer called for. The heroines of the late 1950s had to have that same kind of naturalness that had earlier come dressed in a dazzling white blouse, atop a tractor. Now, it wore a quilted jacket, sheep-skin coat and overalls. These were unremarkable girls with curls and plaits and plain, sweet faces; they were thin, awkward and could have been plucked at random from a crowd in the street. They were the girlfriends of long-armed, clumsy boys with insipid features - the type played by Aleksei Batalov. The only remarkable thing about them was their absolute mediocrity. A close-up shot in the cinema was like a blow-up of a passport photo - one person, no different from any other.

But the image of the heroine in the 1950s had a different meaning than that of the 1930s. It represented a conscious break with the past. That is why this author continually uses the adjectives 'unremarkable', 'simple', 'sweet'.[12] The heroes and heroines of the 1930s had been clear and untroubled; they knew what was good and what was bad, they understood the purpose of their lives and they were ready to give them up for the Motherland and for the revolution. But the inspirational abstraction of these ideas narrowed in the 1950s to an individual concern and a concrete person. The focus shifted away from the heroic past to the prosaic present. The unremarkable, ubiquitous heroine was ready to offer help to someone who had been treated unfairly, or who was in some kind of trouble. This feeling of selfless pity for another person was absent from the films of the 1930s. The anonymity of the heroine who does a good deed for another person created in the audience a feeling of trust in her, and this could be transferred to a neighbour, a workmate or the person sitting in the next seat in the cinema hall. The task of the film's story was to demonstrate decency in a variety of situations. The purpose of the film was to do the same in real life - to try to re-establish personal trust after the denunciations of the 1930s and the disclosures of the 1950s.

As had happened in the past, this new-style heroine, a *Mashen'ka* type, first appeared on the periphery of the film's story, as the unsuccessful competitor in a love triangle in which the victor was a heroine of the old type. Then, in the 1950s, an attempt was made to bid farewell to the old stylized beauties, and to put an end to the sharp contrast between the screen and real life. So alongside Aleksei Batalov's 'unremarkable boys' appeared 'unremarkable girls' played by Liliana Aleshnikova, Inna Gulaya and Nadezhda Rumyantseva. They brought a quiet light, a femininity and diffidence into ordinary, everyday things. There was a continued allegiance to aspects of the 1930s heroes - the fact that they were simple, of the people, and unburdened by a surplus of knowledge -

but unlike those of the past, these new heroines were not idealized, only poeticized. They were granted a personal life: they cooked supper, rocked crying children to sleep and darned socks. They were allowed to be ordinary. The girls played by Inna Makarova and Nonna Mordyukova were the ideal heroines of the 1950s - simple, strong, somewhat rough, and not burdened by an excess of intellect.

Inna Makharova took up where Zoya Fedorova had left off, and played a wilful, cocky, sometimes vulgar, but inwardly wholesome girl. Her films were a combination of comedy and drama. Although in the past she had shown an heroic aspect to her character (as in *The Young Guard*, 1948), in the films of the new era she flaunted her roughness (as in *High*, 1957). The bravado of her heroine was initially presented as a somewhat unsophisticated, naïve attempt to preserve inner freedom and independence, but it turned out to be a cover for the deep inner wounds and defencelessness of an orphaned child.

Nonna Mordyukova reproduced Makarova's heroine in a rural setting. But there was a new slant: signs of sensuality appeared in the heroine, who began wearing lipstick (though shyly), and this sometimes got close to the brink of vulgarity. Yet if Mordyukova had been around in the 1930s, her heavy beauty, her large, strong body and sculptured face would have committed her to noble, heroic parts. Indeed, it had been with this kind of role that she made her debut (in *The Young Guard*).

But the times continued to change. Before long - with the arrival of the 1960s - Nonna Mordyukova and Inna Makarova fell victim to a new development. Their naïve spontaneity, their openness and their unpolished sensuality would come to seem vulgar and stupid in that era, which used the intellectual prowess of the hero to arouse emotion and sympathy in the audience. For a long time, they, and other actors of their ilk, were unable to find a new, 'positive' screen image for themselves. They were forced out of centre stage to play comic supporting roles of a rather negative kind. This was Inna Makarova's fate in *Village Doctor* and *Rumyantsev's Business*. Later, despite the comic veneer, she tried to convey a sense of the dramatic destiny of her heroine, and identify this with her own fate - the tragedy of becoming superfluous as times change. (An example of this can be found in *Women*, made in 1966.)

Such actresses were still sometimes given the starring roles in films about the past. Their simple, now obsolete type, with the bright curls, the round, Russian face and the too-lively prance, was used as a way of emphasizing the era. Hence, in the film *My Dear Person*, made in 1958, Inna Makarova played a 1930s heroine once again, a girl who dreams of becoming an actress like Lyubov' Orlova but ends up as a 'simple geologist' who finds happiness with a 'simple doctor' (played by Aleksei Batalov).

Mordyukova also had to go through this demotion. In *No Return,* made in 1973, she loses her husband to the bride of his young son – having fallen in love with her during the war, he abandons her in peace time for a slim young woman of the 1960s. Later, in 1981, she suffers the ultimate humiliation: in *The Relatives,* the beautiful Mordyukova appears as a fat woman with a huge Fellini bosom, covered with a ripped T-shirt bearing the image of the Russian Olympic Bear, Mishka. In her hair is the remains of an outgrown perm, her teeth are coated with metal. In place of the simple, healthy beauty of the past is a grotesque monster.

Alongside the 'unremarkable type' of the 1950s heroine, a gradual reassertion of the 'beautiful woman' began to take place. To begin with, she did not appear in films about everyday life, but in those based on folk-tales, in musical comedies or in historical films. This was a defensive reaction against the death-blow dealt to the film beauties of the past. The hero of the picture *Dima Gorin's Career* (1961) cut the forehead, lips, mouth and hair from photographs in a magazine and glued them together to create the portrait of an ideal woman, a synthetic beauty, a pin-up girl. The living incarnation of this ideal was Tat'yana Konyukhova, dressed in the quilted jacket of a brigade leader. A number of other actresses, besides Konukhova, 'salvaged' the image of the beauty from a former era, to put it back on screen at the end of the 1950s.

Irina Skobtseva functioned as a connecting link between the simple heroines (*Annyushka,* 1959; *A Summer to Remember,* 1960), and those who were simply beauties (*Othello,* 1958; *War and Peace,* 1965). The latter were played by Iya Arepina, Alla Larionova and Natal'ya Fateeva, among others. All of them could have been defined as Soviet pin-ups, if only the stories in which they appeared had not been so far removed from those of their American counterparts. Their existence merely posed the question: why can't a simple woman also be beautiful? But invariably they had to play egotistic, flippant *femmes fatale,* who force the 'positive' heroes and bosses to suffer on account of their love for them. The beauties of the 1950s were not caricatures, as they had been in the 1930s, but their beauty 'aroused' suspicion. Even if they were not psychologically 'dethroned', as in the 1930s, these women were not the ones who walked up the aisle with Party executives.

The beauties brought the triangle back to the cinema. Natal'ya Fateeva, in *Battle en Route* (1961), attracts the 'positive' hero and even gets him thinking adulterous thoughts; but, faithful to his family code, he returns to his unremarkable wife.

The faces of the Soviet pin-up girls of the 1950s came close to the image of the 'cover girl'. They appeared not only in magazines like *Rabotnitsa* (*The Woman Worker*) and *Krest'yanka* (*The Peasant Woman*), but also in fashion and soap advertisements. Beauty for its own sake was semi-rehabilitated; it did not have to be reinforced by scenes of great industrial progress. (Today this is still more the case. In connection with the current commercialization of the Soviet cinema, there is a search for beautiful actresses and photographic models. Even beauty contests have been held. An incredible leap!)

By the late 1950s, the type of hero and heroines of the 1930s - dogmatists, conservatives, bureaucrats, Stalinists - had definitely been dethroned by the vagaries of fate. Their once-clear faces were now furrowed with wrinkles. Directors, fearing the inadvertent presentation of the old clichés, invited comic actors (like Yurii Nikulin) and character actors (like Rolan Bykov) to play the parts of 'positive' heroes, until a new stereotype could be found which did not produce negative reactions.

For the first time, the hero's external appearance and his fate did not necessarily go together. The hero might not be particularly handsome but he could still be a noble person. The heroine might be beautiful but turn out to be an egotist. The hero might have a fine face but be a dogmatist. Here were the first timid steps towards a more complex characterization. At this point, however, it was still a simple riddle which was solved rather quickly. A beautiful appearance went with a negative character; a plain appearance went with a positive character. But, in subsequent years, this urge for greater divergence between the face and the character, between the type the actor portrayed and the functions he or she served, became still greater (though it was still a far cry from women like Garbo). The riddle - the correlation between the type and the 'role' - became more complicated.

THE 1960s: FAREWELL TO SIMPLICITY

Until the 1960s, it was unheard of to have a hero from the intelligentsia, unless it was in an historical or biographical film. Even then, the peasant origins of a 'people's genius' like Michurin or Belinskii were always emphasized. In the 1930s, an actor who had the appearance of someone from the intelligentsia would play the role of a foreign spy or a secret saboteur for the White Guard. In the 1950s, these roles changed to that of presumptuous individualist and cynic. In the beginning of the film the deluded heroine is infatuated with him, but she eventually comes to prefer the plainer but 'positive' hero. (One example of such a hero is the character played by the handsome Vasilii Lanovoi in *Graduation Certificate*, 1954.)

In the 1960s, however, the hero or heroine was often from the intelligentsia. The simple worker was forced off the screen for a good ten years. The new heroine was more refined, reflective and nervy. The notion of beauty also changed for both men and women. Tender, loving heroes took the place of

the rustic strong men of the past, and thin, fragile, Europeanized girls took
the place of those strong and splendid Slavic beauties. This refinement and
intellectual complexity became a feature of heroines from all social strata –
from actresses to peasant women.

A significant role in the alteration of the heroine, and in determining what
her new appearance would be, was played by Tat'yana Samoilova. When
Samoilova's face appeared on the screen, it struck two blows – one to that
smoothness of feature so loved by cinematography, and the other to
'unremarkableness', to the modest inexpressiveness of the everyday heroine.
She herself was not lucky in the cinema, but she was a preview of what was
to come in subsequent decades.

The arrival of this essentially new heroine in the Soviet cinema was, to begin
with, neither accepted nor understood. Yet Samoilova's strange, asymmetrical
face had at least made it possible. The camera of Sergei Urusevskii (in *The
Cranes are Flying*, 1957) found an individuality in this face which had not been
depicted on the screen for a very long time. It became clear that the cinema
had outgrown the old type of heroine, even if she had the perfect, harmonious
face of Tamara Makarova, or Inna Makarova's sweet, simple one. Safe,
'conflictless', middling faces, which expressed no sense of mystery, ceased to
be interesting. The camera began to concern itself with uniqueness and enigma,
with the mystery of the inner life which existed behind the external façade.
For the first time in Soviet cinema, women could be mysterious, alluring and
unreadable. And the heroine played by Samoilova was allowed to make
mistakes. That she chose to love the man who was not the real hero, as was
obvious to everyone, but the scoundrel – and even to insist that she was right
to do so – caused a sensation. The camera rose from the feet to the face, moving
into 'dangerously' close range, revealing the roughness of the skin and errors
in the make-up. A combination of light and shadow emphasized the mystery
of the face, and the 'correct' arrangement of lights, the kind used in portraits
displayed in the windows of photo-studios, was abandoned.

There were a number of international attempts to use Samoilova as a
representation of the Russian woman. Hungarian, French and Italian directors
cast her in a variety of roles, from the heroic to the wretched (for example,
Leon Garras Goes in Search of a Friend, 1960; *Alba Regiya*, 1961; *They Went After
Soldiers*, 1964). Yet they were not successful. Samoilova's fate as an actress did
not turn out well, and *Anna Karenina*, made in 1967, was her last significant
work. Yet she acted as a catalyst. Having anticipated a new type of epoch, she
then speeded up the consolidation of its heroine. The actresses who came after
her – Alla Demidova (*You and Me*, 1972), Inna Churikova (*No Ford Through the
Fire*, 1968) and Margarita Terekhova (*Mirror*, 1974) – were further and further
removed from the old generalized model of heroine.

The 1960s did more than amend the old types; they introduced completely new ones. 'Rebels without a cause', of the James Dean mould, began to appear: Zbignev Tsibul'skii, for example, and his light-headed girlfriend - frail, young and divine, with clear eyes, a child's tender features, plump lips and an undeveloped body - the opposite of the pin-up. While Oleg Tabakov slashed his sabre against the furniture in *A Noisy Day* (1961), others, such as Nikita Mikhalkov, Nikolai Gubenko and Stanislav Lyubshin, went strolling through the midnight streets of Moscow in the 'Moscow films' by Marlen Khutsiev and Georgii Daneliya (*Stepping Through Moscow*, 1924, and *I Am 20*, made in 1965). Their girlfriends smoked cigarettes with great meaning, and bought single apples from a stall opposite Aleksandrov Garden to display their independence. They stood between childhood and adult life, like weak echoes of the youth wave in Western Europe.

The stabilization of Soviet society had made possible the appearance of such heroes, with their prolonged childishness, their freedom from the burden of the past, the era before 1956. But now, the young heroes greatly extended their range of possible subjects. Firstly, they stretched the spatial limits of history, thanks to their restlessness and their urge to move around the country without constraint - from the capital to Siberia, the virgin lands, the desert, and the far north. These places were just being opened up, not only by people forced to migrate there, but also with the help of young enthusiasts, socialist versions of 'easy riders'.

Secondly, film heroes no longer had to contribute to the revolution and fulfil the plan, as their predecessors had done. They liberated the plots by introducing unessential actions and occupations: loafing around on the street, going to the race-track, eating in restaurants (the puritanical 'positive' heroes never did this), attending poetry readings and young people's 'hang-outs'. They were able to clown around and be eccentric to provoke their society of 'fathers'. So the genres in which they appeared became more varied. They were not only quaint comedies and drama, but tragi-comedies and farce. Irony was their emblem, and this was a far cry from the merry but far-from ironic heroes of previous decades. In the next decade, however, this 'boy' type was devalued. Either he moved on to adulthood and became a careerist, or he was despatched to the genre of adventure - history, revolution, science fiction or folk-tale.

The 'girl', on the other hand - the Soviet Lolita - remained anchored in the cinema for a long time. She was a domestic version of Audrey Hepburn, Claudia Cardinale, Brigitte Bardot. The 'nymph's gallery' of the Soviet Union was made up of Anastasiya and Marianna Vertinskaya, Zhanna Bolotova, Ol'ga Gobzeva, Lyudmila Savel'va and Marina Neelova, with the later additions of Natal'ya Bondarchuk, Natal'ya Belokhvostikova, Elena Solovei and Elena Koreneva. It is still being extended today, with new names and faces fulfilling the same functions. The 'girls' were the creations of the capital, the metropolis; they had refined manners and came from good homes, from the 'great families' of actors and academicians. Like the 'boys', they were not burdened by their historical biographies. They were born after the war, and entered life swathed in a romantic veil, coated with irony and a certain practical cynicism. They assumed they had the right to read people with their flashing intuition and their quick reaction to hypocrisy which they were sure was never wrong. With a child's categorical certainty, they divided everything into black and white, fake and genuine.

To some extent, the 'girl' was a continuation of the type in Turgenev's novels – the personification of the ideal, in a reality which was far from it. Yet she was also endowed with a modern childish femininity. Her eroticism (and she was, certainly, endowed with this) was aestheticized, made somehow incorporeal. Possibly this is why her sensuality was permitted on screen. She was far freer than her predecessors; she did not have to be a wife or bride of the hero, but could be his companion, in a relationship that had not been registered in a ZAGS [marriage] office. This was progress indeed, in comparison with the puritanical morality held aloft in the 1930s.

Zhanna Prokhorenko gave an unusual interpretation of the 'girl' in *Ballad of a Soldier* and, later, *But What If This is Love*? The character she played came from a simple home and wore a tattered dress. But, in general, the young ladies from the metropolis (such as those played by the Vertinskaya sisters) were refined, nervy and well educated, and switched their jeans for the ball-gowns of the Russian aristocracy with remarkable ease.

Some of the 'girls' also experienced a 'devaluation' of the type, and were transformed into a symbol of spoilt, shallow city people, who hindered the hero's moral development. This was expressed by his impulse to set out for romantic, provincial, undeveloped places. But if he actually arrived there, he found a alternative 'girl from the sticks' awaiting him. In this new triangle, the hero had to make his choice, just as the journalist, in Sergei Gerasimov's film of that name, had to choose between Zhanna Bolotova and Galina Pol'skikh. The romantic 'girls' remain, up to the present day, one of the leading types of heroine in Soviet cinema. The popularity of Tat'yana Drubich (since her debut, at the age of 12 in *A Hundred Days After Childhood*, made in 1975, until *Assa* in 1988), the doll-like girlfriend of older heroes, can be partly explained by the fact that it is only possible to find a Soviet woman who has not been broken and ruined by the burdens of everyday life while she is still in her girlhood. The 'girls' enter the lives of 40-year-old heroes, the 'boys' of the past; they remind them of their departed youth, the compromises they have made. They perform the function of a refreshing moral spring. And they are able to compete successfully with the newer heroines, those 'strong and strange' women who Tanya Samoilova's brief career anticipated.

The type of heroine of the previous generation, beginning in the 1930s, had been adjusted to the new times in an interesting way. A 'simple' heroine was made more complex through the introduction of a riddle into the plot. The monumental, sculptured, classically correct face, which had been the standard of beauty in the 1930s, became pointed, taut and with sharply defined features. The heroine's lot was loneliness and unhappiness in love, she had a thinness which seemed like a physical defect or a sign of some secret illness. There was the hint of a complex, burdensome fate. Instead of open joy and smiles there was concealment, silence and a discreet mime-game which hinted at a secret; and a divergence between the face and what lay behind it. Past enthusiasm at meetings was now interpreted as false over-excitement, almost hysteria. The standard of these times, and conformity to it, was a drama of the suppression of the personal in the name of the communal.

Such a role was played by Maya Bulgakova in *Wings*, made by Larisa Shepit'ko in 1966. The heroine was imbued with fate, enigma and a new *raison d'être*. Her face did not give the impression of beautiful, strict, chiselled perfection, but of something shrivelled, set and old-fashioned. Her features were pointed, her face was devoid of humanity. The thinness was perceived as unwomanly, she was a 'straight plank'. She was an anachronism, a non-modern woman who had blundered into modern life. She was a former pilot, now chained to the ground, in conflict with the younger generation (who, in her job as director of a vocational training school, she had the task of teaching), and in conflict with her adopted daughter, one of the 'girls' (played by Zhanna Bolotova), whose choice of husband she failed to understand. She herself tried to find an heroic hero of the old type in the thin, balding person of Evgenii Evstigneev, but failed.

The devaluation of enthusiasm and of the open personality called into life a whole generation of new actors, who were plain or sometimes even ugly. The Hollywood stars of this type - Dustin Hoffman, Jack Nicholson, Barbra Streisand - found their parallels in the Soviet cinema in the form of Anatolii Solonitsyn, Aleksandr Kalyagin and Alisa Freindlikh. The plain actor combines the authenticity of everyday unattractiveness, the unremarkableness of the real person (just one from a crowd), with a strong individuality. This gives his face significance, the impression of an intense inner life. If even this strong personality is suppressed and the hero appears to be a failure, there is still a suggestion that perhaps he could become a Schopenhauer, a Dostoevskii!

Balding men and emphatically uninteresting and unattractive women who are 'without figures', with no hint of sensuality, and with sharp facial features - the nose was too big, the cheekbones unaesthetically wide - swept away the image of the 'film-hero' and 'film-heroine' and made it possible to introduce heroes who were not actors into the cinema. These became popular in the 1960s. They had to bring to the screen their own personalities, which in itself tells of a re-orientation in the cinema: the distinct type had been replaced by a stress on individual originality. The main roles in films were given to men who were by profession directors, poets and script-writers. Fewer women who were not actresses appeared in films. But all the same, these real people paved the way for the new screen heroines of a new decade.

THE 1970s: THE PLAIN STARS

In the second half of the 1960s, sharp changes took place in the public mood. The Thaw was over. The wave of romantic, honest journalism and political poetry carried off with itself the boy hero as it went. The era of literary prose had arrived: the era of analysing changes which had or had not happened. This era needed a new hero – one capable of reflection. The hero and heroine suddenly aged ten years, and became wiser by a whole lifetime. They were self-absorbed, they acquired an air of tired disillusionment, they became more sober. The generation began to divide into active and passive heroes, and by the 1970s there was a reappraisal of the relative value of these types. The active, attractive, sporty hero, after his brief rehabilitation on the screen in the 1960s, found himself once again with a negative image; he makes his career on unacceptable grounds, using unacceptable methods. The passive hero, on the other hand, is morally unsullied, but is unsuccessful. So the heroine found herself in a difficult situation, not knowing which man was worse, and often ending up alone.

The women on the screen are divided into strong and weak women. The emancipated woman, who gives herself to her work and establishes herself in a career, is punished for this with loneliness. Lyudmila Gurchenko, having lost her youthful sparkle, appears as the first image of female emancipation in *Old Walls* in 1974. She plays the director of a factory, but her professional success has not made her happy. She has lost her femininity and become hard, an 'old maid'. She eventually finds late love at a holiday resort, in the form of an elderly lorry driver.

Professional success on the screen, then, is accompanied by an unhappy personal life. In another example, from Lana Gogoberidze's *Some Interviews on Personal Questions*, made in 1979, the heroine is a journalist who has given too much to her job and ends up losing her husband. In this respect, Soviet women of the cinema are no luckier than their emancipated Western counterparts. Love takes its revenge on these heroines in their declining years, which led the writer Klimontovich to make a witty remark about the appearance of an 'aged Eros' in the Soviet cinema.[13] He also drew attention to the strange paradox that when a strong, childless woman who has established her position in society does find herself a partner, it is invariably someone who - in contrast to her - stands on the bottom rung of the social ladder: a metalworker, a driver, a blue-collar worker, a petty administrator, and so on. Also, unlike her, he is burdened with children (he is a widower, perhaps), a sick mother or a fondness for alcohol. The tensions which such a situation would be likely to produce in real life are glossed over on the screen. In *Moscow Doesn't Believe in Tears,* for example, made in 1981, the worker turns out to be a great intellectual, who is more valued in his own circle than an Academician would be.

These stories about strong women who are deprived of love can be seen as the first expression in art of the 'real' emancipation of women which was first proclaimed in 1917, but even now has yet to be realized in so many areas of life. *Old Walls*, although shot in the middle of the 1970s, follows the same outline as the pre-revolutionary picture *The Woman of Tomorrow,* and has the same cautionary warning: 'Before you cross the threshold of the nursery and the kitchen, glance back and think again! Loneliness is the price you will pay for self-realization.'

But the 'weak' cinema heroine - who had not made a career for herself - was seldom happier. She was depicted as an intellectual, whose actions had to reflect increasing complexity and paradox. The screenings of complicated classics - of Tolstoi, Dostoevskii and Chekhov - prepared the actresses for these parts. But the same thing happened in modern stories. The unremarkable heroines have become more complex. If, in the past, they played incidental roles, they were now allowed to stand centre-stage and 'soliloquize'. This is the heroine who has grown out of Tat'yana Samoilova's seed. It has been developed into concrete forms of women, with different characters and fates, by actresses such as Inna Churikova, Irina Kupchenko and Margarita Terekhova. Yet, in each case, they fulfil the same general function - they affirm their right to be individuals and to flaunt a non-standardized beauty, even to the point of being ugly or eccentric. One has to admire the strength of character of these women, the extent of the independence of their judgements and of their emancipation. Their femininity is cold and rational, they give almost the impression of frigidity. But they are, after all, the heroines of cold times. Especially since their partners are hardly supermen.

The deepening of the difference between the type and the character, which began as a simple contrast in the 1950s of someone who is 'not beautiful but good', still continues. The faces of the heroines of the 1930s and the 1950s have been transformed. The old type of 'simple girl', as played by Iya Savvina in *Asya's Happiness* in 1965, has become too deceptive, while the unremarkable pseudo-simple type has become the heroine of tragi-comedy, whose task is to continually expose the disparity between the face and the function, and so confuse the expectations of the audience. This is not a simple but over-talented person, as in the 1930s, nor a simple and ordinary one, as in the 1950s, but a simple person who is not like everyone else: an eccentric, an oddity. However, the simplicity has become commercialized, turned into a genre, used in soap-opera comedies, as in the case of Natal'ya Gundareva. This has led to the gradual inflation of this popular type (for example, *A Sweet Woman,* 1977).

The Slavonic beauty Katerina Izmailova, who played the leading role in *Lady Macbeth of Mtensk District* in 1989, and the Russian Tsarina in the American television series *Peter I,* has brought the 'Russian type' to the international film market, but with a few slight alterations – the addition of enigma *à la Garbo,* of sex appeal.

The development and liberation of the plebeian type, with its prominent cheek-bones, has been given to the heroine of Inna Churikova, created by Gleb Panfilov, her director and husband. In doing so, Panfilov has assigned this main role to a comic actress more usually given the part of ugly eccentrics. Her heroines go through strange, bewitching transformations. An awkward girl becomes a talented painter. A clumsy textile worker ends up revealing her talent by playing Joan of Arc on stage.

But such a heroine, loaded down by a mass of social and physical inadequacies, achieves success with great difficulty amongst the millions of people who make up the Soviet cinema audience. Only when she was clothed in the silvery furs and elegant gowns of Vassa Zheleznova in Panfilov's film *Vassa* (1983) (based on Maksim Gorkii's play) did Churikova receive the recognition of the audience.

Unlike the film critics, who admire the talent of Churikova and the fact that the new heroines do not follow a norm, the audience mourns the disappearance of the simple type. While the intellectuals and the thin, complex young women have been suffering on the screen, the cinema halls have become empty. There is a conflict between the mass character of the audience and the personality presented in films – an unstandardized personality, which is often doomed to failure even on the screen.

12 THE MYTHOLOGIZATION OF SOVIET WOMAN: *THE COMMISSAR* AND OTHER CASES

Elena Stishova

I have been working on this essay for some time now. I kept a folder in which I collected cuttings and sketches, I gave a paper at an international symposium on how the image of the Soviet woman had been presented on screen. But most of all, I myself - my personal fate, my character, my very existence in this world - am the rightful subject matter of this article. I am a product of the epoch, a figure in this historical drama. True, I am not so representative as the heroine of the film *The Commissar,* which is so well known throughout the world today. I am a descendant of the revolution's new image of womanhood, while she was one of its founders. But before the October revolution in Russia, it is hard to imagine such strict determinism, first of all in the relations between an historical cataclysm and humankind, and later between the state and the person. We are all the descendants of commissars; like it or not, we are all genetically connected with the events of that October. And as for me, I am the daughter of a commissar of the Civil War in a quite literal sense - there is no metaphorical meaning in my case.

The commissar finds her antecedent in the woman of the pre-revolutionary Russian underground movement. From time to time, this movement brought itself to public attention through almost sacral acts of violence against important dignitaries; and alongside the names of men, we find those of women blazing in the firmament. Women like Sof'ya Perovskaya, for example, whose life's path ended with the gallows; Vera Figner, who for twenty years languished in Schlusselburg castle; Vera Zasulich, who attempted to assassinate the Governor of St Petersburg . . . They introduce the Pleiad of women of the Russian revolutionary movement. The October revolution itself adds to their number the brilliant names of Inessa Armand, Aleksandra Kollontai, Larisa Reisner. And the more modest name of Nadezhda Krupskaya, the wife of Lenin. The Great Communist Utopia, God's kingdom on earth, gathered under its banner some extraordinary women, who fervently believed in the cause.

But, at a different twist in the historical process, you notice on the streets of the Soviet capital a brigade of road workers in orange overalls. For the most part, these workers are women. These are the truly tragic figures of the mystery of the Great Utopia. When you see how they lay hot tar on the road, struggling with their heavy shovels, you understand: in such a social context, poems about 'The Beautiful Lady', such as Aleksandr Blok wrote at the start of the century, could no longer come into being. And if someone tried to write them it would be nothing but literary hypocrisy.

Perestroika has brought about a renewal in all possible aspects of our life. For example, for the first time in the whole history of Soviet society, we have begun to conduct beauty contests! The young documentary film-maker Tat'yana Khvorova, making a film about one such contest, went straight from the stage to the street with her camera. And she saw women in workmen's clothes, repairing the road by hand.

This juxtaposition of images offers a symbol of our contemporary existence. We are trying with all our strength to compete with the image we have of the West. But we are always held back by poor quality: the asphalt is laid haphazardly, there is no concrete base underneath it.

One can also read a second meaning into these episodes. And it is precisely this second meaning which is important for the subject we are discussing, though I am sure that the film-maker was thinking of nothing but social connotations when she brought together these two images. These scenes bear witness to the fact that the Great Utopia has come full circle. On the one hand, we have a beauty contest, full of half-naked girls - this is nothing but a return to the bourgeois values we once rejected. On the other hand, we have a break with those repetitive values of barracks socialism. Work is presented not as 'a matter of honour, glory, valour and heroism', but as the most vulgar exploitation of women.

When the great Russian poet Nikolai Nekrasov bemoaned the appalling burden of women in his great poem 'Russian Women', could he have thought that the triumph of the social justice he dreamed of - that precisely this, the creation of a society of a new type - would lead to the self-liquidation of his beloved heroine, to the denial of her feminine essence? Statistics which have been made available under *perestroika* bear witness to this fact: there are more children in orphanages today than there were after the Second World War. The fact that 'orphans' exist who have living parents is also a fruit (albeit one full of worms) of the Great Utopia; its indirect, or maybe even its direct, result.

You will say that I have wandered too far from the theme I set for this essay. But it is not I, but rather the theme itself, which leads me away from the straight line of my subject. Everything that is connected with the image of the Soviet

Zinaida Sharko in *Long Farewells*
(Kira Muratova, 1971/1987).

Sovexportfilm

Inna Churikova in *I wish to Speak*
(Gleb Panfilov, 1976).
Sovexportfilm

OPPOSITE ABOVE: Raisa Nedashkovskaya, Nonna
Mordyukova and Rolan Bykov in *The Commissar*
(Aleksandr Askoldov, 1967/1988).
Sovexportfilm

OPPOSITE BELOW: Nonna Mordyukova in *The Commissar*
(Aleksandr Askoldov, 1967/1988).
Sovexportfilm

Sofiko Chiaureli in *Some Interviews on Personal Questions* (Lana Gogoberidze, 1979).

Sovexportfilm and National Film Archive, London

Sofiko Chiaureli in *Some Interviews on Personal Questions* (Lana Gogoberidze, 1979).

Sovexportfilm and National Film Archive, London

Leila Abashidze in *Turnabout*
(Lana Gogoberidze, 1986).
Sovexportfilm

OPPOSITE: Aiturgan Temirova in *Snipers*
(Bolotbek Shamshiev, 1985).
Sovexportfilm

Natal'ya Negoda and Andrei Sokolov
in *Little Vera* (Vassilii Pichul, 1988).

Sovexportfilm

woman, whether she be a private individual, the author of a composition or its heroine, is linked by the common character of her historical soil and historical fate. We did not order this on the basis of our own desire – it was given to us. But several generations have now experienced it; they have passed through a series of stages, from conscious choice and enthusiastic acceptance, to conscious rejection and protest. The woman who embraced the revolution as a longed-for liberation from domestic and social oppression, from male chauvinism, has turned out now to be no less enslaved. Is it not a devilish parody on the struggle for women's emancipation, and for social emancipation generally, when we see our statistically-average Soviet woman tumbling out of a rush-hour bus, clutching two bags she can scarcely lift? Is it not irrelevant to remember that Russian literature of the so-called Golden and Silver epochs (the nineteenth century and the first decade of the twentieth century) elevated women to a height which was only equalled in the Renaissance period, with its Cult of Beauty? The woman of Russian literature is a jewel of creation, a spiritual ideal; in the words of Aleksandr Pushkin, she is 'the purest image of purest charm', 'a genius of pure beauty'.

Art, speaking with the gutter language of the revolution, the language of the street – or, in the words of one poet, the 'rough language of the poster' – turned away from absolute moral values, giving priority to class values. Such a 'change in optics' was a fruitful one for art at that particular moment. The inherent values of this alternative art were destruction, the breaking of old stereotypes. This was a great shock to the staid academic culture and gave rise to much self-reflection. But the swift arrival and complete victory of a crass ideology in the Soviet Union, which had happened already by the second half of the 1920s, led to unforetold consequences. The artistic burst came to an end. In its place, new priorities were consolidated – that of class, of Party-mindedness and of the people – which became an integral and essential part of every piece of creative work. The norm. The normative aesthetic which took shape is known to posterity as 'Socialist Realism'. Was this artistic form, which was decreed from above but supported from below, reflected in those films which are of particular interest to us – those which explore women's themes? It was, of course – in the form of an unrestrained ideologization of everything and everyone. If the film was about prostitution (and the world's oldest profession had grown enormously, something which the authorities made no attempt to keep secret until the mid-1930s), then the heroine was portrayed as a victim of 'accursed capitalism'. She was, of course, led from the streets by a member of the Komsomol, and in the end she was forged anew and became a shock-worker. (Just such a film was *Prostitute*, made in 1927.) Even such a sin as a man raping the wife of his son was given a class slant in the film *Peasant Women of Ryazan* (1927). The offender turned out to be a class enemy, a kulak, and was denounced as such at the end of the film.

The cinema became an apologist for collectivization, which went hand-in-hand with the suppression of the individual and the personal, even up to the point of the displacement of private life as a legitimate subject for portrayal on screen. This was taken to its logical conclusion in the film *A Simple Case*, in which the hero emphatically rejects the family and private life completely. 'Our family is the army,' he declares, 'our family is the country.'

In this context we might mention the plan for the film *Women* (1932-3), which has been preserved in the archive of the great Esfir' Shub. Her screenplay, which was written in conjunction with the writer Boris Lapin (who later died at the front), is a magnificent presentation of 'ideocratic' thought. In an article written in 1933, Esfir' Shub explained her reasons for embarking on this project: 'I want to make a film about women because this subject demonstrates, with the utmost persuasiveness, that only a proletarian revolution, only these new labour conditions and new social organization, *can finally enable us to put an end to the "woman question"*.' (The emphasis is mine - E.S.)

At around this time, a new revolutionary mythology was taking shape, and had already begun its transformation into an official model of morality. It reached its full height in the feature films of the second half of the 1930s, such as *Member of the Government, The Bright Path* and *Circus*. But at the beginning of the 1930s, the idea of loving communism, of giving one's service for the sake of the bright future, was still alive. These, and other new values created by the revolution, were adhered to sincerely and fervently by the majority of the population. But there is a fatal contradiction between the mythological consciousness (that of the mass) and the artistic consciousness (that of the individual). This is, indeed, the major contradiction of the Soviet epoch, and it remains unresolved to this day; in fact, it has been getting stronger. Artists, even distinguished ones, and even some with real genius (such as Eisenstein), have helped to create these new values, unconscious of the implications. This phenomenon of the rejection of humanist values as an act of free will, of the rejection of their own creative and ethical 'self' in the name of some notion about the well-being of all in the far-flung future, has no antecedent in history. German cultural figures, those who took on the cause of fascism, were all the same rooted in the firm soil of national revenge; they had concrete reasons for their choice, such as the economic successes of the Third Reich. In this country, however, it was based on pure faith, pure religion, which did not require any kind of proof. Here, we formed a collective soul, that 'collective consciousness' which eventually turned into a material force.

In the script for *Women*, one can observe the dominant qualities of the ideocratic consciousness, the mythology of the Soviet woman. In the introduction to the film, the director intended to demonstrate the distortion of the image of womanhood which had been created by the culture of the past. Leonardo's Mona Lisa was dismissed as an 'egotistic grinner'. Also discredited was the melodramatic image of the fatal beauty, 'the woman of the alcove' of the Great Silents. The woman as object of pleasure was, of course, a disgrace, and had to be expiated.

The heroines which Esfir' Shub assembled and paraded before us were living women, not fabrications. They were, in her view, the embodiment of correct social roles, which women had received thanks to the October revolution. One of the characters is a shock-worker in a factory, who lives in a workers' hostel and is also taking courses in politics and English. She converses easily with visitors to the factory, and is able to carry on an informed conversation about literature. Such was the image of woman, a fully-developed personality in an epoch which had consigned the 'eternally feminine' to the rubbish dump of history, along with other eternal values which were now defined as bourgeois prejudices.

Reality was presented on screen as a design for an ideal life, drawn up by the artist. Today, when we are experiencing the ultimate bankruptcy of the Utopia (not only in a moral sense - that had already begun in the 1960s - but also in a political sense), many films made at the end of the 1920s, in the 1930s and even in the 1950s, have acquired a new value. We see in them not reality caught in a glass, but more often than not a quasi-reality, detached and varnished. These films represent a matrix of Utopian consciousness of the most refined, the purest type. They are a monolith, a totality.

In the film *KShE*, made in 1932 (the initials stand for 'The Komsomol - The Leader of Electrification'), Esfir' Shub arranged a series of scenes shot in factories and on the construction sites of electricity power stations, so making a hymn to the new life and to its values - social equality and freedom from the power of capital. The masses constitute the hero of *KShE*. Soviet cinema of the 1920s has been applauded for its scenes of the masses, due mainly to the work of Sergei Eisenstein. Esfir' Shub, having studied under the great maestro of montage, also knew how to incorporate scenes of the masses into her films. The mass scenes in *KShE* are expertly filmed, especially when one considers that this was a documentary film, a piece of journalism, and not something intended to entertain. Its artistic strength rests both on the mastery of its production, and on the film-maker's passionate, devoted faith in the ideas and ideals which the film proclaims.

My generation experienced the end, the final gasp, of the 'great style' of this agonized epoch. It is true, however, that by then it had more to do with Stalinist pomposity than with the genuine passion of the masses, called on to create a new life after the October revolution. The cinema audiences of today now shrug their shoulders when they see with what ecstatic rapture the camera describes female labour on a conveyor belt, producing electric bulbs. Someone who knew nothing about the Stalinist five-year plans, and had never heard of the enthusiasm of the masses, would view with bewilderment the scene where workers at a meeting are discussing with such passion the time-scale for one of the electricity plants. Only a few years were to pass and these inspired builders of a new life, waving their fists above their heads, would be demanding the death penalty for innocent people, the first martyrs of the revolution, thrown into the docks by Stalin's clique. Documentary scenes have been preserved for posterity which bear witness to those times.

The contemporary researcher who is studying the cinematography of the past cannot fail to notice, nor to value, one other feature which is characteristic of the totalitarian epoch. The film-maker always identifies with the heroes (i.e. with the masses) who are engraved on the screen. The film-maker is always the all-powerful spokesperson of the world which he or she celebrates. It is the discourse of the film-maker which indicates most clearly this complete merging with the object portrayed, the virtual dissolution of the director into the theme. One can forge a document; but a film-maker's discourse cannot be forged, it is the matrix of the personality. We are not talking here about the competence of the film-maker, nor even about art; we are talking about the subconscious of the artist.

In the films of the 1930s to the 1950s, including those which were placed on the shelf as ideologically faulty, we do not find a single instance in which the film-maker reflects on the history and fate of humanity as the plot unfolds. It was only in the first half of the 1960s that films marking truly revolutionary, truly grandiose changes in the artistic consciousness began to appear. This was already almost a decade after the 20th Congress of the CPSU, when Nikita Khrushchev had first informed the world about the crimes of Stalin. It is an irony of fate that the emergence of this new type of film coincided with the end of the Thaw, with the fall of Khrushchev and the reversal of his policies. Some of these films did appear on the screen, however, if not right away and after considerable cuts and corrections had been made to them. Examples include Andrei Tarkovskii's *Andrei Rublev*, Igor Talankin's *Day-time Stars*, Gleb Panfilov's *No Ford Through the Fire* and Elim Klimov's *Adventures of a Dentist*. But at exactly the same time, in 1966-7, a partial restoration of Stalinism began, accompanied by an outburst of ideological vigilance amongst Party and state officials. This led to the much-publicized trials of Andrei Sinyavskii and Yulii Daniel, the firing of the editorial board of the journal *Novyi Mir* (led by the poet Aleksandr Tvardovskii), and a number of other actions aimed at frightening the intelligentsia. In a totalitarian society, it is advisable to shake one's fist at poets and artists every now and then . . .

The films which were banned included some which were later hailed as masterpieces, after they had been locked up in a safe for twenty years, seemingly with no hope of them ever being seen on screen. From the torture-chambers of Goskino were eventually extracted Aleksei German's *Trials on the Road,* Larisa Shepit'ko's *Country of Electricity,* Kira Muratova's *Long Farewells* and, last but not least, Aleksandr Askoldov's *The Commissar.* We will look at the latter in more detail shortly.

The banning of films in the 1960s and 1970s was done according to the same repressive methods Stalin had used in the past, the only difference being that there was no trial and sentence by a judge. As before, the accusations had an ideocratic tone (they were generally founded on a single motif: 'ideological heresy'), but it was now harder to make out that the film-makers had a criminal cast of mind. This is because at that time, at the end of the 1950s and in the 1960s, the so-called 'author's cinema'* had begun to appear in the Soviet Union. The battle against this was, essentially, a battle against the film-maker's discourse. It was not possible to conceal other projects into the themes, problems, fables and literary adaptations; the trained nose of the bureaucrats sniffed out any sedition without fail. Attempts at such projects were closely watched and 'led'; reprisals followed and they had no chance of going on to completion.

This is the situation in which the persecution of *The Commissar* took place. We should be careful not to make too much of the artistic perspicacity of the functionaries, the apparatchiks. The film was accused, in the final analysis, of Jewish nationalism, although not in so many words. Against the background of the Arab-Israeli conflict which had flared up in 1966, and the position taken by the Soviet government in response to this, the fate of the film could not have been any different. Nor, it goes without saying, could the fate of the recalcitrant film-maker. He was denounced from the Party pulpit, and excommunicated from the 'church' - in other words, he was expelled from the Party.

The accusation which was levelled against him was more than enough to justify reprisals. And perhaps, partly for that reason, since they had already reached their verdicts on the basis of such concoctions, the accusers did not pay much attention to other aspects of the film which were surely no less criminal in the eyes of officialdom. This was, indeed, the first Soviet film which questioned that most sacred of things: the ethics of the revolution.

Askoldov placed eternal values firmly above class interests. At that time this was unthinkable insolence, a challenge to the holiest of holies. Later, however,

---

*Editor's note: This concept originated in French film theory. The 'auteur' theory means that a film is seen very much as the work of one individual; it is virtually stamped with that person's signature.

Mikhail Gorbachev legitimized such a priority when he brought 'eternal values' into the fold of socialist pluralism.

One thing which complicated the film-maker's discourse in *The Commissar*, and brought confusion to unsophisticated minds, was the poetic style chosen by the director. Askoldov recreated on celluloid the expressive language of romantic prose of the 1920s. The style of *The Commissar* is also reminiscent of the delicate black and white images of Soviet epic films of that time. Yet this is in no way a mere copy of the poetry of an earlier time, but rather its re-birth. In 1989, the camera-operator Valerii Ginsburg received the professional award of the Union of Cinematographers of the USSR for Best Camera-operator of the Year – for a work made twenty-three years earlier. As for Askoldov, one could say that he made use only of the 'alphabet and morphology' invented by the leading figures of revolutionary cinema; his 'syntax' is all his own. I would also suggest that he takes a somewhat polemical stance on the cinema classics of the past, and the inevitability with which they portray the victory of the 'mass'.

The Commissar was based on a story by Valerii Grossman, the author of the now acclaimed novel *Life and Fate* (*Zhizn i sud'ba*), who was arrested by the KGB in the same year the film was made. As I have noted, Askoldov arranged his subject in the spirit of the tradition of classical Russian prose. At the centre of the composition he placed a mother and child, a Madonna and Christ. Their fate became the measure of morality against which the events in the film were to be judged.

The story is as follows. It is the time of the Civil War and the heroine, Klavdia Valilova, is the commissar of a regiment. Her husband has been killed in battle. Already pregnant at the time of his death, she awaits the birth of her child in a small town in south-west Ukraine. The town had been all but destroyed by the Whites, but the Red forces have managed to establish a weak hold over it. She is placed in the apartment of the tinsmith, Efim Magazanik. The world of the commissar had consisted of two tones, everything clearly divided into black and white; now, she is plunged into the patchwork-quilt colours, diversity and noise which make up the world of this poor Jewish family. 'You think that to give birth to a child is as easy as a war? Pif, paf and it's over?' asks Maria, the young wife of Efim and mother of six children. 'No, excuse me, it's not so simple.' And she begins to teach the commissar.

When 'Madam Vavilova' was first billeted in his impoverished household, the tinsmith went wailing round the whole street, loudly abusing the local authorities: to think that they were not able to find anyone richer than Efim Magazanik! But only a day passes before the couple are cheerfully sewing a dress for the mother-to-be, who has no other clothes than riding breeches, a soldier's shirt and even soldier's underwear. A transformation takes place before our eyes. The bright cotton dress and headscarf soften the powerful features of the commissar. A hidden beauty surfaces in this inscrutable, ascetic face. A different, feminine manner slowly awakens in Klavdia Vavilova. It had been patiently waiting for its time, and that time has now come.

The film contains a particularly powerful image of birth. During the torture of labour, the commissar is haunted by the memory of a cannon stuck in the sand – an obsessive, clinging image, as if she is in fever. She is straining alongside the men, pushing and pushing the unyielding metal, red-hot under the scorching southern sun. The Michelangelo-like backs of the men are dripping from exertion. The wheezing horses are in a lather, the breathing of the soldiers comes in painful gasps. But the ground, cracked from the sun's worship, slips from under their feet. A wounded Red Army man appears before her, with a bandage covering his eyes, begging for help. She sees the sea-shore, and she herself walking with the father of her child. And cavalry riders with drawn sabres. In the final burst of pain, she sees her husband dying, and a herd of horses, riderless, driven mad by the roar of gun fire, wandering round in no direction . . .

'Efim! We've had a son!' Maria cries joyfully from the threshold.

The simple words, the homely voice, return us to reality. Glory be to God, a woman has given birth to a son! But in this feverish world where the mystery of birth has just occurred, other laws are in operation. The woman who gave birth was Clio herself, the muse of history, and it was not a child but the revolution which she carried in her womb and ultimately delivered.

For the commissar, revolution and religion are the same thing. She earnestly confesses her revolutionary faith. She christens her son at the font of the Civil War. Indeed, the revolution acts as his midwife. Klavdia proudly carries her infant through the town square, where the Orthodox cathedral, the Catholic church and the synagogue all meet – a symbolic passage of the Bolshevik Madonna past the places of worship of alien faiths.

This stroll ends in a chance meeting with her comrades from her regiment. No longer fitting the image of a commissar, but appearing now in the forgotten guise of an ordinary woman – and even with an infant in her arms – she becomes embarrassed, confused and depressed. Pressing herself against a stone wall, the commissar sobs bitterly over her son. She sees clearly what will happen – that her unplanned motherhood will end in tragedy.

This comes when the Whites, after a short breathing space, renew their offensive. The troops of the Red Army are forced to retreat. The commissar, with her babe in arms, is faced with a choice – either to settle in this little town until better times, or to leave her child with the family with whom she was billeted and take her place again in the battle. She chooses the latter.

We have all heard of such stories, we have all read about them. For my generation, of course, they were connected with the Great Patriotic War, not with the Civil War. But a single ethical law prevailed in both cases – the priority of the social over the personal, of the common good over one's own desires. There were women who followed their husbands to the front, or went alongside them, leaving their children in the care of people they knew – or even people they did not know. The citizen's duty overrode the maternal instinct. The social being took precedence over the natural being. The world of feelings was subordinated to the world of ideas. The question of whether this was good or bad did not arise in the mass consciousness for many years; indeed, a re-evaluation is only now beginning. The contradiction between feelings and duty was incorporated into the system of ethical ideas of the revolutionary era, with duty in the paramount position. This was subsequently carried into the excesses of Stalinist ideology.

The 1960s were a time of smashing myths and killing old gods. The handwheel of reflections began to unwind our consciousness and our culture. Only then, with the establishment of a new historical phase and a new level of self-knowledge and self-consciousness, did it become possible to take a more distanced, more philosophical look at our revolutionary past. This new way of seeing had to penetrate the mythologized ideas about revolution which had formed into a rock-hard catalogue of stereotypes of themes and images. Drama and dramatization now came to light at a depth where they had not even been sought in the past.

Askoldov was the first to utter aloud what had still not yet been properly formulated, and to which ears were totally unaccustomed. He was branded a heretic. He had behind him, however, the history of all revolutions, with their iron and unchanging law. What is this law? That the idea which has taken hold of the masses, and turned into a material force, forms its own ethical code; that the private life and the private concerns of the individual are subordinate to the concerns and the interests of the Collective Task. Human feelings, if they hinder the performance of the Collective Task, must be swept aside. 'The person who loves a son or daughter more than me is not worthy of me . . .' – this was said by none other than Christ, who has become the symbol of self-renunciation and love for one's neighbour in world mythology. And as we have noted above, the revolution takes the place of Christ for the commissar.

The everyday, the momentary and the eternal are intertwined in the story, bound together into a knot of philosophical problems. To resolve them is not within the power of Efim, who accepts fate as it is, nor of the commissar, who lays down her own life in order to change the fate of humanity, to change the path of history. Indeed, all of the wisdom in the world would not be able to resolve the quarrel between the commissar of the Civil War in Russia on the one hand, and contemporary humanity on the other. For history is immoral.

The film does not attempt to judge its heroes. It only outlines two versions of female behaviour in those extreme times of revolutionary turmoil. Klavdia places, above all else, 'the truth, for which one should not be afraid to die'. She leaves her child, and goes off to die for the world revolution – that is, for an abstract idea. Maria, on the other hand, the local beauty who takes over the mothering of the commissar's son (when you already have six, why not a seventh?), lives her own private life. She bustles about the kitchen, messes around with the children; in other words, she adheres to those values which have been dismissed by the revolution as prosaic and petty-bourgeois.

The lives we lead today do not serve to censure the commissar. However, it is clear that Maria has been rehabilitated. Both of these female images in Russian and in Soviet culture (and not just in terms of their representation on the screen) are now subjected to retrospection and introspection. In their mirror is reflected both the humanistic tradition of Russian culture and the sacrificial suffering inherent in revolutionary ethics.

It would seem that Maria's time has come – both in our own lives, and in that of our culture, which has been suffering from an 'asthenic syndrome'. (Such is the diagnosis which Kira Muratova made, in her film of that name.) Yet my 90-year-old mother, an ex-commissar of the Civil War, insists that 'socialism will win!' – despite the obvious collapse of the socialist system in Europe. 'You will see!' she prophesies. Commissars hold out to the very end.

13 THE 'WOMAN OF THE EAST':
THE PORTRAYAL OF WOMEN IN KAZAKH CINEMA

Dilyara Tasbulatova

Ask anybody what 'national character' actually means, and you will not get a convincing answer. When Serik Aprymov, a young director from the studio Kazakhfilm, depicted Kazakhs as eccentrics in his delightful short film *Two on a Motor Bike*, everybody began debating: is this our national character? Is eccentricity one of our distinguishing features? And, since eccentricity means deviation from the norm, does this not violate the very meaning of the concept of 'national character'? One could almost imagine someone drawing up a secret list enumerating all the qualities of Kazakhs which should not be transgressed. And as for women . . .

The woman in the cinema of the East has been cast like a majestic statue of the Mother, the Bride, the Heroine. She is almost a parody – of an 'Eastern' type – of the mythologies put forward by the European Soviet cinema in the 1940s. The Russian cinema had a different mythology for each era. In the 1920s, it was 'the enthusiast'; in the 1930s, the wife of a Party hack; in the 1940s, the soldier; in the 1950s . . . and so on. This continued right up to the 1980s, with its *Little Vera*s and *International Girls*. The dramatic construction, the general spirit and the male characters of the Eastern cinema more or less successfully duplicated the stereotypes created by 'the centre'. The characters played by women, however, never varied. The woman of the East was exactly the same now as she had been years ago, despite the fact that in real life she had certainly been changing, together with life itself. Why is this?

The answer, I believe, lies in the religious roots of the people, which are much stronger in our men than in our women. And with few exceptions, it is men who make films. In the imaginations of men, woman is still the keeper of the hearth, the mother, the crutch. And at the same time, she is also the lowest of creatures, totally dependent, without a mind of her own.

A Moslem, even if he is officially atheist, is a highly orthodox creature. This is still the case whatever outer form he takes. He can be a 'rocker', an

Academician or speak three European languages – it does not essentially change anything. At least not for women.

It is precisely this quality – this insuperable orthodoxy – that does not allow him to look at his surroundings with a sober eye. Instead, a certain self-satisfaction (which is, in my view, generally present in Moslems) colours his view. It acquires a tone of elevated romanticism, an almost ingratiating sweetness. All of this, essentially, points to absolute indifference. A Moslem is always indifferent to women. (This is, incidentally, the secret of his irresistibility.) So why should he not be indifferent to his representation of them? This, perhaps, explains the dominance of the stilted, stereotypical female characters which flood our screens.

Very occasionally a vivid female character suddenly appears. This is due almost to a miracle, or to mere chance, or to the warmth and talent of a particular actress. Gul'zia Bel'baeva's portrayal of the heroine of the film *Raushan the Communist* is one such example. Bel'baeva is a subtle and genuine actress, whose own life resembles that of her characters. She plays the part of a 'progressive woman', one of the 'enthusiasts' in the headlong dash towards the 'new life' which took place in the 1920s. The story, by the writer Beimbet Mailin, is nothing exceptional. (Mailin, incidentally, was an unswerving supporter of the revolution, even in the 1930s. It goes without saying that he was ultimately executed.) It is concerned with the conflict in a relationship. The wife is a member of the Communist party, but her 'backward' husband has little faith in the common 'bright future'. This is a conventional tale, which has often been used in Soviet art. But it took on a new meaning in this film, the first by director Damir Manabaev. It became a social conflict, born of these terrible times, but one which did not overshadow the human substance of the relationship between the heroes.

Bel'baeva's Raushan is not like the wild heroines of that time. They preferred the love of abstractions, such as 'world revolution', to all other attachments. Raushan, on the other hand, treats her husband with an understanding which moves the audience, with sympathy, warmth and with no trace of superiority.

If this role had fallen to any other actress, she would have taken pleasure in playing a young Amazon 'torn between her feelings and duty' (as we like to put it). In this unnatural war, of course, duty had to triumph. But the warmth of Bel'baeva twists the film onto another track. Its message turns into this one: that a person's humanity is not so easy to abolish. Whether the director of the film actually had this in mind, or whether he achieved it involuntarily due to the performance of the actress, I cannot say.

The Soviet cinema of the 1950s had an urge to mummify life, to give it a set form. The spirit of these times is captured in the highly conventional image of the sublime and suffering Mother. Yet suddenly, for reasons unknown, it began to fill with currents of new life. It succeeded in overcoming dramatic trivialities. *Tale About a Mother,* directed by Aleksandr Karpov, is an example of this trend. Amina Umurzakova, the 'Little Mother of the Kazakh Cinema', played the part of an old mother (though she was not herself an old woman), who, with heartfelt emotion, receives notice of her son's death. The director's desire to create a 'symbol' collided with the simple-hearted portrayal of the woman by the actress, who took a compassionate hold of her heroine – it is said that Umurzakova cried when she watched her own performance on the screen! In spite of poor direction, a conventional plot and a number of banal difficulties, Amina Umurzakova's performance earned sympathy from the audiences of many countries. This shows that sincerity will always win our hearts, in spite of everything. However, Umurzakova is a particularly rare actress who can find a way of raising herself above even the most odious dramaturgical material, be it the symbolic Great Mother or the enterprising old woman in Shaken Aimanov's unpretentious comedy *Angel in a Skull-Cap.*

But . . . Gul'zia Bel'baeva's performance of Raushan, and all the roles played by Amina Umurzakova, focus on one trait of the female character, and demonstrate a certain archetype of the woman of the East. She is invariably charitable, self-sacrificing and concerned exclusively with worries about family and children. This image, with no contradictions, forms the basis of the Moslem understanding of woman. But art should not exist as a mere illustration of somebody's wishes, even if they be the wishes of the Prophet himself. (The Japanese, for whom tradition is sacred, still produce many films which show the mutiny of the human spirit against the fetters of prejudice. And this mutiny is often conceived in the soul of women . . .)

One of our best writers, Mukhtar Auezov, wrote a story about a young widow who takes a vow of chastity. The story ends, of course, with the violation both of the vow itself, and of decency in general. In the 1950s, no director would have dared to screen such an 'outrageous' tale. That era demanded rather different ideals. But in the beginning of the 1980s, a young director, Ermek Shinarbaev, turned it into a short film, casting Natal'ya Arinbasarova in the leading role. (She had once been famous for her performance in A. Mikhalkov-Konchalovskii's film *The First Teacher,* in the role of Altina.) Arinbasarova is a very talented actress, absolutely unrestrained, and somewhat Europeanized. But in truth, she plays only an eroticized version of the familiar image. She writhes on the bed and mercilessly beats herself, in a literal sense. But the film fails to explore the moral self-flagellation with which this courageous woman coped for a whole seven years – the term of her abstention. The young director, perhaps to his own surprise, made an extremely erotic film, although the original story implied nothing of the sort. Eroticism had been only a metaphor for freedom, and it was not so much the body declaring its rights, but the soul which wanted to break out of the chains of prejudice.

Eroticism in general is a curious subject for discussion. In accordance with the fashion which has recently spread across our country, we Kazakhs also try to place a bed scene in every film. But the filming of erotic scenes is a complex matter, and only works if a certain cultural level has been reached. (This is particularly essential concerning the relations between men and women.) The Moscow press has tackled this subject mercilessly. But the problem lies not in the bed scenes themselves. It is much more complex than that. It is funny to see how the ingratiatingly sweet, dull, almost nauseatingly virtuous heroine ends up in bed with some ill-starred actor stubbornly trying to look like a playboy. The director, having paid tribute to the fashion, then hotly contends in art council meetings that this is the most 'courageous' scene in the film, and that he will not allow it to be cut. But to shoot an erotic scene does not signify that a taboo has been overcome. On the contrary, clumsy eroticism (which borders on pornography) shows more strongly than ever that rough, indifferent and arrogant attitude towards women of which I have already spoken.

I find it hard to believe that it is possible to make a bad film which contains successful sex scenes. To my mind this is nonsense. It would be better to do without such scenes. In any case, the public is not as stupid as we may sometimes think. It quietly forgives inaccuracy and stupidity whenever the human body is not the focus of attention. But if you do not have enough taste and sensitivity in your portrayal of love on the screen, your reward will be sarcastic laughter.

After his more schematically stylized film of Mukhtar Auezov's story, Ermek Shinarbaev made a charming film based on a script by the famous writer Anatolii Kim. *My Sister Lyusya* happily departed from the mould of postwar themes, to sketch for us a complex female character. Aigul', in a fine and expressive performance by the talented actress Khamar Adambaeva, bears a rare female quality - mystery. Aigul' is silent almost the entire time, breaking this silence only to make an occasional insignificant remark. So her 'national' qualities - kindness, delicacy and femininity - are not actually declared; the words she speaks are not adequate for this. These qualities emerge, instead, out of the very fabric of the film. Khamar Adambaeva slips imperceptibly into the sequence, moving across the frame, seemingly unaware of her 'Eastern exceptionality'. In short, her performance is not literary, but cinematographic. If you wish, you can read into it anything you like. She is Mother, in the highest sense, the faithful Wife, whose husband has not returned from the war, and of course she is a metaphor for all Wives and Mothers. Yet all these various general images (each filled with pain) are present in the film in a half-concealed form. They do not lie on the surface. This is mainly thanks to Adambaeva's performance. Her 'elevation to the pedestal' is immersed in daily life. The pathos - if there is any - does not wear on your nerves (probably because it is imperceptible). And if you cry over the sorrows of the women on the screen, your tears are not insincere, they were not squeezed out of you. Aigul' is the first to break the ice of our mistrust towards all these noble heroines - we were so tired of their irreproachability, their coldness and inaccessibility.

Aigul' was created at the time of the war. That means she was created at the same time as those other women whose ruthlessness and iron wills have been glorified in films on the theme of war. *Snipers,* by the Kirgiz director Bolotbek Shamshiev, narrates the heroic deeds of a young Kazhakh woman, Aliya Moldagulova, who perished in the war. This picture claims to be an epic; it glorifies, with Roman severity, the inflexibility of the woman fighter. The heroine is continually counting the number of Germans she has felled. But the film-maker does not pause for even a moment to think of what a mutilating effect this is having on her young soul, and how unnatural, how absurd, her thoughts are. Can murder ever be just? Is it really possible to delight in such terrible actions? Later, Andrei Tarkovskii was to show what a destructive influence war has on a child's soul in *Ivan's Childhood.* Yet Shamshiev does not suggest any such thing. *Snipers* is just yet another film on the theme of war, which illustrates, more or less well, the familiar views which have been pressed on us so diligently since our childhood, by means of official propaganda. There are clumsy attempts to 'humanize' the heroine: she is very fond of a little cat, which she carries around with her everywhere, and she is in love with a young man (an 'unseemly' matter in times of war). But these attempts ultimately fail. The reason, perhaps, lies in the cold dispassion of the actress (Aiturgan Temirova). But most probably it is because *Snipers* was 'made to order' - filmed to celebrate the anniversary of victory.

It makes for an interesting symbiosis, when the 'national character' comes together with the mythology of totalitarianism! I find it hard to imagine Aigul', Shinarbaev's heroine, in the scenes portrayed in *Snipers.* And yet both are of the same era; both are of the same people.

In general, times have changed for the worse for Kazakh women. Today, that intrepid young woman whose humour, strong character, beauty and talent was for centuries a source of inspiration to our story-tellers is not to be found in novels or films. The Moslems, of course, are reactionaries, in my view. But they treated the daughters of the khan, the aristocrat, absolutely differently to more simple girls. The khan's daughter was always seen as equal to men. The Kazakhs have an ancient tradition, called *aitys* - a kind of musical competition. Two singers, a man and a woman, would sit opposite each other, with dombras in their hands, and improvise in verse. One asked a question; the other answered. One cracked a joke; the other rejoined. One made a witty remark; so did the other. An *aitys* could be extremely long – sometimes it would last a day and night. These ancient games of wit have not passed away without leaving a trace; we still have to keep an eye on the tongues of some of our modern young women. But in films you do not find women like this. Such humour is not in fashion these days. Times change – what else can one say?

There is an exception. Twenty years ago, the director Sultan Khodzhikov (who passed away recently) screened an epos called *Kyz-Zhibek*. The heroine was a khan's daughter, a resolute young woman of sharp intellect, who everyone fell in love with not only because of her beauty but also because of her obstinacy, her sharp tongue and her talent. However, this operatic, decorative and over-blown version of the epos was not able to fully capture the outstanding quality of the heroine. The quiet, delicate beauty of Meruer Utekesheva, who played the role of Zhibek, was only outwardly aristocratic; perhaps she did not have the inner fire of the woman she was portraying, which so fascinated the orthodox Kazakhs.

Has it turned out that people of our times are more conservative than their distant ancestors, who were able to celebrate the outstanding nature of women? Those unknown story-tellers celebrated a strange, extraordinary young woman who does not even enter the heads of our present-day screen-writers. It would seem 'untypical' to them. To them, clichés which they have taken – how ironic – from the Koran completely satisfy the demands of 'realism'.

But imagine for a moment that we have a matriarchal society, and that film directors are now exclusively female. What kind of man will they portray as 'typical'? Will they conjure up a wise old man, solemnly uttering aphoristic banalities? Or will they have in mind an Eastern version of the superman-type? I have a very high opinion of female intellect, but nonetheless, there are more than enough films in such a mould made by our women directors.

At the risk of provoking their anger, I have to express my doubts about the validity of emancipation when it comes to film directors. I do not understand what 'female cinematography' means. I concede that there are exceptions, however – notably Kira Muratova and Vera Khitolova. I do not mention Tat'yana Lioznova or Aida Manasarova, since their films cannot be described as specifically 'women's films'. They attain the level of an average male director, but go no higher. Larisa Shepit'ko, on the other hand, is worth three men, but in her case we need not talk of some 'fateful' division of humanity into men and women. Shepit'ko never demanded any female privileges for herself; she always worked like a man, not sparing herself. She would never have had this strange idea (as it seems to me) of creating a women's film studio, a few of which now exist in the republics of the former Soviet Union. The idea is absolutely incomprehensible to me. Does it mean that all women with film diplomas in their pockets, with no exceptions, will be given the means to make films, including those women who were not good enough to compete with men? If so, it will merely become a philanthropic organization, dispensing charity, in this case on the grounds of sex. This is an interesting idea, very interesting . . .

But on the other hand . . . if a woman is very talented, she is talented precisely as a woman. Her manner is female and feminine, and can never be mistaken for that of a man. I mentioned Kira Muratova with good reason. She is the only woman director in our country whose films explore human relationships from a genuinely female perspective. A male director (like Antonioni, for example) is more inclined to be ruthless; he engages in a cooler analysis of feelings. Kira Muratova is full of compassion and mercy. Her mockery always has a warmth, her irony is without malice. Her view of things is reassuring. And the sadness which runs through it is always respectful.

Perhaps a talented person, male or female, is always more expressive, more vivid than others. Hence, a woman of genius is somehow more of a woman, a man of genius is more of a man. But the most curious thing is that their heightened power of insight (which is an inalienable feature of genius) also gives them greater understanding of the problems of the opposite sex. Fellini's films always contain a multitude of women – mothers, prostitutes, friends, acquaintances, film-stars. They are an integral part of his world view. The brilliant Liliana Cavani, in her film *The Night Porter,* paints a picture of a relationship between a man and a woman with rare honesty. In order to do this, she had to be able to penetrate the very depths of male psychology.

Another outstanding woman, the writer Lyudmila Petrushevskaya, balances on the verge of a 'male' sober realism (which resulted in her being denied publication for a long time, charged with being 'over-critical' and 'shallow'), over which soars her female kindness and powers of observation. Because of this combination, the characters she depicts glimmer with a multiplicity of qualities in one and the same instance, in the course of a single sentence. No act has a single meaning; each one is difficult to appraise. Herein lies the fascinating secret of her prose.

If we speak of women's art, then, we need to place women's powers of observation, their delicacy, their desire to portray the nuances of events, characters and actions, in the centre of discussion. We need to include that undefinability which hovers over every sequence in Kira Muratova's films, that peculiarly female, over-flowery speech and those verbal digressions which appear in every phrase written by Lyudmila Petrushevskaya.

Otherwise, all this talk about 'emancipation' has no meaning. Or it would, at any rate, come down to the fact that the route to emancipation means trying to carve one's own path, in a direction which differs from that of men.

And so, what is this 'national character'? It seems to me that everybody gets endlessly worked up about the sketchiness of heroes portrayed in Kazakh films. And yet, when the first film appeared on our screens which did not show mere inventions but instead real, living people, taken from the 'very depths of the masses', there was a tornado of indignation, hostility and even threats.

This story requires a detailed, step-by-step account. If you remember, at the very beginning of my article I mentioned the director Serik Aprymov. In the short film he made as a student at film-school, he gave us some unusual national types. When he had the chance to express himself in a full-length film, Serik deployed his talents to the full: he returned to the place of his birth – the village Aksuat, in the Semipalatinsk region of Kazakhstan – and made a film which was honest, bitter and dreadful. But his gloomy prophesies were, as always, concealed beneath a fond, sad, ironical smile, beneath a delicate humour, a grace peculiar to him. His human heart beats through all this, brimming with love for his humble, ill-starred fellow-villagers, immersed in their petty worries.

His charming smile, his gentle mockery, have always attracted people to him. No one expected such an impudent trampling on their 'norms' and 'traditions', such 'cynicism' and 'slander', from this 27-year-old boy. This may sound odd, but we now have our own Salman Rushdie – somebody in the village of Aksuat carries a loaded rifle with the intention of killing the author of this 'libel'. As usual, none of his opponents have actually seen the film; they know about it only through hearsay. In contrast to Rushdie, Serik did not encroach on the Koran. He only showed the truth of village life. For this, 'honest fellow-citizens' will never forgive him. What provoked such a stormy protest?

The story is that of a young man who returns to his native village after serving his time in the army, to find that everything has changed beyond recognition. (In fact, it is his perceptions of life which have changed.) The tale is imbued with the tragedy of life, concealed beneath the guise of dreary commonplace events. *The Last Stop* tells the story behind simple troubles. The idiocy of 'normal' life, which Serik only touched on in his first short film, takes on tragic lines in this film. The author does not peddle the tragedy; he is never aggressive towards his audience, he does not allow himself to be maudlin or over-sentimental, he does not wring out their tears. There is always an atmosphere of complete calm, whatever events are taking place – the absurd drinking bouts, the absurd village gatherings, the dispirited and miserable debaucheries, the accidental suicide of one of the heroes (which takes place with none of the appropriate attendant circumstances). This sense of calm heightens the injury.

The ability to dramatize life is a normal attribute of an artist. This makes life seem less insipid, more meaningful; it gives it a higher destiny. It is an attribute of the artist to exaggerate events, to twist them - in accordance with the laws of dramaturgy - into a 'ball of passion', to make a rhythm from events, to recreate life. But to do this - to transform life from its usual lazy rhythm - is not everyone's aim. And the course of Serik's film is like the course of real life. Serik does without scenes which shock; he does without special sound effects. He also evades the classical distribution of functions between the characters. In his film, four friends gad about their native village during the course of a twenty-four hour period. They are not at all what you would expect of a group of friends. One is a romantic, one is a layabout, another a womanizer and the fourth is a careerist. The composition of the group is somewhat arbitrary; it has little importance. All four are weighed down by the oppressive atmosphere of village life from which there is no escape. This abnormal, pitiful and useless existence is thought to be completely normal, even predestined. Yet it is not fate which leads to the suicide of one of them; it is simply chance. It is not a lack of personal energy, but circumstances which impel the heroes to remain here. (There is just no good reason to move their entire families from the place where they have lived since birth.) And is it not spiritual emptiness which has determined their style of life.

Then what is it? The camera in Serik Aprymov's film provides the answer. In the hands of Murat Nugmanov, it flies over this God-forsaken place. The air is heavy with inconsolability, poverty, the limitations of life. It is as if there is absolutely nothing beyond the village of Aksuat - just the scorched desert, where each of us is destined to perish. This film says more than those thousands of official figures and reports which tell us that people in huge tracts of Kazakhstan live below the poverty line. And yet, for reasons which are not clear, the film gives out a strong sensation of the energy of life, in spite of its misery.

The inhabitants of Aksuat village have not been written off. Their dreary motions may be directed nowhere at present, but can this last forever? Milos Forman once showed us a similar desolation of feelings, a similar meaninglessness, in his film The Love Adventures of a Blonde. And yet in that film too, some kind of super-energy - possibly coming from the director himself - soared over the film. It could be sensed even through the stupidity, the vanity, the lack of tenderness which characterized the relationships between the heroes. It shone through the idiocy of life in general. However strange it sounds, a sense of hope was lodged deep inside this very idiocy. When it comes down to it, life is always meaningless - even in a situation of 'fundamental freedom'.

Laughter resounded throughout the cinema halls where Last Stop played, until, somewhere in the middle of the film, the suicide occurred. The laughter abruptly stopped when we saw in the distance a figure leaning over the corpse, and heard his indifferent and business-like voice intone: 'The skull is completely smashed in . . .'

It is hard to imagine that a modern film-goer, even one who has seen such violent films as *The French Connection*, will be able to sit back calmly and peacefully on hearing these words – even though the director chooses not to show us the smashed head, nor the dead body. The audience has become accustomed to 'sumptuous', shocking violence, wrapped up in chic. It is not used to death which seems so ordinary, which is not accompanied by cynical visual images aimed at shocking, which is not melodramatic. Depending on the genre, death in the cinema is portrayed either romantically or cynically. But either way, it still produces compassion and agitation in the cinema hall. Yet Serik Aprymov does not give us the chance to pull ourselves together after the death in his film. He moves straight into the next sequence. Hence he does not allow us to give full rein to our feelings; he acts as if we had none. This absurd death is just one of a series of absurdities, which, as a whole, make up life. Such an honest, sober attitude, which is usually termed 'realism', gives the film its deep meaning.

I wrote my first review of the film immediately after its première, and at that time I had no idea of the furore which awaited its director. We can now begin to understand why his film aroused such indignation – an indignation which went way beyond the bounds of a 'minor scandal'.

First of all, it outraged people's 'finer feelings'. Clearly no hypocrite, Serik spared women no more than men. Whereas his male characters were devoid of ideas, his women were overly 'available'. This is a serious infringement on ideas about decency. But as I have already mentioned, it is only indifference to women on the part of male directors which has resulted in such artificial, fictitious heroines, whose behaviour is strictly regulated by unspoken rules lodged firmly in our minds. When, at last, a courageous man dares to speak the truth, everyone screams: 'Slander!' Hypocrisy, it would seem – which in my view is characteristic of Moslems – played the fateful role here. Everybody knows that the norms of village life are far from irreproachable, yet to speak of this aloud is considered 'improper'. Hence, the ingenuous frankness with which Serik viewed the world was the most offensive thing. People saw in it an evil intent.

Love, death, heroic deeds, the enthusiasm of ideas . . . It is forbidden to look at these concepts with the free and simple approach used by Serik. (Daniil Kharms once said that he hated such words as heroism, pathos, and morality. It would seem that Serik feels the same.) Probably this is why I still have not seen the self-aware, full-blooded, vital women who appear in *Last Stop* in a single other Kazakh film. Men have a tendency to go to extremes, they see women either as saints or as whores. But Serik's women fit in neither category.

Perhaps as a man, Serik would have preferred to have portrayed the ideal woman. But as an artist, he could not close his eyes to the truth. Yet the real marvel is that he loves his heroines, in spite of everything. Someone once said: 'It is not enough to accept people as they are; we also have to love them as they are.' To love a licentious young village woman who casually sleeps with the protagonist from time to time; to love an old woman who quietly puts up with her son's drinking bouts; to love the quiet girl who had been virtually in bed with her lover when his friends came round, and then primly refuses to drink with them; this is all understandable. But Serik also loves the fat woman who killed her illegitimate baby to hide her 'sin'. His love is not the condescending love of a righteous man towards a sinner. There is neither sexuality, nor philanthropy in his love. Simply, he understands this woman.

However, it was women who felt most insulted by the film. Their menfolk took it on themselves to defend their women's 'honour'. These were the very men whose unreasonable attitudes had made women's lives so insufferable, so weighed down with hardships.

The director himself sees the reaction to his film as natural. He bears no hostility towards his opponents. He merely allows himself a gentle laugh, as if to say that people find it difficult to deal with unaccustomed truths. But *Last Stop* is no malicious satire. It is only a look at life, imbued with both bitter sorrow and love for his fellow-villagers.

It is not without reason that I have begun and finished my article with the creative work of Serik Aprymov. We can endlessly discuss the nature of the national character; we can hold scores of press conferences on the subject. But only the genuine emotional experience we get from watching real, deep 'national' art can begin to lift the veil of mystery which wraps itself around too-familiar concepts. Nobody, after all, really knows what is meant by 'The Russian Soul', 'The Mystery of the East' or even 'Self-determination'.

Perhaps I have breached what is acceptable by suggesting that the history of the Kazakh cinema has only just begun since these new, young directors have made their appearance. But it has been very difficult for me to find in the films of the past anything approaching frankness and openness, anything which suggests some novelty of opinion. It is, of course, a truism that the more talent goes into a film, the more complex and delicate its reflections on the reality of its people. There is, occasionally, an exception – one comes across a fairly average production which contains something valuable, like a precious gift which had long been lost. But such finds have almost never appeared in Kazakh films, whatever has been said about them. Women have been particularly unlucky. Now, with the arrival of directors such as Serik Aprymov and Rashid Nugmanov, we can at last hope that our complex, secret inner life, invisible from the outside, will be represented on screen. I mean by this the lives of women - women of the East - about whom hardly anything is known, anywhere in the world.

14 SUBLIMATIONS FROM SOCIALISM

New Images of Women in Soviet Cinematography in the Era of *Perestroika*

Marina Drozdova

In this article I will be attempting to analyse the network of social relationships in which women were depicted on Soviet screens in the era of *perestroika* and *glasnost*. Despite the proliferation of sex scenes in these films, I would argue that the cinema is not offering us real erotic images. It is not depicting real sexual energy; real sexual relations are still hardly ever shown on the screen. Sex represents the sublimation of rather different urges.

Real sex also did not appear on screen before *perestroika* of course. Soviet society in the 1970s was glued together by the sublimation of the personal into the social, the 'citizenly'. Monogamy, as a trait of consciousness, was used as a sign of a person's loyalty. Total loyalty was demanded. This was the ideal from the ideological point of view - that all people would be as one. One thought, one coat, one metre of living space, one lover. If someone wanted two of something, that would constitute pluralism, that would suggest the possibility of choice. But when choice was appropriate, from the point of view of ideology, it was made for us by our valiant Party. And the Party did this happily, even with enthusiasm.

Under *glasnost*, people began reflecting on social and ideological issues much more than they did in the silent, impotent period of stagnation. These reflections are sublimated, on screen, into erotic relations. The taboo about depicting such things has dissolved. But all the same, we should be aware that 'pure' erotica has yet to appear on the Soviet screen.

I have chosen the film *Tractor* as a starting point from which to reflect on the new images of women in the cinema of *perestroika*. It was made in an independent studio, or rather a micro-studio, in 1985. It appears, at first, to be an example of 'Soc-Art', the Socialist Art Movement.* A tractor moves

*Editor's note: This was a non-conformist underground art movement which began prior to *perestroika*, and which parodied the official aims, slogans etc., of the Soviet system and exposed the absurdity and hypocrisy beneath them.

through a field. We hear a woman's voice, a monologue. She is telling us how much she loves her work as a tractor-driver. Her words consist of a series of clichés of the kind that we have heard on the radio and television or read in the editorial columns of newspapers since childhood.

But there is a twist. Her tale of her working day, of her love for her tractor, is related in a clearly erotic way, with distinctly heavy breathing. This short film adheres to the aesthetics of socialist art, but takes it to absurd lengths. In doing so, it parodies brilliantly the ideological system which was forced on us: the complete immersion in work for society; the love for the abstract concept of work; the way *work* is spelt in block capitals, as it has appeared on so many banners. The film also parodies those cinematographers who made propaganda, who produced those stereotyped images – woman as servant of the state, as the Builder of the New Society, as though her intrinsic value consisted just of this. The cinematographer wanted both to reach a mass audience, and to avoid confrontation with the accepted norms of society.

Despite the propaganda, real life looked, of course, rather different. And now that *perestroika* has enabled life to be shown on the screen, it turns out to have been overflowing with libertines, profligates, prostitutes, drug addicts, criminals, mothers who abandon their children, and so on. Those who still cling to the idea of purity in mind and soul now exclaim: 'Why is there so much filth on the screens?' In a system of strict ideological control, such people existed outside the law; it is only natural that they now rush to fill in the gaps in our social consciousness.

It is not so much that new faces are appearing on the screen than that the old dictate of monogamy, which suited the totalitarian model, has vanished. Pluralism in the field of ideas has spread to other areas. Before, any attempt to stray beyond the parameters of monogamy in any form – a new feeling, a new passion, a new endeavour – had to undergo not only an abstract moral appraisal, but was also considered socially disloyal. Such heroines were labelled 'negative' – they were outsiders, petty-bourgeois, and so on. Now, women are suggesting (if only on a subconscious, indirect level) that they have an instinct for polygamy. Even if this is not entirely justified, at any rate, the right of such women to exist is now acknowledged.

This is the story told in the film *Forgive Me*. A 35-year-old woman, an engineer by profession, learns about the unfaithfulness of her husband. In order to somehow cope with her sense of injury and injustice, she tries to find a lover of her own. But this attempt, which she makes in order to spite her husband, does not turn out as planned. In the final scene she is raped by three teenage louts. The film on the one hand represents a new frontier: the heroine is breaking new ground in her attempt to find a way out of her conventional but thoroughly false relationship with her husband. Yet some of the old

conventions still appear. The author of the screenplay, V. Merenko, an adherent
of traditionalist drama, has seen it as his duty to punish the heroine for the
very possibility of thinking of doing something which defies conventional
relationships. She is punished not by a process of emotional repentance or soul
searching, but through simple, animal pain. (The psychology of the screen-
writer reminds me of that of the grandmother of a friend, who was want to
sigh, 'only bad comes from people having different attitudes . . .')

The heroine of I. Talankin's film *Autumn, Chertanovo* is completely,
consciously committed to polygamy – both because this is in her nature, and
because her so-called 'amorality' gives her a way out from the false spiritual
atmosphere in which she lives her life. She has a husband, a physicist, and she
also has a regular lover, a driver, someone from an absolutely different social
stratum. In addition, she has a number of one-night stands. This woman's
network of relations is the subject of the film and this is something completely
new in Soviet cinematography. But the way in which it is realized, i.e. the level
of the dramatic composition, is reduced to a completely primitive treatment.

P. Todorovskii's *International Girl* was the first serious film about prostitution
in the Soviet Union. Its plot is as follows: the heroine is a foreign-currency
prostitute (as long as the rouble continues to have such poor spending power,
foreign-currency prostitutes will continue to occupy a special place in their
profession) who works at the same time as a medical sister in a hospital. She
marries one of her 'clients', a businessman from Sweden, and goes to live with
him in Stockholm. Yet she desperately misses her homeland. In the end, on
her way to the airport to fly back home, she is killed in a car crash. This film,
apart from the obvious novelty of its subject matter in Soviet cinema, fulfils
a dual function in ideological terms. This is obvious from the very first scene.
Above all, there is the unlikely image of the main heroine. Why would a foreign-
currency prostitute, earning several times the basic annual salary of an ordinary
worker in one night, also take on one of the toughest and least well-paid jobs
in our country, as a nurse in a hospital? The film-maker tries to persuade us
that she does so in order to hide her real life from her mother, with whom
she lives. The mother is a crystal-pure woman, who has taught Russian
literature to schoolchildren for her entire working life and would never be able
to deal with the truth about her daughter. She would, furthermore, be
dismissed from her job if the truth came out. However, although the director
does not explain this to us, we understand that he needs to give the heroine's
image a positive side for his own sake. He does this in order to justify her
existence, to give us a chance to think that she is not completely 'bad'. If she
did not work in a hospital, we would not have any evidence that a prostitute
might actually have a soul . . .

It would appear that the heroines of whom I have been talking must be fully preoccupied with their sex-lives. Yet, on the contrary, the subjects have been absolutely de-eroticized. This is symptomatic of the Soviet Union. Intimate life is ousted by social and ideological considerations. These have taken up all the space in our distorted society for themselves; they have substituted themselves for the world of intimate relations. Only the biological and physiological aspects of these relations remain, and in those simple forms which the poorest, perpetually put-upon people might allow themselves. Look, from the point of view of sublimation, at those subjects which I have talked of above.

The heroine of *Forgive Me* is an honest wife and honest worker. When she finds that a hole has been smashed in the wall of her marriage, she sublimates her sense of betrayal into socially unacceptable behaviour, which takes the form of sex.

The heroine of *Autumn, Chertanovo* also does not need erotic impressions and experiences as such. These constitute a sublimation of the fact that there is an absence in society of people who are really interested in one another. Sexual adventures are, for her, simply a way in which she can somehow produce in people some kind of response. In this way, she avoids both being left in a complete vacuum, and in a state of painful longing.

In the film *International Girl,* the language of sex - a sex devoid of spirituality and sensitivity - is placed alongside the language of daily life. Swear-words imbued with sexual imagery (known as *mat* in Russian) are used in everyday speech in order to convey the idea that state institutions are organs of violence. It is said, for example: how they 'fucked' me in that shop!* This means that you were thoughtlessly, stupidly humiliated, and that this had nothing to do with you, with anything you had done, that you were in a state of complete submission (you had wanted to buy, for example, two chickens, but the sales assistant insisted that you only had the right to buy one). The culmination of the film is an episode in which the coitus of the heroine with a series of clients is interspersed with a parallel montage of episodes in which she is metaphorically 'fucked' by the state, by all of its bureaucratic institutions - from the office which formalizes the documents needed to travel abroad to the emptiness and maliciousness of a shop selling foodstuffs. And it turns out that the sexual life of the prostitute in the film is merely the sublimation of the desire to have a normal life, such as is denied women who have the misfortune to be born in a country which is eternally constructing something or other.† Through the payment she gets for her sexual services, she is able to buy something closer to normal living conditions.

---

*The Russian verb is *zatrakhat'* - literally 'to bang'.
†This alludes to the 'construction of socialism' (a common pre-*glasnost'* political slogan); also to Stalin's rapid construction of industry from the 1930s.

This idea is also expressed in the words of one of the heroines of the documentary film *How Do You Do?* by S. Baranov and S. Tusev, which is 'dedicated' to Moscow prostitutes. The woman explains that she does not consider it to be shameful to work as a prostitute in our country. Is it not more degrading, she asks, to spend one's whole life chasing one's tail like a mouse in a wheel, trying to earn a wage which is far from enough to provide a decent standard of living? To be constantly torn in pieces by conflicting demands – the needs of a child, the tedious, mindless burdens of daily life which drain you of all your strength, and work which is not valued and poorly paid?

The heroine of V. Aristov's film *The First Hundred Years are Hard* is a 20-year-old country girl, who stumbles into erotica while daydreaming. Recently married, she is already bored by her faithful, loving husband, by the claustrophobic, patriarchal village where she lives and by her monotonous existence. So she escapes into a series of decadent fantasies. She is dressed in exotic outfits, and romantic heroes appear before her. But in reality, there is nowhere for her to go. Sexual adventures are not a real alternative for her, they are just something else which is unattainable. The young woman realizes that her fate has been pre-determined. Even if she tries to go against it, to wilfully destroy her own life, fate will nevertheless lead her further and further away from what she desires – that beauty, that freedom of feeling which is already inaccessible. Eventually, it turns out that she was not even in charge of her own fantasies – they were the result of a nervous disorder brought on by pregnancy.

Little Vera, directed by Vasilii Pichul, is the first Soviet film with a heroine who embodies eroticism 'without any distracting reflections, from the first to the last sequence of the film ... in the fullest, deepest substance of her instincts' (so wrote the well-known film critic M. Yampol'skii). Critics have tried to link the film's box office success to the originality of its theme, the depth of its social analysis, its director. This melodrama, with its bedroom scenes and the family whose members are constantly at each other's throats, takes place against the background of the degeneration of the working class, represented by Vera's parents. All those endless slogans about the hegemony of the proletariat planted the idea in the mass consciousness that the working class was not simply the backbone of the country, but the panacea for all moral ills, that the working class was not simply the most progressive class, but was also absolutely healthy in all its spiritual relations. In the didactic films of the 1950s, every representative of the proletariat who appeared on screen was presented as an angel. During the Thaw of the 1960s, and the following two decades, some directors attempted to challenge this stereotype. They did so successfully, but their films got no further than private showings for the censor.

This explains the explosive strike delivered by the young film-makers, Pichul and his wife M. Khmelik, who wrote the script.

However, it is not the social aspects of the image of Vera which are paramount, but the fact that she is the very embodiment of an erogenous zone. It is interesting to note that some popular film critics reacted to *Little Vera* almost like the censors. The animal-like instinctiveness of the heroine is presented in these articles as the indication of an absence of spiritual values. In this way, film-goers were encouraged not to concentrate on their emotional response to the film, but to elevate that response into the familiar old social values. Yampol'skii himself sums up the view of the authors of these articles: 'The logic runs as follows: if spirituality was present, then the eroticism would have been sublimated into something good and soothing (perhaps a sense of citizenship?), and all would have been well. Since there is no sublimation, this means there is no spirituality. Since there is no spirituality, this means that the film-makers . . . must be posing the problem of the absence of spirituality through the character of Vera'.

While we are on the subject of *Little Vera*, it would be interesting to recall two films dating from the end of the 'period of stagnation', the heroines of which can be seen to some extent as forerunners of Vera. The film *Strange Woman*, by Yulii Raizman, was also a unique phenomenon in the Soviet Union, despite the mediocrity of its dramatic style, on account of its sensitive portrayal of the heroine. She is a factory-worker and takes part in some sort of phantom 'socialist competition'. (Our administration was very taken with such things for many years.) But her spirit is occupied with a search for abstract, idealized sensation, although she does not know in which man she will find it, or if it can be found in any man. The only thing she has achieved is that she has become ashamed and afraid of herself. But why? It is difficult to determine whether she is actually looking for erotic fulfilment or for emotional passion; in any case, the censor, from the moment the first frame was shot, did not allow even the possibility of thinking about unsublimated eroticism.

The other precursor of *Little Vera* was the hero of the film *Dear, Dearest, Beloved...*, directed by Dinara Asanova. In this film, a 16-year-old schoolgirl, who has fallen in love to the point of insanity with a man who has rejected her, steals a baby in order to win him back by pretending it is their child. She was perhaps the first heroine to appear on the Soviet screen who existed, for the most part, outside of social boundaries - she lived according to her own private morality, constructed around her individual desires, her own 'I want'. She opened the way for a galaxy of young anarchists and nihilists.

The schoolgirls and slightly older heroines of the films *Temptation, The Husband and Daughter of Tamara Aleksandrovna, Arsonists* and many others, perceive their escape from amorphous social relations in an adherence to the ideas of total freedom and total individual power. Like gourmets, they sample various ways of showing their resentment towards society, and make no attempt to hide it. As the plot unravels (and the plots of these films do not differ greatly from one another), they constantly and scandalously make clear their attitudes to everything around them, be it the PTU,* family, friends, loved ones or bed partners. Almost all of them have suffered a kind of numbness from childhood, which was passed on to them from their parents, who had long ago given up in the face of the constant falsity and the inadequacy of their way of life. They quickly move from a position of reflection and decide on extreme action, as defined by the verbs 'to betray', 'to beat', 'to envy', and even 'to kill'. Already, by the age of 14 or 15 years, they are trying to put on adult masks, but they are not really taking part in real life, only playing a game of life. They provoke anger in themselves, instinctively aware of its cleansing power. Almost all of them have a complete absence of sexual morality, but as a rule, this is merely an outer display of freedom. These indifferent couplings (it is difficult to call them romances or liaisons, because one always perceives in them a one-off character) are sublimations of ideological, social extremism. The deformation of consciousness has led to a situation in which pure eroticism is perceived by the young generation as simply an easy means of self-expression, a way of getting something or other, and so on. Nowadays, what is valued is a lack of loyalty. We avail ourselves of the achievements of the sexual revolution; they embody it. Propaganda has turned into a boomerang. The eroticization of ideology has found an echo in a totally ideologized eroticism. Once again, a lack of freedom. In our search for a 'natural', spontaneously free woman, we come up with only the heroine of Little Vera.

The last point on the subject of the various depictions of sublimation is the film by Kira Muratova, The Asthenic Syndrome. It is concerned with a woman's growing realization of her strength, and the opposite experience of a man. The film portrays utmost aggression on the part of the woman, and utmost passivity on the part of the man. But what is it really about? With the linguistic acumen of a Vladimir Nabokov, translated into the language of cinematography, the director gives a powerful description of the appalling state of Russia at the end of the twentieth century. Even in the fourth year of perestroika - the film was made in 1989 - bureaucrats threatened to cut off its access to the screens on the grounds that it was full of unbridled swearing. But they were really afraid that the film turned all of Soviet reality inside out, in a way that permitted no appeal. It demolishes all the symbols of life in our society. The metro is the refuge of an exhausted crowd; the queue is the arithmetic of daily life; the family is the basic cell of this society, going from one queue to another;

*A PTU is a technical school offering post-school education of a notoriously low level.

patriotic chatter is a substitute for the desire and ability to know the real facts. The film also looks at the question of what kind of moral code should be adhered to by a society (rather than a mass of unconnected individuals).

The film begins with a sequence shot in black and white. A woman is attending the funeral of her husband. She is in a state of abject despair. She takes out her grief on everyone around her, even to the point of almost getting into a fight on her way home. Instead, she picks up an unknown man, and invites him into her home. Then she enters a state of hysterics, and throws him out. With this scene, the story ends. But it turns out not to be the end of the film, only the beginning. The screen lightens again, the camera moves back, and we discover that we have been watching a film in a small movie theatre. A man sitting in the middle row of the auditorium gets up and leaves; he turns out to be the hero of the plot which is only now about to unfold.

The man is a writer and a teacher of literature in a school. He is diagnosed as having 'Asthenic Syndrome' – a nervous-psychological disorder which involves growing weakness, disturbed dreams and the collapse of motivation. The word 'asthenic' is a taken from the Greek, and means 'without strength'. The protagonist has the appropriate stereotypical moral notions of a normal person: the strong must help the weak, good must fight against evil, and so on. He performs reflex attempts to do these things. Yet he is already half dead, even in his consciousness of dogma. These attempts, then, merely disguise the reality – that he long ago deviated from these ideas. He still thinks that it is necessary to hide what is going on under the slogan 'good versus bad'. But nobody around him conducts themselves according to these principles; on the contrary, they are motivated by their own drives and instincts. In this respect, they are living in reality, while he is the sick asthenic.

M. Yampol'skii, whom I have already referred to, analyses all the events in this film from the standpoint of sexual inversion. The absolute passivity of the man is a counterbalance to the absolute aggression of the woman, the heroine of the 'film within a film' with which the picture begins. This inversion of sex roles, as a sign of the complete perversion of culture, is the main feature of the most scandalous episode of the film, which produced waves of indignation and brought rows of film-goers to their feet. In the final scene, one of the heroines, sitting on an empty seat in a metro station at night, is swearing to herself. Suddenly she turns her face and 'directs her "verbal torrent" directly at the audience'. As Yampol'skii writes, 'The fact that this swearing – a verbal expression of sexual aggression – comes from the lips of a woman, and not a man, is a manifestation of this inversion'. The episode, as with many others, 'is not simply an everyday scene which one happens to chance on, but takes on the character of a sharp psychological provocation'. Some film-goers, more quickly than others, respond to this provocation by breaking into laughter. It serves as a distinctive version of shock-therapy.

The tendency to reflect the radical views of women on all of life's problems is gaining strength. It is vividly reflected in films made in the style and spirit of youth culture, which used to be a phenomenon only of the underground. Now this is a thing of the past, although in the 1970s and 1980s it influenced a whole generation, or rather, a section of a generation. Hippies, *samizdat* literature, rock music – these were its spiritual component parts. Self-irony; *vsepofigizm*, a slang word meaning 'pointless – it's all the same'; the transformation of life into an image of life, a game – these are the favourite principles of behaviour. *Assa*, by S. Solov'ev – a detective story about the young mistress of an elderly mafia boss who falls in love with a young poet – is a quiet adherent of the post-punk era. *The Black Rose is the Emblem of Sorrow, the Red Rose is the Emblem of Love*, also by S. Solov'ev, was described as 'a romantic kitsch-farce, with fights and chases, fainting fits, and super-human love' by B. Grebenshchikov, the Number One Soviet rock-star, who wrote the music for the film. The story, whose main characters are a 14-year-old schoolboy who is the descendant of a noble family, and his 25-year-old wife, is merged on the screen with farcical reflections on the tragic aspects of our history.

The Needle, by R. Nugmanov, is a story about how a neo-knight (a 'dandy of the post-punk period', as one of the reviewers described him), tried to persuade his former lover to give up drugs; but, trapped in her world of illusions, which enter her body through a hole in the vein, she is inaccessible to him.

The documentary film by G. Gavrilov, *Confession: Chronicle of Alienation*, was the first film to appear on Soviet screens which made a serious attempt to analyse the tragedy of drug addiction. It deals with several years in the life of a family of drug addicts. The heroine takes drugs right up to and after she gives birth. She and her husband, who are not even 30 years old, are committed hippies; but, of course, to be a hippy in California and to be a hippy in a communal flat in Moscow are two entirely different things. Here, every rebellion entails much crueller consequences. The heroine can be seen as the next stage of female self-awareness – she has completely turned away from society. In her we can see what became common in the 1970s, that is an 'internal immigration', as it was called, a retreat into one's self.

These films are known as 'author's cinema', and in the period of stagnation they existed completely outside of the commercial market. The authorities tolerated the existence of 'authorship' – i.e. the imprint of the film-maker's own signature, his or her own style – but not the expression of different opinions and positions. A film-maker trying to express his or her own point of view was automatically deemed to have crossed over into the ranks of the 'other-minded', the dissidents.

The films are permeated with the aesthetics of the neo-avant-garde, of the absurd, postmodernism and surrealism, breaking out at long last from the confines of socialist realism. (The VII Plenum of Soviet Film Directors declared socialist realism to be a cultural phantom, dead at last!) They have put forward a principally new dramatic approach, new direction and new artistic technique. And attention logically was focused on different faces.

In particular, 'author's cinema' put completely new images of women on screen. But one must bear in mind that the heroines of these films do not always, throughout the action of the film, embody in themselves specific female destinies. On the contrary, they often personify the philosophical ideas and abstract thoughts of the writers of the screenplay.

One example is A. Sakurov's film *Sorrowful Indifference*, a fantasy-rebus based on ideas from George Bernard Shaw's 1917 play *Heartbreak House*, which was a symbolic representation of the breakdown of European civilization. The play underwent considerable re-writing in the film; the conflicts and mood of the play, pervaded by a sense of spiritual apocalypse, were transformed into a theatre of the absurd. The female images destroy all the stereotypes about female consciousness which have been created over so many centuries. Taken together with the other characters, they demonstrate the decay of the 'social person', but taken separately, they represent the negation of the female essence. All of the traditional ideas about women are turned on their heads: motherhood, beauty, intellectual emancipation. This negation takes place at various levels. The external appearance of the heroines represents a constructivist collection of characteristics which have already become void.

The next stage of sublimation is when spiritual emptiness imitates emotion. This is the situation in Kira Muratova's film *A Change in Destiny*, which is based on a story by Somerset Maugham, 'The Letter'. The story tells of a white woman in a colonial country who murders her lover, who has been unfaithful to her with a native woman. It is full of feeling and exotic colours. But Muratova's version quite deliberately adopts a cold, preaching tone. The character of the heroine represents an extreme point on the road beyond morality – she can be described as morally frigid. She does not experience regrets, and lives in a way that is out of step with the world around her. She feels nothing, but knows that it is necessary to imitate passion, right up to the melodramatic murder, which she carries out in a mechanical fashion.

It is foolish to generalize about the heroines of 'author's cinema'. But one can note, all the same, that they are linked by certain common traits: reverie, a thoughtful liberation of tastes, a pensive callousness. These women are portrayed in various stylistic ways, but all reflect a personality-type which has been deformed by society. The film-makers do not declare the pegs on which to hang their films; they do not declare their names. But they portray a society before which people, in the final analysis, are defenceless.

The theme of the distortion of personality has also been explored in documentary films. The heroine of the documentary by N. Obukhovich, *The Fourth Dream of Anna Andreevna*, is an elderly village inhabitant. She considers herself something of an ascetic, but it is not Christian but socialist ideals which gathered in her soul in her childhood years. Christian saints and communist saints – Nikolai Ugodnik and Vladimir Il'ich Lenin – exist side-by-side in her consciousness. Real history does not exist for her. In its place, there is the illusory future of the Kingdom of the Good, embodied in Communism, as proclaimed by its theoreticians at the end of the last century and the beginning of this one. She directs her prayers to politicians of the ruling party, so tainting herself with the blood of innocent victims. The film's heroine is an ideal citizen, from the point of view of the propaganda which has had such a powerful impact on her. She is a monster, however, in the eyes of any intelligent and thinking being.

The film's title contains a reference to a famous chapter in the novel by the Russian revolutionary Nikolai Chernyshevskii, *What Is To Be Done?*, written in the 1860s. That chapter is entitled 'The Fourth Dream of Vera Pavlovna', and tells of Utopian imaginings, of the bright future of the commune of progressive women.

' . . . The women displayed great steadfastness in their faith', wrote Aleksandr Solzhenitsyn in his novel *The Gulag Archipelago*, when telling of the suffering of thousands of religious women who refused to give up the faith which had led them into the camps. Anna Andreevna is their antipode, as far as the object of her faith is concerned. But her psychological make-up reinforces Solzhenitsyn's words.

The heroine of the film *The Fourth Dream of Anna Andreevna* is not a new face on our screen, as such. She is a loyal, peaceful, happy worker, familiar from films of the past. The new angle with which the film focuses on her, however, reveals an image which was formerly concealed. It demonstrates the mixing together of traditional, humanistic values with the startling overlay of abstract ideas, which, as history has shown, can be used to justify any crime against real humanity.

In this way we have returned again to the theme introduced earlier in this chapter – the replacement of one thing by another. In this case, we are talking of sublimation in a more global sense. Real feelings, emotions and ideas are replaced by surrogates linked to the conditions of life. The theme of substitution is an important one these days, in both journalistic writings and in artistic reflections on the processes torturing our country. This is because the substitution of one concept for another forms the basis of any ideological strategy. In order to make sense of the results to which it has led, one has to analyse all of the details of the substitution. Woman in all ages has been seen as more direct and more emotional. The muse of history - Clio - is female. Woman carries within herself the contradictions, the strangeness, the unpredictability of history; its illusions, its dark deeds.

Woman is, of course, the face of society. This face, at present, is wearing a rather wry expression. Let us hope that her features will become smoother in the not-too-distant future.

PART III

Women Behind the Camera

THE EXPERIENCE OF WOMEN WORKING
IN THE SOVIET FILM INDUSTRY

In the previous chapters, we have seen how Soviet women film critics responded to the images of women presented on screen. Now, we turn to the creators of those images.

In the first chapter, Maria Vizitei offers us a glimpse inside the hallowed halls of VGIK, the All-Union Institute of Cinematography in Moscow, which was the world's first film school. Vizitei is a recent graduate of VGIK herself, having studied in the faculty of film criticism. In this essay, however, she is primarily concerned with the experience of women who have tried to establish careers in an area of the film industry which, unlike her own, remains predominantly male - that of directing. She looks at the difficulties women face in getting accepted for training in this faculty; once there, at the constant struggle to be accepted as equals by male classmates and instructors; and at the advantages and disadvantages which accrue from their gender when they eventually try to find work. Vizitei also addresses the changes which *perestroika* has brought to VGIK, and to the film industry as a whole, and the effect these have had on women.

The next chapter offers the personal stories of a number of women who have already established their names in a variety of fields within the film industry. Three of the women are directors: Lana Gogoberidze, Kamara Kamalova and Marina Tsurtsumiya. Two, Marina Goldovskaya and Tat'yana Loginova, are camerawomen, although Goldovskaya does also direct. The final interview is with the script-writer Maria Zvereva, who has since been elected to the post of Vice-President of the Union of Cinematographers. This is the first time in Soviet history that a woman has appeared in the top echelons of the Union leadership.

These women differ considerably in their ages, their nationalities,[1] and in the areas of the film industry in which they have made their careers. Nonetheless, they are connected by one common thread: they are all graduates of VGIK.

VGIK was founded in 1919. Around 1,500 students are currently studying there, under the tuition of more than 250 instructors.[2] As well as teaching, many of the instructors are actively engaged in their profession. This means that students are able to gain first-hand experience by helping on their instructors' films. Courses range from four to six years, and cover all aspects of the profession – acting, directing, camera-work, design, script-writing and film criticism.

The impact which the Soviet Union's disintegration will have on VGIK is as yet unknown, but this was the situation to the end of the Soviet era. Most people in the Soviet Union who wanted a career in the cinema had no alternative but to study at VGIK. All of the republics which made up the country had their own film studios, but few had training facilities. So VGIK operated a quota system, setting aside a number of places for students from each of the other republics. The decision as to who got these places was made in the national republics, under the auspices of the local film studios. Successful candidates would usually return to work in these studios after completing their studies. The quota system ensured that students for whom Russian was a second language were not forced into an unfair competition with native speakers, and that there were always enough qualified people to work in the local studios.[3] Non-Russian students were also able to apply directly to VGIK, and take part in the general examination system.

The quota system did not work to the advantage of aspiring women film-makers. This was especially the case in the southern republics, where traditional notions about male and female roles were at their strongest. Almaz Melikova, an Azerbaijani film critic, explains that Azerbaijanfilm, the state studio in her republic, decided who got the quotas, and that it was dominated by men who could not contemplate the idea of women in any cinema profession apart from acting.[4]

The national studios differed considerably in size and output. Until now the Armenian studio has generally produced one or two feature films per year; the Georgian studio around twenty. The Russian republic has inevitably been the most prolific. The studios of Moscow alone make several hundred films each year.

Perestroika sent the film industry into a state of flux. Before, completed films were submitted to a panel consisting of representatives from Goskino (the State cinema organization) and the directors of various studios. They were judged according to two criteria, artistic merit and box-office success, and given two separate ratings. If a film was considered to be of particularly high artistic merit, or if it did especially well at the box office, it earned a bonus for the director, screen-writer and camera-operators. The difference between commercial and artistic cinema was thus acknowledged, and an art film was not expected to have the same box-office success as a commercial film.

Perestroika changed this. The practice of *khozraschet*, or self-accounting, was introduced in the film industry as in other branches of the Soviet economy. Studios now had to balance their books and ensure that their films were commercially viable. Many people in the industry feared that this meant the death toll for artistic cinema in the Soviet Union.

What of women's role in the Soviet film industry in these changing times? There are no legal impediments to women making a career in any aspect of the cinema. All the same, they have had to battle against a volley of psychological and practical problems. Many of those who tell their stories in the following pages talk of the prejudice of male instructors at the selection stage, which makes it harder for women to be accepted into the film institute. Once there, they receive less encouragement and support than their male colleagues.

When they graduate and begin work, they have to juggle a particularly demanding job with the extra domestic responsibilities they have as women. The majority of women film-makers have chosen to have children, although they agree that this is not a profession in which they can easily be accommodated. As we have seen, the Soviet Union has long had a strong pro-natal climate, and women who choose not to have children have been considered both selfish and unnatural. Many talk of the strong sense of guilt they have experienced as they tried to divide themselves between two conflicting sets of demands, and ended up feeling that they succeeded at neither. The time which has to be spent away from home on location, the round-the-clock demands which the film makes at various points of its production cycle, turn women into, as script-writer Natal'ya Ryazantseva puts it, 'nomads with children'. It is necessary to give at least a decade of one's life to mastering the profession, she adds, and these coincide with a woman's prime child-bearing years. [5]

This is not made easier by the fact that until relatively recently, Soviet ideology promoted an idealized image of the Soviet woman as exemplary worker, wife and mother. Comparing their own lives with those of the superwomen beaming out at them from the pages of Soviet women's magazines (such as *Rabotnitsa* [*The Woman Worker*], and *Krestyanka* [*The Woman Peasant*]) only compounded their sense of failure.

As we noted in the introduction to this book, it is important to bear in mind the distinctive cultural and historical context in which Soviet women have lived their lives and formed their ideas. Official declarations of women's equality, contrasted with the over-burdened reality of their lives, led women to reject the very concept of equality. It was just a fraud, a euphemism for a double workload. Instead, they looked back over their shoulders at a romanticized vision of the past when women did not have to work on building sites but were pampered and protected by chivalrous menfolk. The rather wistful comments in some of the contributions to this book about female beauty, delicacy, fragility and innate tenderness can be seen as an understandable, if regrettable, backlash.

More surprising, perhaps, are the complimentary references to 'a man's hand' when describing work by women film-makers. In a society which has consistently devalued women, however, it is not so strange to find women undervaluing themselves. As a Soviet woman journalist once commented, 'Ideas about masculine superiority run very deep . . . even emancipated women sometimes betray a tendency to recognize masculine properties of intelligence and character as standard, as the point of reference for both sexes. Tell, for example, one of my successful colleagues that she writes like a woman, and she will be offended. It is another matter if one says, "You have a masculine cast of mind" - what great praise!'[6] This is, no doubt, what lies behind the controversy over the concept 'women's cinema', and the general reluctance of women film-makers to accept the term in relation to their own work. Lana Gogoberidze is the one exception, and it is probably no coincidence that she also enjoys the highest reputation amongst current women film-makers. She can afford to be more relaxed about her status.

Ryazantseva suggests that the film industry could be restructured so that it does not demand so much of people. There would be more female directors if the profession did not 'demand a horse's strength, nerves of steel and a high tolerance of continual stress'.[7] This would also improve the quality of films, she adds, since these attributes 'are rarely combined with artistic gifts'. However, this 'humanization of the industry', as Ryazantseva calls it, seems unlikely to appear now; the new profit-oriented climate which characterized the final years of the Soviet Union seems unlikely to diminish as the country reforms itself into a Commonwealth.

15 FROM FILM SCHOOL TO FILM STUDIO

Women and Cinematography in the Era of *Perestroika*

Maria Vizitei

The All-Union Institute of Cinematography in Moscow - known by its Russian initials, VGIK - is almost a legend in Soviet cinema. The competition for entrance to all of the film schools in the country is fierce, in particular the Karpenko Institute in Kiev, the Tbilisi school of Theatre and Cinema and the Leningrad Institute of Theatre and Cinema. Yet the explosion surrounding every admission to VGIK's faculty of directors can only be likened to a natural disaster.

Those who enter VGIK come from all over the country. They even come from those cities which have their own film schools. In fact, the majority of those who dream of studying at VGIK come from Leningrad and the republics of Georgia and the Ukraine - in other words, the very places which host the prestigious film schools mentioned above.

Why, then, are they so anxious to enter VGIK instead of their local schools? What is the attraction of this old, uncomfortable building which is forever under repair and forever leaking, built in the style of 'Stalinist classicism', with its small auditoriums and halls weighed down by heavy columns?

Many new students, when they first enter this Holy Land of Soviet cinema, expect to find some hitherto unglimpsed oasis from the tales of Scheherazade. This is, after all, the school which nurtured the best in Soviet cinema. The greatest directors of the country studied and taught at VGIK. Sergei Eisenstein and Mikhail Romm, Aleksandr Dovzhenko and Lev Kuleshov, climbed the stairs of the institute and gave lectures in its auditoriums. The director Sergei Gerasimov ran what was VGIK's best workshop for both actors and directors for many years. To this day, the lectures given by the great masters Eisenstein and Romm are remembered by the older teachers at VGIK. Many graduates of the institute, even those of later generations, have written books of reminiscences about themselves, their fellow-students and their teachers.

Such is the competition for places that to dream of entering the directing faculty at VGIK is almost as unrealistic as a Stephen Spielberg film. Tales abound about the sacraments carried out behind the closed doors of directors' workshops. Yet all the same, seventy years after its foundation, the institute is now in something of a decline. It is not so much a majestic cathedral now as an overcrowded cloister. The teaching staff is not what it was twenty years ago; some of the best have died, while others have left the institute in order to concentrate on film-making or research. Alas, not all of the masters of cinematography are in a position to combine active work in the industry with teaching. All the same, these old walls have been able to protect within themselves the most important thing, which does not diminish with time: a thirst for work and study and an almost obsessive desire to create. It is this which keeps VGIK alive, and which attracts ever new generations of dreamers.

To enter the directing faculty of VGIK (or, indeed, any other faculty) is, then, still not easy. For every six to ten places there are eighty to 100 applicants. Of these, one third are women. No special allowances are made for women. All the same, there are a couple of so-called 'women's faculties' in the institute – economics and film criticism – which have a particularly high number of women applicants. Even so, young men wishing to study in these faculties are still given preference. I do not mean that they can enter without passing the entrance exams; but if a male applicant has the same marks as a female applicant, he stands a better chance of being accepted.

The film-acting and theatre workshops are generally made up of equal numbers of men and women. There is an obvious reason for this: every male actor needs a female partner for dance sequences, exercises in stage movement and *ploshchadka* (the name given to the study of stage acting). In the script-writing faculty, there is also no great difference in the number of male and female entrants. Here, a candidate's ability is the decisive factor. Similarly, the faculty of cinema criticism has a large number of women. Still rare in Soviet cinematography, however, is the female camera-operator. If a woman succeeds in entering this faculty, she arouses the greatest interest. (Apart, of course, from the interest generated by the prettiest actresses.)

Yet it is still more difficult for a woman to enter the directing faculty. Adding together the figures for the documentary and feature-film workshops, around three to five women are accepted each year. There have been some notable exceptions, however. For many years there was a workshop based around science-fiction films, run by A. M. Zguridi. He paid particular attention to women, and there were usually as many of them on the course as men, if not more. It is difficult to explain this unusual disposition towards female directors on the part of a great master. Yet it should be noted that not one of his pupils has ever let him down. (Marina Tsurtsumiya, incidentally, who is interviewed in the next chapter, is a graduate of A. M. Zguridi's workshop.)

Another director and teacher, A. Naimov, who for many years was the leading workshop master for feature films at VGIK, never accepts women on his course. I am sure that this is not so much a conscious bias against women, but more to do with stereotyped ideas about male and female roles. To recognize real talent in the midst of those hundreds of applicants is not easy. All the same, a teacher is more inclined to take a chance with a male student who shows promise, even if he did not do particularly well in the exams. A female student will not be accepted 'on credit', however.

For a woman to be accepted onto a directing course, she needs to be not only talented but also resourceful, sharp-witted and strong-willed. She needs not only to be successful in the exams, but to prove that she is able to work as an equal amongst equals with the male students, or, indeed, that she is even better than them. And, of course, it is useful to be pretty. After all, students have to act in almost all of the directorial studies of their classmates. The director Marlen Khutsiev, one of the most loved, respected and trusted masters at VGIK (he is said to be one of the fairest and most impartial of teachers), accepts females into his workshop as a kind of 'reserve army' of partners for male students in the *ploshchadka*, or stage training. And all of them are pretty.

This is not, however, the final demand which is made on female applicants. I have already noted that people come to VGIK from all parts of our multi-national country - its walls are stormed by Latvians, Belorussians, Yakuts, and so on. And, of course, when the selection is made, there is the constant risk of offending the national cadres who have been sent by the various union republics according to the quota system. There are always fewer women occupying these reserved places; once again, if there is a man and woman from the same republic competing for the same place, the man is more likely to be chosen.

I myself did not succeed in entering the directing faculty. This was not because I was unable to do as well in the exams as the male applicants - not at all. The whole time it seemed to me that I was competing in two competitions: a general one, in which everyone took part; and a special female one, in which we female applicants competed against each other. We did this because we understood that however talented we might be, we would not be selected from the general pool of applicants.

Those women who do enter VGIK are not always the most talented, the most original or the most familiar with the cinema. The secret of success lies in strength of character, persistence, clearness of purpose and level of energy. Otherwise, trembling with a combination of fear and the desperate desire to study at VGIK, they will be defeated by the battle tactics of the successful entrants. And yet, experience shows that such a selection process works. For the Soviet woman, getting into VGIK is actually the easiest test in her fight to become a director. She will need to use the same qualities to the full when she is working in Soviet cinematography, if she is to prove that she is as capable or even better than the men in the industry.

Since film directing is still an unusual profession for a woman, and one which presents particular problems, I will be paying particular attention in this chapter to the experience of women in the directing faculty at VGIK. However, I would first like to say a few words about the faculty of film criticism, from which I myself graduated, along with many of the contributors to this book.

Film criticism, and the education of film critics, is experiencing a difficult time at present. For many years, real film criticism simply did not exist in VGIK, or even in Soviet cinematography as a whole. What the term came to mean in the Soviet context was simply a complimentary description of films. The study of cinema theory constituted nothing more than reflections on the basic processes which take place in the making of films. As is well known, our art and our artists - and this includes film-makers - were able to depict only what they were allowed to depict; they analysed only what it was possible to analyse. All this led to a great similarity of style, to film-makers becoming 'peas in a pod'. A general framework was created, which it was forbidden to break out from. Those who dared to do so were severely punished.

I think you can imagine what the teaching of film theory and film criticism was like in the institute, if it was conducted by those who forbade, misunderstood and rejected. It was at this time that the so-called 'official film research' was established, founded by cinema theorists such as N. Lebedev, R. Yurenev and S. Komarov. Its basic qualities were tendentiousness, narrowness of approach and conservatism.

With the passing of time, things did change in the study of the cinema. Yet the basic methods of study, the formulation and presentation of material, remained much the same. It is only since the advent of *perestroika* that film critics have not been compelled, when writing their theoretical pieces, to criticize the film-makers of the capitalist countries; they have not had to talk of a crisis in foreign cinema, and to seek the roots of this crisis in capitalist society. Just three years ago, no student at VGIK would even have been able to dream of writing the dissertation for his or her diploma on Tarkovskii, on 'The Depiction of Religious Faith on the Screen' or on 'Soviet Avant-garde Cinema of the 1920s and 1930s' - still a virtually unresearched theme in the Soviet Union. Today, however, such theses are finally being written; they are even being published. Yet since for so many years the Faculty of Film Criticism scarcely changed at all, it will require no little effort to bring about what is needed - a complete transformation.

This is not to say that all film research and criticism has been without value.

In the 1960s, a number of new names appeared in the world of film criticism, some of whom have contributed to this book: Maya Turovskaya, Neya Zorkaya, Elena Stishova and Alla Gerber, among others. They were part of the *Shestidesyatniki*, or 'those of the sixties' – the new intelligentsia which emerged in the Khrushchev period. Although no longer young, these women still represent the best of film criticism in the country today. With great courage and skill, they set about destroying the old stereotypes, and forcing the conservatives to worry about their reputation in the cinema world. Hence, it can be said that there was something of a revolution in film criticism, even before *perestroika*, although it did not reach the walls of the 'best cinema school in the world' (as the institute is described in its literature).

Of course, these film critics, like society as a whole, were unable to retain the full strength of their initial youthful optimism and hope for the future throughout the period of stagnation. Yet their voices continued to be heard. They provided the foundation for a new generation of film critics, who have taken on one of the major roles in the process of change and development of the cinema in this country. Together with their spiritual parents, they are helping to create a new cinematic structure, a new cinema language, and new journals and books about the cinema. Among them is M. Yampol'skii, whose work Marina Drozdova makes reference to in her chapter in this volume.

The changing times have not only demanded corresponding changes in film criticism, they have transformed the whole educational structure of VGIK. For one thing, there is now much greater communication between the faculties. In the past, there was co-operation only between the faculties of directing and camera-work; now, there is fairly frequent contact between all of the faculties. Until recently, the curriculum was constructed in such a way that first-year students could work only with other first-year students. All kinds of restrictions generally prevented the younger students from working with people in the more advanced classes. If they did come together on a film set, the first-year students felt redundant and often left without having done anything. The young directors, inevitably, had no interest in using a first-year camera student, who had never even held a camera before. Script-writers wrote 'into a vacuum', since the subjects given them by their teachers were completely devoid of interest for those making the films. And there is no point in even mentioning film critics: who would want to have a student critic around, whose understanding of film theory was stuck in the 1950s?

Yet VGIK has now taken up *perestroika*, or reconstruction, which has been taking place in the country as a whole, and has turned it into a reconstruction of itself. The stormy 'round table' discussions organized by the more active students may not have achieved much; but the old curriculum has, all the same, begun to quietly change, and students are being liberated from the old narrow framework of rules. Now, first-year student directors can invite camera-operators from any year of the course to film with them, and can get economists from the economics faculty to act as administrators on their films. Artists, be they from the first to the sixth year of study, can work on their stage design in real studios. Film critics and theoreticians can write on whatever themes interest them in the institute's newspaper. Still, they need the permission of the faculty, the workshop leader and the dean before they can do their inviting. Yet it is, at last, possible.

Let us now return to the situation for women directors. The entrance exams are behind them. The members of each workshop begin their gradual acquaintanceship with the profession. Only now do they begin to think about the path they have chosen for themselves in life, the difficulties they will have to face, how much they will have to learn and understand. Only now, when they have embarked on their first year, do the future women directors realize that all of their problems lie ahead, and that the examination trials were the easiest stage of all. They quite possibly find themselves the only women on their chosen course; yet displays of coquetry and female weakness will not help. They harness themselves to work - documentary filming, stage work, rehearsals with actors, stage movement, voice projection . . . In the first year the directors usually do the acting in the pieces staged by their classmates, and rehearsals have to take place at home or in the corridors of the institute and in the breaks between tests and exams. Students get no help with solving their basic practical problems, the hunt for a free auditorium and for props and costumes, the positioning of the lights or the choice of music. Women directors now find that no one notices they are women. Their male colleagues do not give up the auditoriums they acquired with difficulty, or the time allocated to them for individual work with a teacher; they do not respond to requests to move the time of their rehearsals. These women are no longer treated as women: they are directors. No allowances are appropriate. There are no special workers to help the students prepare a stage set, so they have to knock together all of the scenery necessary for the filming of their sequences themselves (though the scenery is, admittedly, quite minimal). They also paint it themselves, and often sew the stage curtains and the curtains for any windows used on the set. Here, at last, is an opportunity for a woman's touch!

The hardest task for the women directors, however, is to make their fellow students believe in their ability as directors, to prove to the class that they are capable of doing everything they need to do as first-year students. Some workshop masters have a stereotyped image of their relationship with a woman; they treat their female student directors as if they were nothing more than partners in a *ploshchadka*. This stereotype imperceptibly, but rapidly, enters the consciousness of the women's classmates. To force young male directors, who already consider themselves to be budding Fellinis, to respect women directors is no easy task. As always, then, the women need to assert themselves throughout their studies in two ways - both as directors, and as women. Many, however, by the middle of their first year, find it easier to throw back at the male students the popular VGIK phrase which, in reverse, was levelled at them when they were seeking help: 'I am not a woman! I am a director!'

While they are still involved in stage work, a new trial is simultaneously heaped on the fragile shoulders of the female students - the shooting of their first film. This is part of their course work, and is called 'a reportage' [*reportazh*]. It consists of a short film on any theme, shot in documentary form. For many students, the shooting of this film is their first experience of the process of film-making. Very often these documentaries reveal the potential ability of the students, their tastes, the extent of their passion for the genre, their views on life. However, the films are often unsuccessful, both because of the students' lack of experience and because they are not yet able to take a commanding role in their profession. They need to present themselves as knowledgeable individuals, sure of themselves and their thoughts, and able to lead a small film collective. Sometimes, it is necessary to shout out in a rough and powerful voice, to chastise members of the crew and to give orders, in a polite way but firmly enough so that they will be obeyed. Many students, especially if they are female, have difficulties asserting themselves in the role of leader. This is not facilitated by the fact that the technical workers in a film crew are usually men who are no longer young, who have spent many years at the studio and who have 'seen everything'. They are not readily going to respond to the orders of a young director - especially one who is also a woman. This may all sound harsh to a reader unacquainted with the system of training at VGIK. But believe me, I have not made up a word.

The relationship between creative and technical personnel in the studio at VGIK is a miniature version of that which exists in professional studios. Hence women directors will continue to meet with these problems throughout their professional lives. Part of the problem is that technical personnel are poorly paid and often consist of people who are indifferent to the cinema. Many also consider that to be part of a group of men led by a woman is degrading.

Yet there are female students who make such a serious and confident statement with their first film that they are ever after haunted by a reputation as a strict and ruthless director. This was the case with my mother, a director of documentary films. In her first year as a student, she developed such a reputation amongst technical crew members as an iron lady whom it was better not to antagonize that when she later began work in a professional studio she found that her reputation as an intractable character had preceded her through the grapevine, and many were afraid to work with her. Now, all of mother's contemporaries have, like herself, grown old and mellowed; their youthful severity and their refusal to compromise has disappeared somewhere along the road. Yet Henrietta Vizitei's reputation as a scandalously demanding director survives at the television studio in which she worked to this day.

The five years at VGIK fly past, between tests, exams and making films. If the women do not get married and have babies during this time (which, incidentally, rarely happens in the directing faculty), they proceed to the third trying period in their advance towards their cherished dream – they have to find a job. The quality of the diploma film is particularly important here. It is not enough for it to merely be good; it has to be very good. It has to demonstrate the professional ability of the director, it has to please both the artistic director and the chief editor of the chosen studio, and it must inspire their faith in the likelihood of the director producing successful films in the future. This is not easy. But if the exams have gone well and the diploma film is really good, the female director may find that all doors are now open to her. Her feminine charm and the expectation that, as a woman, she will be especially conscientious will win over many artistic directors of studios. Some studio directors, given the choice between a man and a woman of equal merit, will prefer to trust a woman to shoot a new film, because it is felt that she can be relied on more. Nevertheless, it is important to remember that many barriers have to be crossed before this trust is won.

There is, however, another side to the coin. Another possible scenario is that the studio director is disinclined to help a woman director since he remembers that women directors can also be wives and mothers. She might – God forbid! – have children, and her husband might turn out to be, let us say, 'capricious'. A woman, even if she is a director, cannot work normally if something is wrong at home. This, in turn, usually threatens to disrupt production schedules and completion deadlines for the film; it complicates shooting trips and expeditions. Some women, of course, manage to solve this problem with the help of grandmothers. All the same, we can confidently assert that as long as young women have tried to make careers in the cinema, ways have been found to deny them work. Hardened in the struggle for equality which they have had to wage at the film institute, young female directors throw themselves 'into the breach' almost like soldiers. If they do this, they usually achieve a certain degree of success. But the severe character which they need to develop in their professional lives is not appropriate at home and in the family. Russian cinema folklore has come up with the following sayings: 'A woman director is a soldier in a skirt'; and 'If a woman is a film director, her whole life is spent in defiance'. These expressions are quite old, but are still as apt today. They refer to the dedication of women directors to the cinema, the cruelly competitive struggle this demands, the constant fight to penetrate the walls of misunderstanding and the difficulties they experience in arranging to go on shoots.

Larisa Shipit'ko, Kira Muratova, Dinara Asanova . . . these are just some of the women directors who are working alongside men in the same studios. Shepit'ko's film *The Ascent,* made twenty years ago, still impresses viewers with its unique style. Asanova was the one director who gave her serious attention, in a wholly masculine way, to the problems of the adolescent. Muratova did not work for twenty years, but still managed to preserve her energies and her desire to work, and has absorbed herself totally in her work once more, now that she has the chance to do so. The efforts of these women show not only that they are no worse than male directors, but, indeed, that they are significantly more professional, brave and talented. The work of each of them deserves individual and lengthy consideration. This, however, unfortunately lies beyond the scope of this chapter.

The *perestroika* taking place in our country has not ignored cinematography. The appearance of new studios organized on the basis of *khozraschet,* or self-accounting, and the creation of new film companies, have broadened the horizons of film-makers. They now have better opportunities to engage in more interesting work, and to make films they could only dream of in the past. Critics can now boldly raise issues which were previously off-limits. Much has changed in the structure of the film industry, and in the relationship between the administrative and creative work collectives. And yet, the problems have not decreased – they have merely changed.

The financially independent studios and companies have met with a problem hitherto not encountered in the film world: the need to earn money from one film in order to make the next. Up till now, the government took care of assigning money to the studios. Now that they have gone over to the system of self-financing, the studios have to think carefully about whether it is worth investing in a particular film, whether they can trust the work of a certain director, and so on. On the one hand, this means that the film companies are interested in finding new blood in young and talented directors; on the other, the director has to be capable not only of making a film which shows genuine talent, but also one which will be commercially successful, which will earn money for the studio and advance its reputation. The selection of directors has, accordingly, become even more severe.

One positive feature of the new self-financing system is that old directors, even those with titles and prizes to their names, no longer have the right to go on making film after film regardless of their quality. Now, titles and age do not automatically give one the right to make films. The administration and leadership of the studios have turned their attention more to cinema language, style and genre. The head of a studio is now likely to go to youth film festivals himself, and to attend the exams at VGIK in search of young talent. He may also have to fight with other companies for the chance to employ a new director who has caught his fancy.

The new economic situation in the cinema has also brought financial benefits to employees. Cinema workers in the Soviet Union have always been poorly paid; when and by whom these miserly salaries were introduced is difficult to determine. Now, however, film studios are able to increase the salaries of their workers, be they technical personnel, directors or any other members of the collective working on a film.

Self-accounting has not only made increases in salaries possible, but it has also allowed the studios to take charge of their own film distribution. This means that they are able to sell the films directly to a customer, and, with the resulting profits, buy good film stock and equipment in order to make better quality films.

The self-accounting system has, then, opened up more extensive economic opportunities. Yet at the same time it has exacerbated creative problems. A general commercialization of the Soviet cinema has begun. Many film studios, in their newfound financial independence, have turned their attention exclusively to the production of entertainment films, or those concerned with current issues, and have completely abandoned the higher art of the cinema. The provision of information and entertainment have thus begun to swallow up all other trends in the cinema. In other countries, the conflict between commerce and art is not so serious. Of course, it is more difficult to get funding for a non-commercial film, but no one denies that an intellectual cinema which attracts only minority interest is, all the same, necessary. This is not the case here.

And so VGIK has entered a new era. New masters have arrived. They aim to destroy the old teaching system and create a different type of professional training, to educate a new generation of directors unlike any that has gone before it. Let us look at the composition of the two new workshops for successful applicants. One consists of fifteen students – four of whom are female. In another, there are eighteen students – and two are female. Yet another attempt on the part of women to storm those old walls has been thwarted. How many more times will this happen?

16 'SOME INTERVIEWS ON PERSONAL QUESTIONS ...'

Soviet Women Talk About Their Experiences in the Film Industry

Lynne Attwood

We will turn now to the personal experiences of women working in different areas of the film industry. The chapter which follows is based on a series of interviews most of which took place in the summer of 1989, either at 'Femme Totale' - a festival of films by Soviet women held in Dortmund in May - or the XVI Moscow Film Festival in July.

Three of the women are directors, from a variety of backgrounds, and at various stages in their careers. The first is Georgian director Lana Gogberidze, who has been described more than once by the contributors to this book as the most significant female Soviet director of the present time. Then comes the Uzbek director Kamara Kamalova. The third is Marina Tsurtsumiya, a Muscovite of Georgian descent, who is a recent graduate of VGIK.

We then move to the most male-defined profession of the film industry, that of camera-operator. Marina Goldovskaya and Tat'yana Loginova, two of the very few women who have managed to scale the walls of this male bastion, give rather different views of what life is like for women inside this macho world.

Finally, we turn to script-writing. This, in contrast to directing and camera-work, is seen as a particularly appropriate choice of career for a woman. In fact, it becomes clear from Maria Zvereva's lively account that the role of script-writer replicates some of the traditional features of female family roles. Female script-writers become the side-kicks of male directors, who often take for granted their contribution to the success of the film. Ironically, since this interview was conducted, Zvereva has taken on a role which is hitherto unknown for a woman - she has been elected Vice-President of the Union of Cinematographers.

These interviews were conducted either in English or in Russian, depending on the preference of the woman being interviewed. I have indicated in each case which language was used. When the conversation took place in English, direct quotations have been slightly altered so that stylistic differences and grammatical errors do not disrupt the flow or impair the meaning of the opinions expressed.

WOMEN DIRECTORS IN THE SOVIET UNION

Lana Gogoberidze

Lana Gogoberidze is one of the most highly praised contemporary Soviet film-makers, and her films have been shown at festivals throughout the world. She is one of the few women directors who is not afraid to be associated with the concept of 'women's cinema', and Maya Turovskaya has described her film *Some Interviews on Personal Questions* as possibly the first real woman's film in the Soviet Union. She was also the first president of KIWI (Kino Women International), the organization set up in 1987 to further the position of women in the film industry throughout the world. Siân Thomas talked to Lana Gogoberidze about her life and work in Moscow in 1987, and I managed to grab her for a breakfast meeting during the hectic XVI Moscow Film Festival in July 1989. The following is taken from these two interviews, both of which were conducted in English.

Lana Gogoberidze was born in Tbilisi, in Georgia, on 13 October 1928. This was just seven years after Georgia was incorporated into the Soviet Union, after four years of fraught independence following the abdication of the Tsar and the collapse of the Russian empire. Gogoberidze decided she wanted to work in the cinema while she was still at school: 'I felt that there was something in my inner life that I wanted to express, and I had a distinctive feeling that I could do this best in films.' This did not prove to be easy, however. When she finished school, in 1946, there was still no film institute in Tbilisi (nor was there to be for another three decades) and aspiring Georgian film-makers had to study at VGIK in Moscow. Yet, for Gogoberidze, this door was closed. Both of her parents had fallen foul of Stalin; her father was killed by the secret police, and her mother spent twelve years in a labour camp. This placed the entire family under suspicion, and their movements were officially restricted. Gogoberidze was not permitted to study in Moscow.

Instead, she enrolled in the philology faculty at the University of Tbilisi. She first studied Georgian literature, and then moved into English and American literature. Assuming the cinema to be a lost cause, she decided on an academic career. She wrote a book about Walt Whitman, and translated poetry from French and English into Georgian.

In 1953 Stalin died, and the travel restrictions were lifted. Gogoberidze finally went to Moscow, and in 1955 she was accepted at VGIK. She graduated in 1959 and has since made nine feature films and three documentaries. She is also the artistic director of one of the studios of GruziaFilm, the Georgian state-owned film company, and teaches at the Tbilisi film institute. She trained five of the current Georgian women directors. Since these interviews were conducted she has become increasingly involved in Georgian politics and is one of the country's most prominent liberals, concerned with helping the country move towards democratic independence.

Gogoberidze works with writer Saira Asenishvili on the scripts for her films, many of which are based on stories from her own life. She is currently working on a film based on a story her mother wrote during her years of internment. Gogoberidze's ethnic as well as her personal background figures strongly in her films and she has always been adamant that her films are Georgian rather than Soviet: 'We are very attached to our ethnic roots,' she explains. 'I don't think this makes us nationalists, however. Simply, we have these national feelings.'

Gogoberidze's mother was also a film-maker before her arrest. She made three films, none of which have survived. 'The films were destroyed,' Gogoberidze explained, 'but recently I discovered that some of the negatives still exist, and I am trying to get prints made . . .' She hopes that she will find a clue to the cause of her mother's arrest in these films: 'She preferred not to speak of these things, and she never returned to films; when she was released from the camp she worked on compiling dictionaries.'

Gogoberidze was only 5 years old when her mother was taken away. She was initially placed in an orphanage, but was rescued by two maiden aunts who brought her up themselves. When she was 17, her mother came home: 'She was somebody I didn't know at all. I had to get used to saying this word *Mother*. At first I was not able to. It was two months or more, I think, before I could say the simple word *Mother*.'

Not surprisingly, the theme of the mother is always very strong in Gogoberidze's films. This is certainly the case in *Some Interviews on Personal Questions*, which has strongly autobiographical tones. The mother of the heroine, Sofiko, had also been sent to a labour camp; one of the most poignant scenes in the film depicts her reunion with her teenage daughter.

In an article in *Sovetskii Ekran* (*Soviet Screen*), Gogoberidze recalled with amusement a male colleague's comment that her film *Commotion* (1977) was her 'first truly manly film'. He evidently assumed that he was paying her a great compliment – as she puts it, that 'to be "manly" is the ultimate goal of a woman's art . . . I smiled to myself at that boundless male presumption (can you imagine the opposite case, of a woman saying to a man: "This is your first truly womanly film"?!).'[1] In fact, many people in the film industry describe Gogoberidze's films as the only unambiguous examples of 'women's cinema'. I asked her what she thought about this. 'I always make films from a woman's point of view,' she replied. 'I never wanted to make films like a man, and I don't understand film directors who prefer it not to be evident from their films whether they are male or female. I always like to be aware of the difference.'

She tries, in particular, to portray strong women characters. 'Women always played such an important role in my life,' she explained; 'not just my mother but the aunts who brought me up, who sacrificed themselves to raise me, this child without a mother or father.' In *Some Interviews*, Gogoberidze wanted in particular to show how the fate of one woman connected with the fate of others: 'That was why I decided to give such a profession to the main character, Sofiko. She's a journalist, and she's putting questions to other women. These interviews are the most important part of the film.' Personal scenes from Sofiko's life are intercut with the interviews, which creates an impression both of women's common oppression at the hands of men, and of the strength and resilience with which they deal with this.

One of the most prominent elements of the film is the conflict between the heroine's professional life and the needs and demands of her family. Gogoberidze sees this as the central feature of women's lives in what was the Soviet Union. She explained: 'In our country every woman works, and there are generally no problems with this. But a problem begins when the woman is really devoted to her work – when she almost sacrifices herself to it. Men don't like it at all if their women give their careers as much importance as their families. This is the case for Sofiko. And her husband is a typical Georgian husband, he can't endure this.'

In the past, the Soviet Union stressed the centrality of work in the lives of all of its citizens, female as well as male. It was, after all, defined as a workers' state. However, since there was no redefinition of the male role to enable it to incorporate a bigger slice of family responsibility, women were still left with virtually all the housework. Educational theorists are now arguing that making women work so much outside the home was a big mistake, and the current generation of schoolgirls should be taught to put work in second place after their families. For women of Sofiko's age, however, brought up to see work as a crucial part of their identities, there is an almost inevitable clash between work and family roles. Gogoberidze's portrayal of this dilemma in her film found a wide resonance amongst women. 'When I was making the film,' she said, 'I didn't realize how typical this case was. I understood it, however, once the film had been distributed and I started getting letters. Hundreds and hundreds of letters, from all parts of the Soviet Union, almost all from women. And the letters all began with this phrase: "This film is about me." The women asked me how I could have known what their lives were like . . .'

About men's limited contribution to domestic life, Gogoberidze suggested that, 'this is a problem everywhere in the world. But things are even more difficult for women in Georgia. Our everyday life is more of a problem than it is for the West European woman. It's harder to get things, and everything takes more time. And our men are not accustomed at all to sharing these difficulties. So too much of the burden falls on the shoulders of women.'

Gogoberidze waivers about how optimistic she is concerning men's potential for change. One the one hand she discerns an improvement in the current generation of men. Her daughter's husband really does share the work, she said, and so too do the husbands of her younger friends: 'There is a hope that men's mentality is changing, little by little . . .' Later in our conversation, however, she wondered if this was only a matter of degree. 'Even for our daughter's generation, men's and women's share of the housekeeping will not be the same,' she concludes with resignation.

Gogoberidze holds contradictory views on the subject of Georgian men's attitudes to women, as she herself acknowledges. On the one hand, she argues that male reluctance to take a share in domestic labour is particularly pronounced in Georgia. On the other, she claims that, 'a very great respect towards women exists in Georgia – not just towards woman in the traditional sense, as mother, but in a more general sense, towards the woman as a social being'. This explains why there is a relatively large number of women film directors in Georgia, she continued; the men in the profession have not closed ranks against them. She justifies this contradiction as something which is itself embedded in Georgian culture. Georgia represents, both geographically and psychologically, the middle ground between Europe and the East, its traditions and attitudes come from both directions. Hence, 'In Georgia we are really very traditional people, and one tradition is that the man is the head of the family. But on the other hand, we have a great respect for women which has come down through the centuries. In the twelfth century, Georgia was an independent country, ruled by a woman, Queen Tamara. And it was the time of the Renaissance of Georgian culture . . . so Tamara is remembered as the queen of independent Georgia.'

Gogoberidze agrees with Maria Vizitei that women have a harder time than men getting accepted at VGIK: 'I'm sure that male directors are more eager to have male than female students,' she said. However, she does not accept that they have to go on waging a continual battle for acceptance. Women and men are treated much the same once they are inside the industry, she insists. The biggest problem women directors face is not opposition from men, but their own lack of self-respect. This will improve when they have more experience at organizing together and supporting each other.

Gogoberidze's own combination of professional and personal life has not turned out too badly: 'My children were unhappy in their childhood that they saw me so little. But now they are 21 and 23, and we are really good friends.

They have told me they think it was good for them, that I had my own life; they had to become more independent, they made their own choices rather than waiting for me to make them for them.'

What does the future hold for women of the former Soviet Union? I asked Gogoberidze for her comments on the emergence of unemployment for women. 'At the moment, almost all women are working,' she replied. 'Many of them are doing heavy physical work, though, and I would not be unhappy if this were to be taken from them. But if they were to lose intellectual work as well, this would be terrible. It could happen, because we have very strong propaganda about women - that they should be at home, have children, be good wives. Even women are saying such things, since life in the Soviet Union is so hard for them because of the "double burden".'

A few days earlier I had met Arkadii Inin, the script-writer of the film *One Day Twenty Years Later,* which attempted to 'rehabilitate' the full-time housewife. I asked Gogoberidze what she had thought of this film and its message. 'I was very angry when I saw this film,' she said. 'It makes the point that the best thing women can do is stay home and have children. But the strange thing is - there were a lot of women who liked it.' Inin had assured me that he had never intended the film to be a piece of pro-family propaganda, but Gogoberidze laughed when I told her this: 'He wrote it, and it is his point of view. In his opinion, women are not really happy to go out to work; only this woman who has ten children enjoys real happiness. This is propaganda, an attempt to turn the clock back to a masculine kind of society where men decide everything and woman is just an object.'

Yet, in common with many other Soviet women, Gogoberidze believes that there are fundamental differences in male and female personalities which derive from their different roles in the reproductive process. She explained: 'I can't remember anything else in my life that can compare with the feeling I had when I gave birth to my first daughter. It wasn't simply happiness . . . It was the feeling that I had fulfilled my destiny. And, really, I think that this is the destiny of women - to give birth to children. Not for every woman, perhaps, but for most of them . . . The possibility of showing tenderness, of understanding another's point of view and of tolerance, are generally more characteristic of women than of men. I think this is inherent, biological . . . The fact that a woman can give birth to another human being makes her more interested in the continuation of the human race. This is why for the woman it isn't simply a matter of words to say she is against war. Everybody is against war, of course. But for woman it is an instinct - a biological instinct. She wants to take care of her children. Even if she doesn't yet actually have her own children.'

I asked Gogoberidze what changes she saw in the film industry, particularly in Georgia, as a result of *perestroika*. 'Until recently we were wholly dependent on Moscow,' she explained, 'now we have become wholly independent. This means that we can choose our own screenplays, decide which ones to shoot, then we have to decide who will direct the film - everything depends on us and it's good to be so free and independent. But we have some fears too. It's a great responsibility - we have to distribute our own films, for example, and although Georgian films are well known now, still they aren't well distributed in our country. Really, we don't know yet how things will turn out . . .'

Kamara Kamalova

Kamara Kamalova is from Uzbekistan. She is the only woman in her republic directing fiction films, though there is one other woman making documentary films and two making cartoons. Kamalova's first fiction film, *Bitter Berry*, was first shown at the X Moscow Film Festival in 1983, where it is was awarded the jury's special prize. Her latest film, *The Savage*, was released in 1989, and looks at the personal experience of Stalinism in Uzbekistan. I talked with Kamalova over a bowl of fresh fruit (a rare treat in the Soviet Union!) in her room at the Hotel Rossiya during the Moscow Film Festival in 1989. The conversation has been translated from Russian.

Kamalova did not come from a cinematic family. Her father was a philosophy lecturer at the university; her mother was a school-teacher. All the same, she was smitten with films from early childhood: 'I was born in Bukhara, which is a small town,' she explained, 'but when I was 6, in 1945, we moved to Tashkent, and I saw my first film there. Like all children I lived through the story on the screen as if it were reality, and I grew up with a "sickness" for films. In Tashkent we lived next door to the Pioneer Palace, and there was a cinema there. I saw every film they showed.'

Despite this distraction, she graduated from school with good results and went to Moscow to study in the physics faculty of MGU (Moscow State University). At this point it had not even occurred to her to go for a career in films. Then, one evening, there was a party at MGU and some VGIK students had been invited. She talked with them, asked them a multitude of questions and left the party with an invitation to visit them at VGIK. That decided her fate. She applied to take the entrance exams, and while she was waiting, spent every available moment in the VGIK library. Her dedication paid off, and she was admitted on her first attempt. She gave up her course at university and settled into her new life, studying with the director Grigorii Roshal'. After graduation she returned to Tashkent, but there were no openings for fiction film directors at that time. For the next ten years she made cartoons, and then got a job working in television. Finally she managed to move into fiction films.

Looking back on her life, Kamalova mused that it was perhaps easier for women in those days. In the early years of Soviet power, there was a strong emphasis on people studying and improving themselves. Accordingly, there were more opportunities for working-class children to go into higher education. The children of factory-workers did not dream of becoming factory-workers themselves, she asserted; nor did the children of collective farm-workers intend to spend their own lives on the farm.

Of course, things were not so easy for everyone. In parts of rural Uzbekistan life was simply a matter of survival. Women gave birth to six or more children, one after the other, and still carried on working in the cotton fields from dawn till dusk. There was obviously little opportunity for them to improve their lives. Although a few collective farms are now headed by women, life has not changed much for most women in rural Uzbekistan. The only difference is that, with improved communications, they now know that not everyone lives like this. Television in particular has given young girls an awareness of the possibilities which exist beyond their villages. The contrast between these and the inescapable confines of their own lives sometimes proves too much: an alarming number of Uzbek women have burned themselves to death in the last few years.

There have always been cases of self-immolation in Central Asia, Kamalova continued. Sometimes this happened for no other reason than unrequited love. Now, it is more often a response to the harshness of life, the repeated pregnancies and the contrast between heightened aspirations and reality.

I asked Kamalova if she felt she had encountered any particular problems in becoming a director on account of her gender. Her answer was an adamant 'yes'. She explained: 'Being a director is not just creative. It also involves working with and organizing large numbers of people – up to sixty or so. Most of these are men. They have an Uzbek mentality, which does not readily accept having a woman in a position of authority. Every man in Uzbekistan thinks he is higher, better than a woman. So it is difficult for a woman to do this job here. She must be very strong.'

Did she feel there was any difference in films produced by male and female directors, I asked? 'It depends very much on the director. Some women directors could be said to have a "masculine hand" – in no way could their films be described as women's films. Larisa Shepit'ko is such an example. But all the same, women are by their very nature more sensitive, soft and emotional. It is they, after all, who become mothers. It is not in their nature to be aggressive or cruel. This has an effect on the films they make. So, yes, one can talk of a difference.' She herself has nothing against the notion of a distinctive 'women's cinema', but she understands why some women directors reject the concept. It is like 'children's cinema', she says; it is thought to denote something inferior. Women have to prove that they can make films at least as good as those made by men, and forming all-women organizations like KIWI may help them do this. Kamalova is optimistic about the eventual appearance in the Soviet Union of festivals dealing exclusively with women's films, and of the development of a independent women's movement. She herself has made a 'woman's film', *That's Not the Way it Was*. This was a comedy about a woman scholar, a strong and resourceful heroine. It was not very successful, however, since the portrayal of this kind of woman does not go down well with Uzbek men.

I asked Kamalova how strongly her ethnic heritage featured in her films. Unlike Lana Gogoberidze, she did not feel it to be that important. Only one of her six feature films has a overtly national theme, dealing with the problem of Uzbek versus Soviet power. The others have all been about contemporary life in urban Uzbekistan, and this subject does not lend itself to nationalist concerns: 'Tashkent is a very European city,' she explained. 'One hears more Russian spoken than the Uzbek language, and the problems of life are much the same as in the Soviet Union as a whole. The actor may have an Uzbek face, and wear Uzbek outfits, but the problems are still Soviet problems.' Of course, the films do implicitly indicate how life in Uzbekistan differs from life in the other republics, but this is not their main point.

Kamalova has reservations about how positive *perestroika*'s impact on the cinema will be. On the one hand there are new themes and issues which film-makers can address, such as sex and drugs, and if they are treated with sensitivity she feels there is nothing wrong with this. Such films can be both informative and artistic. However, many film-makers are just jumping on what they hope is a lucrative bandwagon.

Perestroika has also not improved the administration of the film business in Uzbekistan. People who get used to enjoying the fruits of office do not easily let go, and those who lost their jobs when the bureaucracy was trimmed were able to use their contacts to find a niche elsewhere. The film world now has its share of these relocated bureaucrats, who know nothing about the cinema but insist on attempting to control it. This leads to conflicts, and to films not being promoted because the directors have fallen out of favour with the new leaders. *Perestroika* will not bring about the necessary changes in Soviet society very quickly, she concluded.

Marina Tsurtsumiya

Marina Tsurtsumiya is a young director who has recently graduated from VGIK. I talked with her at the Gorkii Studios in Moscow, where she was then working. (She has since branched out as an independent film-maker.) The interview took place in Russian.

Tsurtsumiya's passion for the cinema began very early. Indeed, she was

introduced to VGIK at the age of 6: 'My mother was studying to be a film critic,'
she explains, 'and there was no one to leave me with at home!' Her father
was trained as a camera-operator, but moved into directing. 'He took me on
shoots with him sometimes when I was still very young, 7 or 8. That's when
I decided that my future would be in the cinema.' In her final year at school,
she applied to the directing faculty at VGIK but was not accepted the first time
round. So she went to the Gorkii studios and got a job as an editor: 'Everyone
knew my father, so this wasn't particularly hard. I worked there for a year and
gained some very useful practical experience, actually splicing the film. Then
I tried again for VGIK. This time the exams didn't terrify me, as they had the
first time round, and I passed.'

She studied with the science-fiction director A.M. Zguridi, in a small
workshop of eight people. (There are rarely more than fifteen in any group.)
'I didn't find that my gender complicated things,' she said, 'but my age did.
I was the youngest, 19 years old, and they treated me like a child.'

She became more aware of gender as an issue when she started work: 'But
in some ways I actually found it easier being a woman. I had to work with
many people, a large number of whom are men. They tended to argue amongst
themselves, but they were always polite to me, they treated me like a woman.'

I asked Tsurtsumiya what she thought of the concept 'women's cinema'. She
said that she was not really aware of any great distinction between films made
by men and films made by women. There were many examples of excellent
'women's cinema', in the sense of films which addressed issues of concern to
women, made by male directors. In the Soviet Union, Yulii Raizman was one
good example; Woody Allen might be seen as his Western counterpart. (We
had just been together to a screening of Allen's film *Another Woman* at VGIK.)
In general, however, she did not find the concept particularly illuminating: 'I
think there are just good and bad films – and I hope mine will be in the first
category!'

Tsurtsumiya was adamant that her own films should not be described as
'women's cinema': 'I think I tend to have a "masculine" way of thinking.
Perhaps this is because my parents wanted a boy! So the heroes of my films
are generally men.' This 'masculine' approach was quite common amongst
women directors, she added, since directing is not generally seen as a woman's
profession, and so was likely to attract women who felt they had a 'male type'
lodged inside them. She offered Kira Muratova as an example: even when
Muratova placed a woman character in the centre of a film, it was not usually
in the capacity of the main hero, the one she fully identified with. When it
was, the character seemed 'internally' more like a man, although 'externally'
female. Lana Gogoberidze, on the other hand, placed real female characters
in the centre of the action, and fully identified with them. If anyone made

'women's cinema' it was Gogoberidze, she felt. I asked Tsurtsumiya what she meant by real female characters: 'A woman is more intuitive, more sensitive, has a greater "sensibility"', she replied. 'For me, this is axiomatic.'

What of the changes taking place in the cinema under *perestroika*? 'The cinema has always been a difficult profession, and this has not changed,' she began. 'People who work in the artistic professions always clash with politics – it doesn't matter what type of political situation they find themselves in. The old clichés may have changed, but we have some new ones in their place. In the past, for instance, it was forbidden to talk about Stalin, or about any really provocative themes – Soviet power, drug addiction, and so on. Now, we *have* to address these issues! This means that the freedom of film-makers to choose their own themes is still limited.'

What themes would she choose, if she had a completely free hand? 'I would like to make films which unite people,' she said. 'We live in a time in which the old barriers are falling. I see people now as citizens of the world. I am a big mixture myself – my mother's mother was from Belorussia, her father was Polish, my father is Georgian, and my life has been closely connected with Germany – I speak good German and have a strong affinity with that country. So I'm not really able to say what nationality I am. I would like to make a film about a person who is born in one place and travels his whole life through different places – and comes to realize that people are, after all, very similar.'

What are the impediments against her making such a film? 'To make the kind of film I want, to choose my own theme, is complicated. I would have to be my own producer. Such a situation is common in the West, but is new to us. In the past, the State paid for everything. In return, they expected films with correct ideological themes. Now we have new possibilities, but also a new complication – the notion that profit can be made from art. We are in big danger of commercialization. Of course, it's possible to make a profit from something like comedy but not from art in general. Some films will not be a commercial success and they should not be judged solely in terms of profit. The government should still provide a subsidy for such films. But the old restrictions of ideology have now been replaced by new restrictions, stemming from the need to make a profit . . .'

CAMERA-WORK

Soviet society – despite its early proclamations of equality for women – has retained very traditional ideas about male and female personalities, and the roles which should reflect them. Directing, as we have seen, is still considered an unsuitable profession for a woman. This is still more the case with camera-work. In such an ideological climate, what draws a woman to such a profession? What is life like for her once she is in it? Does she face continual resistance on the part of male colleagues? As we will see, there are no simple answers to these questions. Marina Goldovskaya and Tat'yana Loginova are two of the very few women who have made their careers in camera operation. Siân Thomas discussed the profession with Marina Goldovskaya in Moscow, and we both talked with Tat'yana Loginova in Dortmund. The interview with Goldovskaya was in English and with Loginova in Russian.

Marina Goldovskaya

Marina Goldovskaya trained as a camera-operator at VGIK, but now works as both camerawoman and director. Like many of the women we talked with, she comes from a cinematographic background; her father was a camera-operator and a teacher at VGIK. Goldovskaya is particularly well known by Soviet viewers for a series of television films which focused on the lives of different individuals. Her most notable achievement, however, is *Solovki Power*, a documentary which she both filmed and directed, and which is discussed at length in Part I of this book.

Goldovskaya does not feel she encountered any male resistance to her choice of career. On the contrary, she sees certain advantages to being female. Men take pity on a woman struggling with the heavy weight of the camera, she said, and this sympathy opens doors, both literally and metaphorically. She explained by means of a personal anecdote: 'A very long time ago, in 1970, I started making a film about a prominent Soviet surgeon, Aleksandr Vishnevskii. He did the first heart transplant operation in the Soviet Union. People do not feel comfortable when they are being filmed - an American cameraman once said that they feel they are sitting in a torture chamber - so I try to shoot them discreetly, so that they hardly notice. This is what I told Vishnevskii I would do. On the first day we were meant to film him in conversation with a prominent French surgeon, who had also done several transplants, and four of his former patients were still living. I think one of them was a priest, and was giving sermons with his new heart. Vishnevskii warned me: "You've promised that you will not be seen or heard, you and your film crew." But when we came into the conference hall, I got carried away - there were so many people, and I wanted to get them all on film, listening so attentively. So I forgot my promises. I put on my lights, I stood on a box so I could see everyone, and the camera was on a tripod, standing very high. And then Professor Vishnevskii opened the door. It was five minutes before the conference was due to begin. He saw me and yelled, "What is this? Go away! You promised me that you would not be seen or heard!" So I took the camera from the tripod. It was a French camera, an Eclair, very heavy and very inconvenient. And I wasn't well that day, I had a temperature. But something snapped in me. I thought, "Well, if you don't want me to shoot properly, I'll show you!" For three and a half hours I held the camera, I didn't put it down for a moment. When everything was over I was exhausted. But I was determined to make him see how tired he had made me. So even though I had no film left, I carried on holding the camera, walking round with it. He called me his *Kisinka* - it's a very nice Russian word, it means "pussy cat" - "Please have a sandwich, please drink something . . .", I said, "I can't, I'm working." People took pity on me - they said to him, "Look what you've done to this little girl!" (I was very young then.) After this, through the two months we worked together on the film, you can't imagine how he tried to help me. I could shoot anywhere I wanted. Nobody else could go into the operating theatre to make shots, but I could.'

Now, after twenty years of work in the industry, Goldovskaya is well used to the camera, and holding it for long periods causes her no real problem. Yet she still encourages the idea that woman cannot carry such a weight: 'Men want to help. When I first noticed this, I realized that I could exploit this quality in men - I could turn it to my advantage.'

Are there not also disadvantages? Goldovskaya was able to think of a few instances of non-cooperation on the part of male colleagues: 'Maybe when I was quite young and just beginning in my profession, the men were rather ironical about my being a camerawoman. And I did at one point think of giving up when I kept on hearing, "You can't be a camerawoman, it's not a job for a woman!" Even after I'd made two or three films, I still came across men who didn't want to work with me. They said, "This is not your business; your business is to have children . . .".'

When her camerawork began to win acclaim, however, the same people who had once rejected her were now asking to work with her. Yet not all of her collaborations with male directors were successful. This led her to the decision to direct her own films: 'Now I have no disadvantages at all - I just work, and that's that. I'm very happy.'

She also concedes that male resistance does have an effect on the number of women choosing this career. 'Many people have the opinion that women should not enter this profession. In our institute I know that teachers do not like women. Every year they take one or two female students, but they say this is because it makes the boys more polite! It's not considered to be a suitable job for a woman. I don't think that's right. All the same, it is true that a woman needs some special qualities of character in order to do this job. She must have good health. She must not be afraid of weights. She must like to work. And I think she must also have some of the qualities of a psychologist, because it's a profession that needs co-operation and communication with other people.'

Goldovskaya has never worked with other women: 'You'll laugh, but my crew consists only of men. I don't know why . . . The crew is very small. I am director and camerawoman; I have a sound engineer, always the same one, he is a friend and we have worked together for ten years. Then there's my assistant. That's all – just three of us.'

Goldovskaya's work has taken her abroad on many occasions. How would she say life differs for women in the Soviet Union and in the West? 'Here, in our country, women are perhaps too emancipated. We hardly have any restrictions at all. If she wants, a woman can become not just a camerawoman, but anything – even a cosmonaut. But this is not always good. Whatever job she does, she still has to come home and do the housework, make the dinner . . . And if her child is often ill, she can't stay home with him all the time . . .' Some husbands are known to take on some of the housework, she continues, but this depends on their characters. Many men just cannot break out of the psychological barrier which tells them that housework is humiliating for them, Goldovskaya concludes.

The conflict between dedication to work and dedication to children seems unsolvable to Goldovskaya: 'Something always loses out; something suffers. Children miss the attention of their parents, particularly their mothers. I think that women should not work as much as eight hours a day, but as little as they can afford to. They will, of course, have less money, but they will be able to regulate their lives better.'

Does she think women would generally prefer to stay at home? 'No,' she said, 'practically all of our women want to work. Firstly, it's dull to stay at home. And secondly, our education, our manner of thinking, our way of life for the past seventy years has made us not even consider the possibility of staying at home. When my child was born, I was entitled to stay at home for a year. But when he was five months old I took on a nurse and I went back to work, because I couldn't bear it any longer. I was accustomed to working, to being with people . . .' She has only the one child (he is now in his early twenties, and works as a script-writer), and now regrets not having had another. She blames her work for this, she liked it too much and could never find the time to take a break: 'But at least I had the one child,' she said sadly. 'I pity people who don't have any.'

Tat'yana Loginova

Tat'yana Loginova is one of just three camerawomen working in fiction films in the Soviet Union. She has made fifteen films altogether, several of which have won prizes at international festivals. Her most recent film is *The Observer,* released in 1989, which had its première that summer at the Moscow Film Festival. Her experience in the profession has, as we will see, been rather different from that of her colleague, Marina Goldovskaya.

Loginova comes from a small town in the northern Caucasus. Her mother was a professional photographer and her father held an administrative post within the film industry. From the age of 12 she began to study photography in a youth group, and at 14 she joined a club for amateur film-makers. The intense pleasure she felt when she saw her few brief films on screen convinced her that her future lay in the film industry.

This decision was reinforced when she came across a photograph of the camerawoman Margarita Pilikhina (who has since died), in the journal *Sovetskii Ekran* (*Soviet Screen*): 'She was an extremely good camerawoman. She did not make many films, but those that she did make have become classics of Soviet cinema. It was a beautiful portrait, of her beside her movie camera. My dream now took on more of a real quality.' When she told her father that she had decided to apply to VGIK, however, he was strongly against the decision. 'He considered that the profession of camera-operator was not appropriate for a woman. Discrimination begins in one's own family . . .' She was forced to enrol instead at a pedagogical institute but she hated it and left the course after only a year. Her father then forced her to go to a mining metallurgical institute where she studied mechanics and higher mathematics. It is interesting to note the cultural variations in what is considered an appropriate female profession! While Loginova was reluctantly studying at this institute, her father was taken ill and died. She talks of this almost with relief: 'Now there was no one to oppose me. My mother understood me, and sympathized with me. It was decided that I would, finally, enrol at the film institute. My desire to do so had grown still stronger, I could not imagine myself doing any other kind of work.' She was not accepted on her first attempt, however, nor even on her second. In the meantime, she continued to work and to improve her photographic skills. 'To enter the institute you need a portfolio of thirty pictures - portraits, landscapes, journalistic shots. So I worked on this. For money, I taught photography to small children. But my mother fed me, I didn't earn enough to do this. And I prepared for the institute.' She gained admittance to VGIK on her third try, in 1965, when she was 21 years old. 'It turned out very well for me. In the second year the students - there were twelve of us altogether - were divided into groups, with three students per teacher. And my teacher was none other than Margarita Mikhailovna Pilikhina. She helped me so much. She watched over me, looked at my work, analysed it, criticized it, praised it . . .'

Loginova graduated in 1971: 'When they gave me the diploma I felt it was a real victory, because amongst the circle of lads in the institute there had been a very strong scepticism directed towards me. Even when I managed to complete the course, they still thought I would have children straight away and would never work. It was very difficult to be surrounded by those men. The whole time I had to do battle, both against them and against myself, in the sense of constantly having to assert myself. This is discrimination.'

Within a month of getting her diploma, with Margarita Pilikhina's help, Loginova got a job at the studio in the republic of Belorussia. Once there, she was immediately set to work on a feature film. 'I was really very lucky because I went straight into camera-work. We have a profession called "Second Operator", the person who deals with the technical side of things. Often people have to do this work for two or three years, acting as assistants to camera-operators. After that first film, I made several others, one right after the other. But it was very hard working with the men in the studio. Again, they had a sceptical attitude towards me. They always doubted that I would be able to do the job properly. In order to win their confidence I had to work very hard, read a lot and be constantly up to date with the latest developments in cinematography.' It took five years of constant struggle and self-assertion before she gained the respect of her male colleagues and they began to deal with her, as she puts it, 'in a normal fashion'. What kept her going through those years was her conviction of her own worth. 'The most important thing is to believe in yourself,' she declared. 'If I believe in myself, I have the confidence to go on.'

Her first film was called *Far from the River*: 'It was set in the year 1937, and was about a small boy who is waiting for his uncle to come back from Spain, where he had gone to fight the fascists.' Unlike more recent films about the Stalinist period, this one did not probe into politics. It was just a simple tale of childhood. 'At that time it wasn't possible to discuss the period openly. We didn't really know anything about what had happened. I was more concerned about the technical side of things, in any case. The quality of our film stock was very bad, the equipment was very bad, and all of my energy went into trying to overcome those problems.'

She had met her husband while still at VGIK, where he was a student on the script-writing course. Her experience of married life was not a happy one: 'Marina Goldovskaya was very lucky in her family life and had a good husband,' she said, 'but this was not my experience. The whole six years we were together, my husband would tell me, "you're not a real camera-operator, nothing will ever come of you, you should stay at home. *I'm* the artist". So discrimination took place on the family level, too. Eventually I couldn't bear it any longer. There were other problems as well – he drank heavily. So we parted, and now we have no contact with each other.'

'I have not married again,' she continued. 'I have never met anyone who could understand my work, my profession . . . I don't know why, but I always seem to meet the type of man who thinks that a wife should centre everything around him, serve him and look after his interests. I've never met a man who understands me. Now I'm at the age when it's probably too late. Maybe when I retire – when I'm no longer working – I'll find myself a nice old man!'

The marriage produced a son, and Loginova found that trying to carry on her chosen profession as well as bringing up a child produced yet another range of problems. 'I breastfed him for the first year, and it's difficult to do so when you are in this kind of work,' she explained. 'Also, a small child needs you to be there the whole time; but working in the cinema means going on long expeditions, sometimes for three months at a time. I was luckier than many, because my mother gave me a lot of help. She took on much of the upbringing of my child. You probably know that if you leave children in our crèches and kindergartens, they always get ill. So my mother looked after him a lot until he reached school age. My mother lives in the south of Russia, and I live in the north, so I've spent a lot of time on planes flying back and forth. Once he started school, it was easier. I can now go away on longer shoots, with more peace of mind. He's at a very good school, an *internat* – that means that when I'm away from Minsk he can live at the school, but when I'm there he stays with me. It's a very small school and it's difficult to get a place there, but it has something of a home atmosphere. During the summer he still spends his holidays with my mother in the Caucasus because that's the peak of the film year and we're always filming. It's not been easy on me either, by the way – sometimes I've thought that if I had to go a whole month without seeing my child I would die! For women, this is very difficult.'

Unlike Marina Goldovskaya, Loginova could think of no advantages derived from being a woman in this male-dominated profession: 'Quite the contrary; I have always experienced opposition from men. Now, things are easier, but only because I have already acquired some authority amongst cinematographers, and they have at last come to respect me. But in general, discrimination against women has been very strong in the Soviet Union. First, my father didn't want me to enter the institute. Then, once I was there, I had to put up with the sceptical attitudes of the men around me. When I started work at the studio, the same thing happened. Then my husband didn't want me to do creative work. And then when I had my child, it was very hard to combine motherhood with this kind of work. These are all heavy burdens on women.'

Given Loginova's condemnation of the attitudes of her male colleagues, it is surprising to find that she does not have a strong preference for female directors. 'I worked on two films with women directors. Perhaps it was easier to talk openly to the women, and this meant that a closer relationship could develop. But if a women director is not good, it doesn't matter how openly I can talk to her; she still can't set up a scene properly, or grasp the real philosophy of the film. If I'm working with a good male director, however, maybe I can't talk to him so easily about intimate things, but we will find a common language and a good film will come of it. Everything depends on whether the person is talented or not.'

What are Loginova's views on the concept of 'women's cinema'? 'I find the term hard to define. Some people say that women are more sensitive than men, can penetrate into the inner meaning of a drama, and Pilikhina, for example, was able to do this. She was a very bright, clear, clean, romantic person. This has been described as "a woman's camera", and it has been said on occasion that because I was her pupil I have a similar style. But in my opinion this is nonsense. There is only good camera and bad camera. There are men who have a great feeling for light or for composition, and there are women who don't have this feeling. Again, everything depends, simply, on talent. There's a Russian term – "God's spark" – that means God-given talent. I think such a thing exists, and whether the person who has it is a man or a woman has no relevance.'

All the same, she continues, 'there are, certainly, films on women's themes. This is what I would call women's cinema – films that deal with women's themes, rather than films which are made by women. Larisa Shepit'ko's second film, *Wings*, falls into this category. The script was also by a woman, Natal'ya Ryazantseva. But male directors have also made good films about women.'

What does the future hold for women in this profession? Does Loginova see an increase in the number of women entering this field? She is cautious about making predictions: 'Every year, VGIK has to take two or three women – that is, if they apply. There have been occasions when they've held the exams and no women have turned up to take them.' Even if more women enter the course, the impediments against them will remain as strong as ever. Children, for example, remain a female problem. Loginova does not even consider the possibility of men taking on a greater role here. Nor does she anticipate an improvement in pre-school childcare institutions. The only hope for a woman is to press her own mother into service – the legendary *babushka,* or granny. 'If there is a grandmother at hand it is so much easier. A woman can have a child and pass it over to her!' Otherwise, her career simply falls apart: 'A very talented woman graduated not long ago from the film institute, but she got married to another camera-operator, and now has three children. And she has no *babushka* to look after them. What can she do? She has to look after the children herself until they go to school, and so she loses five or six years of work experience. But children have to be born! There are many talented young women who, because of their family situation, can't continue with their work. How do you help them? I don't know the answer.'

SCRIPT-WRITING

Maria Zvereva

On first glance, Maria Zvereva seems to be an unbelievably prolific writer. In 1989 alone, five films based on her stories were screened for the first time. However, three of these turn out not to be recent works, but to have been rescued from obscurity by *glasnost'*. Like other literary and cinematographic works, many of Zvereva's scripts, and the films based on them, sat on censors' shelves for years.

I talked with Zvereva over supper at her apartment, just round the corner from the beautiful Novedevitchy (New Maiden) Convent. Her apartment is a rare example of Stalinist housing. Little public housing dates from that time, since Stalin was too preoccupied with more monumental projects such as blast furnaces, statues and metro stations. Yet the Stalinist apartments which do exist have huge rooms and high ceilings, and a feeling of space which is a rare luxury in the Soviet Union. 'Yes, I've always thought I had one thing to thank Stalin for . . .' Zvereva said ironically. She speaks excellent, lively and colloquial English and much of what follows is a verbatim transcript of her own words.

Maria Zvereva was born in Moscow in 1952. Unlike many of the film-makers we talked to, her family was not involved in the cinema. Her mother was a lawyer, her father a writer of short stories. Although he did not work in films, she claims to have got her inspiration from him. He died in 1966, when she was only 14, but under his tutelage she had already begun to write. At the age of 13 she was publishing short articles in the special children's section of *Komsomol'skaya Pravda*, the newspaper of the Communist Youth League, and when she was 17 she had a story accepted by the journal *Yunost'* (*Youth*).

Since her passion for writing was almost matched by a passion for the cinema, she eventually set her mind on a career that combined the two. This did not mean turning her back on her literary skills: 'Our screenplays are much more like novels or prose writing than they are in your country. They are works of literature. We have to write in a more emotional way, we have to convey an idea of the person's thoughts, feelings and so on. It must be possible to read the scripts with enjoyment, as well as see them performed on screen. The best are published, and are very popular. One magazine only publishes screen plays.'

Unlike the other areas of the film industry we have looked at, script-writing is not primarily a male domain. However, that does not mean that being accepted for training is easy: 'Competition is very tough. Only thirteen people are accepted each year at VGIK to study script-writing, and there are a hundred or so trying for each place. First of all, you have to send your stories for them to see. This is done in April. By the end of May they have whittled the number of applicants down to two hundred – so more than a thousand have already been shed. Their next task is to find out if you really wrote the stories, or if you got a friend, your father or someone else to do it for you! This makes for a funny competition, but it works. All the applicants are put in one big room, and they have to stay there for eight hours. They are allowed to leave to use the toilet, but not for anything else. In these eight hours they have to write a short novella. They are given a choice of five or so topics or ideas to work from. Some of these just consist of the last two lines of a story – they have to fill in what goes before. The examiners are usually the script-writers who will subsequently be training the successful candidates, so they are choosing their own students.'

The course at VGIK is divided into distinct stages. Each year the students work on developing one particular skill. 'We begin with the writing of short, "silent" novellas – a great number of short stories without dialogue, to concentrate on the portrayal of emotion. In the second year, we begin work on dialogue. In the third year, we work on the adaptation of books for the screen. But as well as this, we also have to study art, theatre, mime, and so on.'

In general, there is not much contact between people working in the different departments of VGIK, which are situated on different floors of the building. Actresses do their best to break down these barriers, though: 'They go dashing up to the directors' floors in their breaks, smoking their cigarettes in the smokers' corner of the directors' corridor, in the hope of meeting and marrying a nice new director!' This is not just for romantic reasons. There is a strong tradition of directors placing their actress-wives in key roles in their films, so there is an obvious advantage in having one as a husband. Students of screen-writing also try to have as much contact as possible with directors, in the hope that the scripts they write at VGIK will actually be filmed. In Zvereva's case, the script she wrote for her final examination did appear on screen.

Although there are many more women in this area of the industry than in directing or camera-work, women script-writers still have to assert their right to the profession: 'Once you have made a name for yourself, it doesn't make so much difference whether you are male or female,' Zvereva explained, 'but in the beginning you encounter much prejudice as a woman. You hear over and over again: "Why don't you want to get married, have a family, instead of trying to do this job?!" ' Many do not survive the pressures: 'Of the thirteen students who train together in any one year,' Zvereva asserted, 'usually not more than two stay in feature films.'

One of the particularly pressing problems is money. 'Script-writers all work for themselves; they don't work for a particular studio and they don't get a fixed salary. It is particularly hard in the beginning because you are not paid anything in advance for your first script. You do it entirely at your own risk.

Once you are known, you can just write five or six pages and submit these to a studio, and if the studio likes these it will give you an advance.'

Even when you are established, the salary is still unpredictable. This is because the fee for a script is paid in a complex series of stages: the total is initially divided into equal halves, then one of these is subdivided into three different sums. The first sum, 45 per cent of the first half, is paid when a studio decides to accept a script. When the script is completed, the next 30 per cent is handed over. When the studio begins filming the script, the writer gets the final 25 per cent of the first half of the fee. Only when the film appears on screen is the final payment made. This is the second half of the total – in other words, a payment which equals all of the previous ones put together. Since it was not uncommon for films never to make it to the screen in the days before *glasnost*, script-writers lived a life of financial uncertainty. In the new financial climate of the *perestroika* period, if the film is successful the writer gets a further payment from the profits. If a writer cannot work for a while, the Union of Cinematographers might help out. When Zvereva took time off work to have her child she was given money by the union. There is now also a separate writers' guild, set up in 1989.

Another of the unpleasant aspects of the job is dealing with autocratic directors. 'During the five years of our training we are told that we are the most important people in the cinema world. The director can change nothing without our permission. Unfortunately, when we leave VGIK and start work, we discover that the director has far more power than that.' Many directors fancy themselves as writers and insist on putting their own stamp on a script. Accordingly, when Zvereva first sees a film made from one of her scripts, she often feels like 'a woman who has given her baby away and then sees it again eighteen years later, after someone else has brought it up and spoilt it. It has the same blond hair, the same blue eyes; but all the same, it is different . . .'

Zvereva does not think that gender has a great effect on the tension between director and script-writer. All the same, when she describes the relationship which develops between the two, it sounds like a rather traditional marriage. Directors are necessarily strong-willed people, she says, and whenever there is a dispute they always win in the end. Script-writers may as well give in immediately. On the whole, she thinks that script-writing is a more appropriate role for women because of the toughness required to be a director: 'Women directors sometimes lose their "womanliness", she explains.

The tension between directors and script-writers can be particularly strong when they are really married. Zvereva's husband of fifteen years is a director, and they have worked together only once. Zvereva jokes that it brought them close to divorce: 'Instead of saying, "Could you possibly change this a little bit . . ." he wakes me up at 5.00 a.m. and yells, "What is this! Re-write it all!"'

The marriage-like relationship between the director and script-writer is compounded by the fact that the writers generally work at home, the traditional domain of the woman. To Zvereva, however, this is one of the more positive aspects of the job: 'One of the joys of the profession, for me, is that you don't have to get up and go to work at the crack of dawn!' Yet it can lead to battles with her family, who think she should combine writing with housework. 'They don't realize that if you're not actually typing a script you're still working on it, in your head. They say "but surely you can do the cooking at the same time, or the washing up"!'

Since she spends so much time at home, Zvereva is lucky to have such a spacious apartment. Soviet citizens were theoretically provided with a set amount of living space per person, but because of the housing shortage in the major cities, this was far from generous. Many people did not even have as much space as they were officially entitled to. In acknowledgement of the fact that script-writers need room to work, the government decreed that they could have a few additional metres of space. Whether they actually got it, however, was due to a combination of luck and connections. There is now talk of privatizing housing, giving citizens the accommodation they formerly rented from the state. This will hardly improve the situation, however; it just means that those living in totally inadequate space will merely own it rather than rent it. The Union of Cinematographers has two spacious houses for the use of members, one in Moscow and another not far outside, and writers can apply for a room when they feel the need for space or peace. Zvereva notes that some men have found other uses for these houses, however . . .

Asked about the concept of 'women's cinema', Zvereva said that she could not discern any real difference in films made by men or women. 'It might be that women can tell us a little bit more than a man about a female character, can add a new dimension, but this isn't always the case. Yulii Raizman, for example, has an exceptional understanding of women. He has been making films for years, he is now about 90 years old, and has almost always placed women characters in the centre of his films.' In fact, people might portray the other sex better than their own: 'It's a bit like being a foreigner and looking round an unknown country,' she explains, 'you sometimes see things with a more perceptive eye than someone who lives there.'

Zvereva acknowledged that she has an antipathy to the concept of 'women's cinema', linked to the fear of being 'ghettoized'. Men in the film industry have a tendency to trivialize anything linked specifically to women: 'They were being particularly ironic about our women's organization, KIWI,' she said, 'they thought it very foolish. One of them said to me, "Why do you need to get involved? You have already made your name, you've won prizes at festivals." He made it sound like a house for invalids!'

One of the most successful films to be made from one of Zvereva's scripts is *Stolen Meeting*, directed by an Estonian woman, Leyda Lajus. It was made in 1981 but only released in 1989. It is about a female ex-convict searching for her son, who was put in an orphanage when she was arrested. The heroine finds that he has since been adopted by a middle-class professional family, and she eventually decides to leave him where he is, despite the pain this causes her.

Zvereva got the idea for the main character when she was looking for a nanny for her child. One of the women she interviewed was obviously telling lies to get the job, saying whatever she felt Zvereva wanted to hear. Yet Zvereva was fascinated by her. She gave her the job, but a week later the woman disappeared, having helped herself to a few of Zvereva's things. Zvereva felt that she was a talented person, all the same; she just used her talent in a negative way.

So she began working her into a story: 'I decided there had to be an emotional struggle, in which two opposing sides of the woman's character were revealed. This was brought out by her relationship with her son. The woman gives him up in the end because she feels she would ruin his life. For the first time ever, she was doing something for someone else. She is like the true mother in the story of Solomon. That was the idea I had for this character, that she proves herself to be a real mother by giving up the child.' Zvereva also conveys the essential goodness of the character by making it clear that she protected the identity of her partner-in-crime throughout her interrogation, although he had been far less generous in his treatment of her. He was the father of the child, although married to someone else, and made no attempt to keep in contact with the boy throughout the years of her imprisonment.

Zvereva wrote the story with Russian characters and a Russian audience in mind. When it was bought by the Estonian film studio, it acquired a strong nationalist flavour. The film was made in both Russian and Estonian, with each language subtitled in the other; this conveyed the bilingualism of life outside of the Russian republic. Russian audiences have complained that the Russian speakers were the nastier characters, while those the audience was supposed to identify with were Estonian. Zvereva agrees that this may be the case, but that is because one is supposed to see things from the point of view of the Estonian heroine. When she and the director were working on the film, they went to a women's prison in Estonia to help them achieve the right atmosphere; she was very aware of the fact that all of the prison officials were Russian, and the prisoners Estonian.

When the film was finished, it was discussed at an Arts Council meeting. Zvereva described the meeting: 'Most of the men who were present said, "We can't stand a woman who can give her child away! We don't want to go inside the psychology of this woman, we can't forgive her!" But we wanted to be this particular woman's "defence council"!' The men who voiced those views, she added, were the kind who would prefer women to stay at home and devote themselves to their families.

Zvereva had tentative plans to write another script for the same director. This would be a modern version of the Romeo and Juliet story, about an Armenian boy and an Estonian girl. 'Estonians are from the north, so the cultures are very different. Estonians don't even want to deal with Russians, and they see Armenians as still worse. We are the "last empire" – we have so many nationalities and we are being torn apart by the tensions between them. I want to show that love can be stronger than nationalism.'

Another of Zvereva's recent projects was the adaptation of a story by her father, Il'ya Zverev, for the screen. Directed by Evgenii Tsimbal, *Defence Council Sedov* was released in 1989. The story had been written during the temporary liberalization initiated by Khrushchev, and it was subsequently suppressed until Gorbachev came to power. It tells the story of a Moscow lawyer who, at great personal risk, takes on the defence of three men falsely accused of treason during the period of Stalin's 'Terror'. Remarkably, the lawyer wins his case, but it turns out to be a hollow victory. The system turns instead to a new set of victims, and puts to death dozens of people who are falsely accused of taking part in this 'miscarriage of justice'.

Maria Zvereva is evidently relieved at the arrival of a new intellectual climate in which works like this can be published and screened. However, she is cautious in her optimism about the future. Like the other women we talked to, she expressed alarm about the commercialization of the cinema. In the past they had to worry about the censor; now, they are repressed by the need to think about a film's profit potential all the time. She also talked about the confusion surrounding the new structure of the industry: 'We had no idea what producers were, for example. Studios acted as our producers, using government money. Now, we are having to quickly learn about these things.'

What of her own future? 'I don't want to take on too much work,' she said. 'I have a family, children and no one will look after them if I don't!' A year after this discussion, she took on the role of Vice-President of the Union of Cinematographers – the first time a woman has ever held a leading position in the union. It is, perhaps, time for her family to learn how to look after themselves.

REFERENCES

INTRODUCTION

1. Quoted by Garth Jowett and James M. Linton, *Movies as Mass Communication* (Newbury Park & London, Sage, 1989), p. 76.
2. *Sovetskoe kino - rezhissery o kino: partiinost', narodnost', sotsialisticheskii realizm* (Moscow, Iskusstvo, 1986), p. 48.
3. Quoted by M. J. Clark (ed.), *Politics and the Media* (Oxford, Pergamon Press, 1979), p. 33.
4. Jay Leyda, *Kino: A History of the Russian and Soviet Film* (NY, Collier, 1973), p. 160; and Clark, *Politics and the Media*, p. 32.
5. Cited by (among others) Leyda, *Kino*, p. 160. See also M. J. Clark (ed.), *Politics and the Media*, p. 32.
6. Quoted by Robert G. Kaiser, *Russia: The People and the Power* (Harmondsworth, Penguin, 1976), p. 15.
7. Tatyana Mamonova, *Russian Women's Studies* (Oxford, Pergamon Press, 1989), pp. 168-9.

PART I: WOMEN, CINEMA AND SOCIETY

1. Quoted by Jay Leyda, *Kino: A History of the Russian and Soviet Film* (NY, Collier, 1973), p. 20.
2. Neya Zorkaya, *The Illustrated History of the Soviet Cinema* (NY, Hippocrene Books, 1989), p. 15.
3. Yuri Davydov, *The October Revolution and the Arts* (Moscow, Progress, 1967), p. 344.
4. Victoria E. Bonnell, 'The Representation of Women in Early Soviet Political Art' in *The Russian Review*, July 1991, vol. 50, no. 3, p. 267.

CHAPTER 1: THE BACKGROUND

1. Historians disagree strongly about the figure, and as J. N. Westwood notes, official and unofficial assessments at the time differ widely. See J. N. Westwood, *Endurance and Endeavour: Russian History 1812-1971* (Oxford, OUP, 1973), p. 156.
2. Lionel Kochan, *The Making of Modern Russia* (Harmondsworth, Penguin, 1978), p. 240.
3. Quoted by T. Selezneva, *Kino Mysl' 1920-kh godov* (Leningrad, Isskustvo, 1972), pp. 9-10.
4. Westwood, *Endurance and Endeavour*, p. 209.
5. Quoted by Kochan, *The Making of Modern Russia*, p. 243.
6. V. Khanzhonkova, 'Iz vospominanii o dorevolyutsionnom kino' in *Iz Istorii Kino*, no. 5, 1962, pp. 120-30.
7. Zorkaya, *Illustrated History of the Soviet Cinema*, pp. 35-6.
8. Ibid., p. 36.

CHAPTER 2: REVOLUTION AND CIVIL WAR

1. Zorkaya, *Illustrated History of the Soviet Cinema*, p. 41.
2. Ibid.
3. Cited by William Blum (among others), *The CIA: A Forgotten History* (London, Zed Books, 1986), p. 1.
4. See Kochan, *The Making of Modern Russia*, p. 269; and Moshe Lewin, *The Gorbachev Phenomenon* (London, Hutchinson, 1988), pp. 15-16.
5. See Gail Lapidus, *Women in Soviet Society* (Berkeley, University of California Press, 1978), p. 48.
6. Ibid., p. 61.
7. Zorkaya, *Illustrated History of the Soviet Cinema*, p. 39.
8. Richard Taylor, 'From October to 'October': the Soviet Political System in the

1920s and its Films' in M. J. Clark (ed.),
*Politics and the Media: Film and Television for
the Political Scientist and Historian* (Oxford and
N.Y., Pergamon Press, 1979), p. 32.

9. Selezneva, *Kino Mysl'*, p. 59.

10. Lev Kuleshov, *Kuleshov on Film*, translated and
edited by Ronald Levaco (Berkeley, University
of California Press, 1974), p. 203.

11. Russell Campbell, *Cinema Strikes Back -
Radical Filmmaking in the United States 1930-
1942* (Ann Arbor, UMI Research Press, 1982),
p. 2.

12. Nadezhda Krupskaya, 'Privetsvie N.K.
Krupskoi III vsesoyuznomy soveshchaniyu
kinokhronikerov', from *Is Istorii Kino*
(Moscow, Isskustvo, 1965), p. 10.

13. See Khanzhonkova, 'Iz vospominanii', p. 130;
and Zorkaya, *Illustrated History of the Soviet
Cinema*, pp. 46-7.

14. *Letopisty nashego vremeni - rezhissery
documental'nogo kino* (Moscow, Iskusstvo,
1987), p. 6.

15. See Yuri Vorontsov and Igor Rachuk, *The
Phenomoneon of the Soviet Cinema* (Moscow,
Progress, 1980), pp. 36-7; also Louis Harris
Cohen, *The Cultural-Political Traditions and
Development of the Soviet Cinema 1917-1972*
(New York, Arno Press, 1974), pp. 40-1.

CHAPTER 3: THE 1920s

1. For more detailed discussion, see L. Attwood
and M. McAndrew, 'Women at Work in the
USSR' in M. J. Davidson and C. L. Cooper
(eds), *Working Women* (London and NY, John
Wiley, 1984), p. 274.

2. See Alexandra Kollontai, *Selected Writings*,
translated and with commentaries by Alix
Holt (London, Allison & Busby, 1977).

3. See M. P. Sacks, *Women's Work in Soviet Russia*
(NY, Praeger, 1976), p. 25.

4. See Lapidus, *Women in Soviet Society*, p. 88.

5. Ibid., pp. 69-70. See also Mary Buckley,
Women and Ideology in the Soviet Union (Ann
Arbor, University of Michigan Press, 1989), p.
82-94.

6. See, for example, 'Pavel Petrov-Bytov: We
have no Soviet cinema' in Taylor and
Christie, *The Film Factory*, p. 259; and Denise
J. Youngblood, *Soviet Cinema in the Silent Era*
(Ann Arbor, UMI Research Press, 1985), pp.
2-3.

7. See A. Petrovich, 'Obzor russkoi
periodoicheskoi kinopechati pervykh

poslerevolyutsionnykh let (1917-1924)' in *Iz
Istorii kino*, pp. 175-203; also Youngblood, *Soviet
Cinema in the Silent Era* (Ann Arbor, UMI
Research press, 1985), p. 2.

8. John David Rimberg, *The Motion Picture in
the Soviet Union: 1918-1952. A Sociological
Analysis* (New York, Arno Press, 1973),
p. 77.

9. Quoted by Vlada Petric, 'Esther Shub:
Cinema is my Life' in *Quarterly Review of Film
Studies*, Fall 1978, p. 442.

10. Zorkaya, *Illustrated History of the Soviet
Cinema*, p. 49.

11. Quoted by Christopher Williams (ed.),
Realism and the Cinema (London, RKP, 1980),
pp. 20-1.

12. See Campbell, *Cinema Strikes Back*, p. 14.

13. N.P. Abramov, *Dziga Vertov* (Moscow,
Izdatel'stvo Akademii Nauk, 1962), p. 45.

14. The Young Pioneers are part of the network
of communist youth organizations, in this
case for children aged from 9-14. At 14 they
go on to the Komsomol.

15. Judith Mayne, *Kino and the Woman Question:
Feminism and Soviet Silent Film* (Columbus,
Ohio State University Press, 1989), pp. 169-70.

16. A. Yurovskii, *Letopisty nashego vremeni:
rezhissery dokumental'nogo kino* (Moscow,
Iskusstvo, 1987), p. 35.

17. T. Selezneva, *Kino Mysl' 1920 godov* (Leningrad,
Iskusstvo, 1972), p. 43.

18. Jay Leyda, *Kino*, p. 224. See also Selezneva,
Kino Mysl', p. 44.

19. See Petric, 'Esther Shub: Cinema is my Life',
p. 431.

20. Cohen, *Cultural-Political Traditions*, p. 52.

21. Peter Wollen, *Signs and Meaning in the
Cinema* (London, Thames and Hudson/BFI,
1969), p. 48.

22. Ibid., p. 39.

23. Quoted by Richard Taylor, *Film Propaganda:
Soviet Russia and Nazi Germany* (New York,
Harper and Row; London, Croom Helm,
1979), p. 95.

24. Adrian Piotrovsky, 'The Battleship Potemkin'
reproduced in Richard Taylor and Ian
Christie, *The Film Factory: Russian and Soviet
Cinema in Documents 1896-1939* (London,
Routledge and Kegan Paul, 1988), p. 139.

25. Wollen, *Signs and Meaning in the Cinema*, p.
36.

26. See Attwood and McAndrew, 'Women at
Work in the USSR', p. 271.

27. From *Novyi Lef*, no. 3, 1928; in translation in *Screen*, Winter 1971-2, p. 86.
28. Ibid.
29. Leyda, *Kino*, p. 264.
30. From a poem by A.N. Maikov, 1856: quoted in Taylor and Christie, *The Film Factory*, p. 255.
31. Ibid.
32. See, for example, Yuri Vorontsov and Igor Rachuk, *The Phenomenon of the Soviet Cinema* (Moscow, Progress, 1980), p. 48; Herbert Marshall, *Masters of the Soviet Cinema* (London, Routledge and Kegan Paul, 1983), pp. 21, 33.
33. See Marshall, *Masters of the Soviet Cinema*, p. 21.
34. T. Rokotov, 'Why is October difficult?' in Taylor and Christie, *The Film Factory*, p. 220.
35. Vorontov and Rachuk, *The Phenomenon of the Soviet Cinema*, p. 49.
36. Mayne, *Kino and the Woman Question*, p. 91.
37. Ibid., p. 97.
38. Taylor, *Film Propaganda*, p. 83.
39. See Victoria E. Bonnell, 'The Representation of Women in Early Soviet Political Art' in *Russian Review*, July 1991, vol. 50, no. 3, p. 270.
40. Vsevolod Pudovkin, 'The Director and the Scriptwriter. Seminar at VGIK' in Taylor and Christie, *The Film Factory*, p. 383.
41. See Youngblood, *Soviet Cinema in the Silent Era*, p. 144; and Kuleshov, *Kuleshov on Film*, p. 175.
42. Yuri Tynyanov, 'On FEKS' (*O FEKSakh*) in *Sovetskii Ekran*, 2 April 1929, p. 10. Reproduced in Taylor and Christie, *The Film Factory*, pp. 257-9.
43. Viktor Shklovsky, 'The Film Language of New Babylon' in Taylor and Christie, *The Film Factory*, p. 311.
44. Youngblood, *Soviet Cinema in the Silent Era*, p. 207.
45. 'Pavel Petrov-Bytov: We have no Soviet cinema' in Taylor and Christie, *The Film Factory*, p. 261.
46. Ibid., p. 261.
47. Aleksandra Kollontai, 'Working Woman and Mother' in Aleksandra Kollontai, *Selected Writings* (translated by Alix Holt), p. 134.
48. See Leyda, *Kino*, pp. 215-16, 245; and Youngblood, *Soviet Cinema in the Silent Era*, pp. 215-16.
49. This story encapsulated particularly well the conflict between 'the social' and 'the personal', so a second version of it was filmed in 1956 by Grigorii Chukrai.
50. Miron Chernenko, '"Sorok pervyi", SSSR (1927)' in *Iskusstvo Kino*, no. 7, 1987, pp. 93-5.
51. N.A. Lebedev and E.M. Smirnova, 'Stanovlenie i rasvitie sovetskoro nemogo kino' in *Kratkaya Istoriya Sovetskogo Kino 1917-1967* (Moscow, Iskusstvo, 1969), p. 160.
52. Youngblood, *Soviet Cinema in the Silent Era*, p. 152.
53. See Paul Babitsky and John Rimberg, *The Soviet Film Industry* (NY, Praegar, 1952), p. 132.
54. Ibid., p. 150.

CHAPTER 4: THE STALIN ERA

1. Lewin, *The Gorbachev Phenomenon*, p. 31.
2. Quoted in Kochan, *The Making of Modern Russia*, p. 282.
3. Figures from Westwood, *Endurance and Endeavour*, p. 296.
4. Geoffrey Hosking, *The First Socialist Society* (Cambridge, Harvard University Press, 1985), p. 166.
5. Ibid., p. 163.
6. Kochan, *The Making of Modern Russia*, p. 296.
7. Lewin, *The Gorbachev Phenomenon*, p. 23.
8. Yurii Bogamolov, 'Po motivam istorii sovetskogo kino', part I, in *Iskusstvo Kino*, no. 8, 1989, p. 65.
9. Ibid.
10. For more detailed discussion, see Lynne Attwood and Maggie McAndrew, 'Women at Work in the USSR' in M.J. Davidson and C.L. Cooper (eds), *Working Women* (London and NY, John Wiley, 1984), pp. 269-304.
11. Quoted by Mary Buckley, *Women and Ideology*, p. 117.
12. Cited by Louis Harris Cohen, *The Cultural-Political Traditions and Development of the Soviet Cinema 1917-1972* (New York, Arno Press, 1974), p. 4.
13. Wollen, *Signs and Meaning in the Cinema*, p. 50.
14. Ian Christie, 'Making Sense of early Soviet sound' in *Inside the Film Factory* (London and NY, Routledge and Kegan Paul, 1991), p. 179.
15. Ibid.
16. Youngblood, *Soviet Cinema in the Silent Era*, p. 222.
17. Ian Christie, 'The Cinema' in James Cracraft (ed.), *The Soviet Union Today: an Interpretative Guide*, 2nd edition (Chicago, University of Chicago Press, 1988), p. 284.

18. Extract from B.Z. Shumyatskii, 'A Cinema for the Millions' in Taylor and Christie, *The Film Factory*, p. 365.

19. See Marshall, *Masters of the Soviet Cinema*, p. 91.

20. Quoted by Marshall, ibid., p. 85.

21. Ibid., p. 86.

22. Abramov, *Dziga Vertov*, p. 134.

23. Marshall, *Masters of the Soviet Cinema*, p. 86.

24. Abramov, *Dziga Vertov*, p. 144.

25. Ibid., p. 146.

26. Ibid., p. 146.

27. Yurovskii, *Letopisty Nashego Vremeni*, p. 40. The reference is to the book *Istoriya Sovetskogo Kino*, published in the Soviet Union in 1969.

28. Campbell, *Cinema Strikes Back*, p. 21.

29. M. Bleiman, writing in *Sovetskoe Kino* in 1933; cited by Selezneva, *Kino Mysl'*, p. 57.

30. See the excerpt of Shub's script in 'Esther Shub's Unrealized Project', translated and introduced by Vlada Petric, *Quarterly Review of Film Studies*, Fall 1978, p. 451.

31. Ippolit Sokolov, 'The Legend of "Left" Cinema' in Christie and Taylor, *The Film Factory*, p. 290.

32. Marshall, *Masters of the Soviet Cinema*, p. 203-5.

33. This was done by Sergei Yutkevich and Naum Keiman.

34. Marshall, *Masters of the Soviet Cinema*, p. 210.

35. Boris Shumyatskii, 'The Film Bezhin Meadow' in Christie and Taylor, *The Film Factory*, p. 379.

36. Marshall, *Masters of the Soviet Cinema*, p. 218.

37. Rostislav Yurenyev, 'From History to the Film' in introduction to the film script of *Ivan the Terrible* (NY, Lorrimer Publishing, 1970), p. 12.

38. See Marshall, *Masters of the Soviet Cinema*, pp. 226-32.

39. This is evidently the view of Mikhail Romm; see 'The Second Summet' in introduction to the film script of *Ivan the Terrible* (NY, Lorrimer Publishing, 1970), pp. 16-19. See also Marshall, pp. 226-32.

40. See Marshall, *Masters of the Soviet Cinema*, p. 228; also Marshall's introduction to Eisenstein's *Immoral Memories* (Boston, Houghton Mifflin Co., 1983), p. xv.

41. See Neya Zorkaya, quoted by Marshall, *Masters of the Soviet Cinema*, pp. 226-7; and Yurenyev, 'From History to the Film', p. 12.

42. Yurii Bogomolov, 'Po motivam istorii sovetskogo kino in *Iskusstvo Kino*, part II, no. 2, 1990, p. 88.

43. For example, Andshei Verner, Polish contributor to a round-table discussion on totalitarian cinema, in 'Kino totalitarnoi epokhi', part II, in *Iskusstvo Kino*, no. 2, 1990, p. 116.

44. I. Vaisfel'd, *G. Kozintsov i L. Trauberg*; excerpted in I.V. Sokolov (ed.), *Istoriya Sovetskogo kino iskusstva zvukovogo perioda*, Part I: 1930-41 (Moscow, Goskinoizdat, 1946), p. 18; see also F. Baranov, 'Tvorcheskii put' Kozintsova i Trauberga' excerpted in Sokolov, ibid., p. 17 (originally in *Iskusstvo Kino*, no. 7, 1937).

45. See I. Vaisfel'd, ibid., p. 18; also G. Kozintsov and L. Trauberg, 'Nash fil'm' in Sokolov, ibid., pp. 96-7 (originally in *Kino*, no. 21, May 1937).

46. Boris Shumyatskii, 'A Cinema for the Millions' in Christie and Taylor, *The Film Factory*, p. 365.

47. G. Kozintsov and L. Trauberg, 'Nash fil'm' in Sokolov (ed.), *Istoriya Sovetskogo kino*, part I, p. 96-7.

48. Theodore van Houten, *Leonid Trauberg and his Films* ('s-Hertogenbosch, Art and Research, 1989), p. 93.

49. Zorkaya, *The Illustrated History of the Soviet Cinema*, p. 149.

50. B. Agapov, 'Vyborgskaya storona' in Sokolov, part I, pp. 100-2 (originally in *Izvestiya*, 28 November 1938).

51. Editorial in *Pravda*, November 1934, p. 1, in Christie and Taylor, *The Film Factory*, pp. 334-5.

52. C. and G. Vasil'ev, 'Zametki k postanovke' in Sokolov, part I, p. 85 (originally in *Chapaev*, a collection of articles about the film published in 1935).

53. B.Z. Shumyatskii, 'A Cinema for the Millions', ibid., p. 359.

54. Youngblood, *Soviet Cinema in the Silent Era*, p. 230.

55. See, for example, M. Otten, 'Dramaturgiya filma (ori varianta stsenariya "Chapaeva")' in Sokolov, *Istoriya Sovetskogo kino*, part I, p. 78 (originally in *Sovetskoe kino*, no. 7, 1935); and I. Dolinskii, *Chapaev* (Moscow, Goskinoizdat, 1945), chapter 7.

56. Dolinskii, ibid., p. 106.

57. O. Yakubovich, *Vera Maretskaya* (Moscow, Soyuz Kinomatografistov SSSR, 1984), p. 18.

58. Ibid., p. 19.
59. The Tur brothers, 'Tsirk' in Sokolov, *Istoriya Sovetskogo kino*, part I, p. 172 (originally in *Izvestiya*, 23 May 1936).
60. See A. Macheret, 'Romantika sovetskikh budnei' reproduced in Sokolov, ibid., p. 205-6 (originally in *Kino*, no. 28, March 1935).
61. Boris Shumyatskii, 'A Cinema for the Millions' in Christie and Taylor, *The Film Factory*, pp. 363-5.
62. Neya Zorkaya in 'Kino totalitarnoi epokhi', part III, in *Iskusstvo Kino*, no. 3, 1990, p. 100.
63. Lilya Mamatova, ibid., p. 107.
64. See Lewis H. Siegelbaum, *Stakhanovism and the Politics of Productivity in the USSR, 1935-1941* (Cambridge, CUP, 1988), pp. 236-42.
65. Mary Buckley, *Women and Ideology in the Soviet Union*, p. 116.
66. O. Leonidov, 'Zoya' in I.V. Sokolov, *Istoriya Sovetskogo kino iskusstva zvukovogo perioda*, part II: 1934-44 (Moscow, Goskinoizdat, 1946), p. 275 (originally in *Moskovskii bol'shevik*, 24 September 1944).
67. N. Kovarskii, 'Doch' rodina' in Sokolov, ibid., part II, p. 276 (originally in *Komsomol'skaya Pravda*, 22 September 1944).
68. O. Leonidov, 'Zoya' in Sokolov, ibid., part II, pp. 275/6 (originally in *Moskovskii bol'shevik*, 24 September 1944).
69. Zorkaya, *The Illustrated History of the Soviet Cinema*, p. 153.
70. Yurii Bogomolov, 'Po motivam istorii sovetskogo kino', part I, p. 64.
71. Zorkaya in 'Kino totalitarnoi epokhi', part III, p. 102.

CHAPTER 5: KHRUSHCHEV AND THE 'THAW'

1. 'The Dethronement of Stalin: Full Text of the Krushchev Speech', published by the *Manchester Guardian*, June 1956.
2. Quoted by Kochan, *The Making of Modern Russia*, p. 316.
3. However beautiful it is, the Moscow metro has recently been described as an absurd symbol of Stalin's totalitarianism. M. Allenov, 'Ochevidnosti sistemnogo absurdizma skvoz' emblematiku moskovskogo metro' in *Iskusstvo Kino*, no. 6, 1990, pp. 81-4.
4. See Tanya Frisby, 'Soviet Youth Culture' in Jim Riordan (ed.), *Soviet Youth Culture* (London, Macmillan, 1989), p. 3.
5. See Buckley, *Women and Ideology in the Soviet*

Union, p. 142, for more detailed discussion of this.
6. Mary McAuley, *Politics and the Soviet Union* (Harmondsworth, Penguin, 1979), p. 256.
7. Cohen, *Cultural-Political Traditions*, p. 4.
8. Zorkaya, *Illustrated History of Soviet Cinema*, pp. 207-8.
9. Westwood, *Endurance and Endeavour*, p. 374.
10. Thanks to Neya Zorkaya for drawing my attention to this line; see *Illustrated History of Soviet Cinema*, pp. 241-2.
11. See interview with Tat'yana Loginova in Part III of this book.
12. Hosking, *The First Socialist Society*, p. 362.

CHAPTER 6: LEONID BREZHNEV: THE 'ERA OF STAGNATION'

1. A confidential report by Abel Aganbegyan in 1965; cited by Hosking, *The First Socialist Society*, p. 363.
2. Some argue that the creation of a Cult of Personality around Brezhnev did succeed. See Mark G. Field, 'Soviet Society and Communist Party Controls: A Case of Constricted Development' in Michael Paul Sacks and Jerry G. Pankhurst, *Understanding Soviet Society* (Winchester, Mass., Allen & Unwin, 1988), pp. 119-46.
3. See Gale Lapidus, 'State and Society: Toward the Emergence of Civil Society in the Soviet Union' in Seweryn Bialer (ed.), *Politics, Society and Nationality: Inside Gorbachev's Russia* (Boulder, Westview Press, 1989), pp. 121-47.
4. See Alix Holt, 'The First Soviet Feminists' in *Soviet Sisterhood* (London, Fourth Estate, 1985) pp 262-3. Also based on personal conversation with Russians.
5. Alix Holt, 'The First Soviet Feminists', p. 239.
6. Personal contacts; plus Mamonova, *Russian Women's Studies*, pp. 168-9.
7. Natal'ya Baranskaya, *A Week Like Any Other*, translated by Pieta Monks (London, Virago, 1989).
8. See Lawton, 'Toward a New Openness in Soviet Cinema', p. 2; and Val Golovskoy (with John Rimberg), *Behind the Soviet Screen: The Motion Picture Industry in the USSR 1972-1982* (Ann Arbor, Ardis, 1986), p. 138.
9. Zorkaya in 'Kino totalitarnoi epokhi', part III, p. 103.
10. Elena Stishova, *Blizkoe proshloe* (Kiev, Mistetstvo, 1989), p. 82.
11. Natal'ya Ryazantseva, 'Ya ne feministka, no

. . .' in *Iskusstvo Kino*, no. 12, 1988, p. 11.

12. Elena Stishova, *Blizkoe proshloe*, p. 82.

13. Zorkaya, *Illustrated History of Soviet Cinema*, p. 252.

14. Ibid., pp. 253-4.

15. M. Zak, 'Opyt kinorezhissury' in *Sovetskoe Kino 1970-e gody*, p. 225.

16. Stishova, *Bliskoe proshloe*, p. 83.

17. Bozhovich, 'Rentgenoskopiya dushi' in *Iskusstvo Kino*, no. 9, 1987, p. 59.

18. See, for example, V. Fomin, 'Ot cheloveka k "chelovecheskomu faktoru"' in *Iskusstvo Kino*, no. 4, 1989, p. 79.

19. Bozhovich, 'Rentgenoskopiya dushi', p. 64 (footnote).

20. Lana Gogoberidze, 'Chestnost' in *Iskusstvo Kino*, no. 5, 1986, pp. 19-20.

21. L. Mamatova, 'Internatsional'noe i natsional'noe v sovetskom kino' in *Sovetskoe kino 70-e gody*, p. 179.

22. Ibid., p. 180.

23. Lawton, 'Toward a New Openness in Soviet Cinema', p. 17.

24. Ibid.

25. Stishova, *Bliskoe proshloe*, p. 87.

26. Ibid.

27. Quoted by V. Kichin and N. Savitskii, 'Sovremennaya tema v kinoiskusstve. Nravstvennye iskaniya geroya' in *Sovetskoe Kino 70-e gody*, p. 33.

28. See Lawton, 'Toward a New Openness in Soviet Cinema', p. 13.

29. See Val Golovskoy, *Behind the Soviet Screen*, p. 142.

30. Zorkaya, *Illustrated History of Soviet Cinema*, p. 298.

31. Kichin and Savitskii, 'Sovremennaya tema v kinoiskusstve', p. 38.

32. I. Lagueva, 'A vse taki-lyubov' in *Komsomol'skaya Pravda*, 8 February 1981, p. 4.

33. O. Dmitreiva, 'Domovodstvo' in *Komsomol' skaya Pravda*, 24 September 1981, p. 2.

34. 'Mnogodetnaya sem'ya': vzglad v budushchee', round-table discussion reported by O. Dmitrieva in *Komsomol'skaya Pravda*, 30 October 1981, p. 2.

35. Personal interview with Maria Zvereva.

CHAPTER 7: 1982–5: THE INTERIM PERIOD

1. Martin Walker, *The Waking Giant* (London, Michael Joseph, 1986), p. 35.

2. Quoted by Elena Stishova, *Look Who's Here! -
a New Trend in the Soviet Cinema* (New Delhi, Panchsheel Publishers, 1989), p. 45.

3. Christie, 'The Cinema', p. 287.

4. Quoted by Lawton, 'Toward a New Openness in Soviet Cinema', p. 34.

5. Ibid., p. 32.

6. Quoted by Christie, 'The Cinema', p. 290.

7. Lawton, 'Toward a New Openness in Soviet Cinema', p. 32.

CHAPTER 8: *PERESTROIKA, GLASNOST'* AND THE CINEMA

1. Russell Watson, 'Why he Failed' in *Newsweek*, 23 December 1991, p. 9.

2. See Gale Lapidus, 'State and Society', p. 134.

3. John Bushnell, 'An introduction to the Soviet Sistema: The advent of Counterculture and Subculture' in *Slavic Review*, Summer 1990, p. 272.

4. See Elizabeth Waters, 'Restructuring the "Woman Question": *Perestroika* and Prostitution' in *Feminist Review*, no. 33, Autumn 1989, p. 5.

5. See, for example, 'My igrali v rumasku' in *Zdorov'e*, no. 8, 1987, pp. 10-11. The article made only oblique reference to the game, evidently assuming that readers knew what it was. Friends in Moscow filled me in on the 'rules'.

6. From an article in *Ogonek*; quoted in Andrew Wilson and Nina Bachkatov, *Living With Glasnost': Youth and Society in a Changing Russia* (Harmondsworth, Penguin, 1988), p. 160.

7. Quoted by Celestine Bohlen, 'East Europe's Women Struggle with New Roles, and Old Ones' in *New York Times*, 23 November 1990, section 4, pp. 1-2.

8. The sociologist Igor Bestuzhev-Lada, for example, has written a number of articles on these lines. See: 'O zhenshchine i dlya zhenshchiny' in *Rabotnitsa*, no. 5, 1985, p. 26; 'Itak, nachinaem' in *Izvestiya*, 31 August 1985, p. 6; and 'Net detei - net i budushchego u naroda' in *Nedelya*, 15-21 August 1988, pp. 20-1.

9. N. Zhakharova, A. Posadskaya and N. Rimashevskaya, 'Kak my reshaem zhenskii vopros' in *Kommunist*, no. 4, 1989, p. 58.

10. Ibid.

11. M. S. Gorbachev, *Perestroika* (London, HarperCollins, 1987), p. 117.

12. Kerstin Gusmaffson, 'Raisa' in *Sobesednik*, 18 March 1990, p. 10.